CW00822878

Skoda 1000 & 1100 Owners Workshop Manual

by J H Haynes
Member of the Guild of Motoring Writers
and I M Coomber

Models covered:

1000 and 1100MB Saloon 988cc and 1107cc
S100 and S110 Saloon and Coupe 988cc and 1107cc

ISBN 0 85696 303 8

© J H Haynes and Company Limited 1977

ABCDE 303
FGHIJ
KLMNO
PQRS

All rights reserved. No part of this book may be reproduced or transmitted in any form or by any means, electronic or mechanical, including photocopying, recording or by any information storage or retrieval system, without permission in writing from the copyright holder.

Printed in England

HAYNES PUBLISHING GROUP
SPARKFORD YEOVIL SOMERSET ENGLAND
distributed in the USA by
HAYNES PUBLICATIONS INC
861 LAWRENCE DRIVE
NEWBURY PARK
CALIFORNIA 91320
USA

Acknowledgements

Special thanks are due to Skoda (Great Britain) Limited for the supply of technical information and certain of the illustrations used in this manual. Castrol Limited provided lubrication details.

We are particularly grateful to Mrs Connie Waddon who kindly loaned us her Skoda 110R Coupe as a project vehicle.

Car Mechanics magazine provided many of the photographs used in the bodywork repair sections of Chapter 12.

Lastly, thanks are due to all of those people at Sparkford who helped in the production of this manual. Particularly, Martin Penny and Les Brazier who carried out the mechanical work and took the photographs respectively; Stanley Randolph who planned the layout of each page and Rod Grainger the editor.

About this manual

Its aims

This is a manual for do-it-yourself minded owners of Skoda MB, S100 Series and S110 Series cars. It shows how to maintain these cars in first-class condition and how to carry out repairs when components become worn or break. Regular and careful maintenance is essential if maximum reliability and minimum wear are to be achieved.

The step-by-step photographs show how to deal with the major components and in conjunction with the text and exploded illustrations should make all the work quite clear - even to the novice who has never previously attempted the more complex job.

Although Skodas are hardwearing and robust, it is inevitable that their reliability and performance will decrease as they become older. Repairs and general reconditioning will become necessary if the car is to remain roadworthy. Early models requiring attention are frequently bought by the more impecunious motorist who can least afford the repair prices charged in garages, even though these prices are usually quite fair bearing in mind overheads and the high cost of capital equipment and skilled labour.

It is in these circumstances that this manual will prove to be of maximum assistance, as it is the *only* workshop manual written from practical experience specially to help Skoda owners.

Manufacturer's official manuals are usually splendid publications which contain a wealth of technical information. Because they are issued primarily to help the manufacturers authorised dealers and distributors they tend to be written in very technical language, and tend to skip details of certain jobs which are common knowledge to garage mechanics. Owner's workshop manuals are different as they are intended primarily to help the owner. They therefore go into many of the jobs in great detail with extensive photographic support to ensure everything is properly understood so that the repair is done correctly.

Owners who intend to do their own maintenance and repairs should have a reasonably comprehensive tool kit. Some jobs require special service tools, but in many instances it is possible to get round their use with a little care and ingenuity. For example a Jubilee clip makes a most efficient and cheap piston ring compressor.

Throughout this manual ingenious ways of avoiding the use of special equipment and tools are shown. In some cases the proper tool must be used. Where this is the case a description of the tool and its correct use is included.

When a component malfunctions repairs are becoming more and more a case of replacing the defective item with an exchange rebuilt unit. This is excellent practice when a component is thoroughly worn out, but it is a waste of good money when overall the component is only half worn, and requires the replacement of but a single small item to effect a complete repair. As an example, a non-functioning dynamo can frequently be repaired quite satisfactorily just by fitting new brushes.

A further function of this manual is to show the owner how to examine malfunctioning parts; determine what is wrong, and then how to make the repair.

Given the time, mechanical do-it-yourself aptitude, and a reasonable collection of tools, this manual will show the ordinary private owner how to maintain and repair his car really economically.

Using the manual

The book is divided into eleven Chapters. Each Chapter is divided into numbered Sections which are headed in **bold type** between horizontal lines. Each Section consists of serially numbered paragraphs.

There are two types of illustration: (1) Figures which are numbered according to Chapter and sequence of occurrence in that Chapter. (2) Photographs which have a reference number in their caption. All photographs apply to the Chapter in which they occur so that the reference number pinpoints the pertinent Section and paragraph number.

Procedures, once described in the text, are not normally repeated. If it is necessary to refer to another Chapter the reference will be given in Chapter number and Section number.

If it is considered necessary to refer to a particular paragraph in another Chapter the reference is given in this form: 1/5:5 (Chapter 1, Section 5, paragraph 5). Cross-references given without use of the word 'Chapter' apply to Sections and/or paragraphs in the same Chapter (eg, 'see Section 8') means also 'in this Chapter'.

When the left or right side of the car is mentioned it is as if looking forward from the rear of the car.

Great effort has been made to ensure that this book is complete and up-to-date. However, it should be realised that manufacturers continually modify their cars, even in retrospect.

Whilst every care is taken to ensure that the information in this manual is correct no liability can be accepted by the authors or publishers for loss, damage or injury caused by any errors in, or omissions from, the information given.

Introduction to the Skoda

Introduced in 1964, the Skoda MB1000 Series was obviously designed as a practical car for the family man, being basic in all of its design features.

An 1107cc version (MB1100) later became available in the same bodyshell. These two models remained basically unchanged until superseded by the S100 and S110 models, respectively, in 1970. De luxe versions of the S100 and S110, with additional fittings, are called S100L and S110L, respectively. In addition, two models having added performance combined with the de luxe features became available in the S110LS and S110R Coupe.

Mechanically, all the models have remained basically the same since the introduction of the MB Series.

The overhead valve engine is situated in the rear of the car, as is the gearbox and combined differential unit (transaxle). The swinging half-axles are independently sprung, as is the front suspension. The bodywork is quite simple. All four wing panels are bolted to the main bodyframe, making for easy removal and repair.

The interior is well appointed. Seats are fully reclining in the front, and the rear seats can be individually folded down or removed completely to provide additional luggage capacity to supplement the front boot compartment. This feature applies to the Coupe model as well as the saloon range.

Most jobs can be tackled with a basic tool kit but there are instances where special service tools are required and the owner mechanic should therefore study carefully any job to be undertaken prior to commencing work, in order to assess his capability of completing the job at home satisfactorily.

Buying spare parts and vehicle identification numbers

Buying spare parts

Spare parts are available from many sources, for example, Skoda garages, other garages and accessory shops, and motor factors. Our advice regarding spare parts is as follows:

Officially appointed Skoda garages - this is the best source of parts which are peculiar to your car and otherwise not generally available (eg, complete cylinder heads, internal gearbox components, badges, interior trim, etc). It is also the only place at which you should buy parts if your car is still under warranty; non-Skoda components may invalidate the warranty. To be sure of obtaining the correct parts it will always be necessary to give the storeman your car's engine and chassis number, and if possible, to take the old part along for positive identification. Remember that many parts are available on a factory exchange scheme - any parts returned should always be clean! It obviously makes good sense to go to the specialists on your car for this type of part for they are best equipped to supply you.

Other garages and accessory shops - these are often very good places to buy material and components needed for the maintenance of your car (eg, oil filters, spark plugs, bulbs, fan belts, oils and grease, touch-up paint, filler paste etc). They also sell general accessories, usually have convenient opening hours, often charge lower prices and can often be found not far from home.

Motor factors - good factors will stock all of the more important components which wear out relatively quickly (eg, clutch components, pistons, valves, exhaust systems, brake cylinders/pipes/hoses/seals/shoes and pads etc). Motor factors will often provide new or reconditioned components on a part exchange basis - this can save a considerable amount of money.

Vehicle identification numbers

The *engine number* is situated on the cylinder block adjacent to the water pump flange (photo).

The *chassis number* is stamped on a plate attached to the bulkhead panel inside the front luggage compartment (photo) on the rear bulkhead next to the engine compartment lid retainer and on the shroud above the radiator.

The engine number

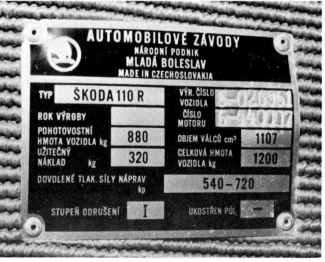

The chassis number

Skoda S100 Saloon

Skoda S110R Coupe

Routine maintenance

The maintenance instructions listed below are basically those recommended by the vehicle manufacturer. They are supplemented by additional maintenance tasks which, through practical experience, the author recommends should be carried out at the intervals suggested.

The additional tasks are primarily of a preventive nature in that they will assist in eliminating the unexpected failure of a component due to fair wear and tear.

The levels of the engine oil, cooling water, windscreen washer water and battery electrolyte, also the tyre pressures, should be checked weekly or more frequently if experience dictates this to be necessary. Similarly it is wise to check the level of the fluids in the clutch and brake master cylinder reservoirs at monthly intervals. If not checked at home, it is advantageous to use regularly the same garage for this work as they will get to know your preferences for particular oils and the pressures at which you like to run your tyres.

Every 3,000 miles (5,000 km) and 6,250 miles (10,000 km)

---

1 Run the engine until it is hot and place a container of at least 8 Imp. pints (4.5 litres) capacity under the sump drain plug, undo and remove the drain plug and allow the oil to drain for at least 10 minutes. Clean the plug and its surrounding area and replace the plug tightening it firmly. Place a tray below the oil filter, remove the nut from the filter body, withdraw the filter casing and remove the element. Clean out the casing, fit a new element and fit a new sealing ring under the nut and also between the filter casing and body, before reassembly. Refill the sump with the recommended grade of oil and clean off any oil which may have spilled over the engine or its components. Check the oil level. The interval between oil changes should be reduced in very hot or dusty conditions or during cold weather with much slow stop/start driving.

2 Check the water pump housing bolts for tightness and also the drivebelt for slackness. Check the fan belt condition and tension between the fan pulley and crankshaft pulley. Check the fan cowling for tightness.

3 Check the coolant/antifreeze mixture in the radiator and top-up if

required. Check for signs of leakage in the radiator cone and the connecting hose joints.

4 Undo and remove the bolt in the centre of the fuel pump cover, lift off the cover, and lift out the gauze filter to clean it with petrol and a soft brush. Renew the cork gasket if it has hardened or broken.

5 The air cleaner element should be inspected, cleaned and serviced.

6 Examine the engine and the transmission unit for leaks and, if found, determine the cause.

7 Check the carburettor slow-running setting as described in Chapter 3.

8 Inspect all hydraulic pipes, hoses and connections for leaks or damage, Inspect the handbrake cable for wear or damage and check the efficient operation of the handbrake. Check the brakes and adjust if necessary. Always test the brakes several times after making any adjustments.

9 Remove the spark plugs, clean them and reset them as specified. Clean the ceramic insulators and inspect the plug leads for deterioration.

10 Check the distributor contact breaker and adjust if necessary. At the same time clean any dirt from the inside of the distributor cap and clean the rotor arm. Apply two drops of oil at the centre of the cam spindle and also through the plate to lubricate the automatic advance mechanism. Smear very lightly with grease the cam surface and apply one drop of oil, only, to the moving contact breaker pivot. Wipe off immediately any excess oil or grease.

11 Check the steering joints and column fixing points. Apply grease to those joints in the suspension and steering units having grease nipples. Check the front hub endfloat, and adjust if required. Apply grease to the cap.

12 Check the pivot bolts on the front and rear suspension mountings and also the bolts between the floor and mountings.

13 The door strikers, locks and hinges, the bonnet and engine compartment locks, hinges and catches, and the rear window lock and hinges should all be lubricated by means of an oil can.

14 Have the front wheel 'toe-in' checked.

15 Check the headlamp beam alignment.

16 Check all lamps, especially the stop/tail lamps, for correct functioning and renew if necessary.

17 Check the windscreen wiper blades for efficient functioning and renew if suspect.

18 Check the operation of the windscreen washer.

19 Check the window winding handles, seat adjustment mechanism, sun visors etc., for ease of movement.

20 Check the alignment of the doors.

21 Give the bodywork and trim a thoroughly good wash and then a wax polish. If chromium cleaner is used to remove rust on any of the car's plated parts remember that the cleaner also removes parts of the chromium and therefore must be used sparingly.

22 Remove the carpets or mats and thoroughly vacuum clean the interior of the car. Beat out or vacuum clean the carpets.

Every 12,500 miles (20,000 km)

1 Carry out the operations for the 3,000 miles (5,000 km) service.

2 Renew the spark plugs ensuring that the gaps are correctly set.

3 Renew the distributor points, if necessary.

4 Check clutch adjustment.

5 Relubricate the fan bearings and the water pump bearings.

6 Renew the air cleaner element.

7 Examine the carburettor flange, the manifolds and the exhaust system for leaks and check all fixings for tightness.

8 Check the starter motor fixing bolts for tightness.

9 Run the car until it is hot and place a container of at least 4 Imp. pints (2.25 litres) under the transmission unit. Undo the drain plug,

clean it and its surrounding area, and replace the plug tightening it firmly. Refill with a recommended grade of oil to the level plug, cleaning off any oil which may have spilled.

10 Check, and top-up if required, the steering box oil level.

11 Lubricate the fan bearings, as described in Chapter 2.

31,000 miles (50,000 km)

1 Carry out all the operations for the 3,000, 6,250 and 12,500 miles (5,000, 10,000 and 20,000 km) services.

2 Check the rubber engine mountings for any signs of damage or deterioration.

3 Inspect the rubber couplings on the driveshafts for any signs of damage or deterioration.

4 Check all the rubber bushes on the suspension for damage or deterioration.

5 Repack the front hub bearings with grease.

6 It is a sound scheme to visit your local main agent and have the underside of the body steam cleaned. All traces of dirt and oil will be removed and the underside can then be inspected for rust, damaged hydraulic pipes, frayed electrical wiring and similar maladies.

7 At the same time the engine compartment should be cleaned in a similar manner. If steam cleaning facilities are not available then brush 'Gunk' or a similar cleaner over the whole engine and engine compartment with a stiff brush working it well in where there is an accumulation of oil and dirt. Do not paint the ignition system but protect it with oily rags. As the Gunk is washed away it will take with it all traces of oil and dirt, leaving the engine looking clean and bright.

Engine oil level dipstick (left) and filler hole (right)

Oil filter element (1) and centre through bolt (2)

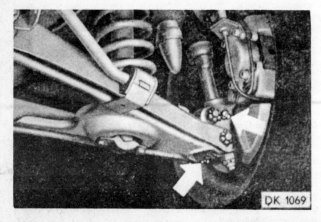

Lubrication nipples for steering knuckle pin and bottom arm bearing

Gearbox oil drain plug (1); final drive plug (2); and inspection (level) plug (3)

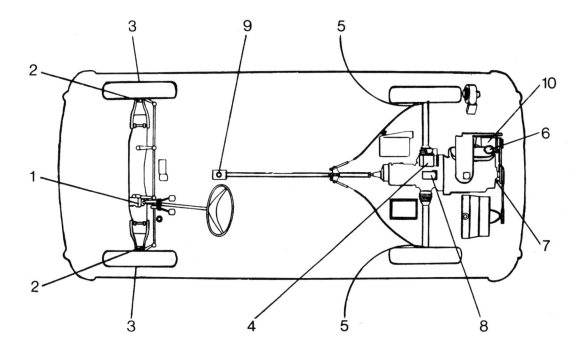

Lubrication chart

Component		Lubricant
1	Steering box	Castrol Hypoy
2	Steering knuckle pins and bearings	Castrol LM Grease
3	Front wheel bearings	Castrol LM Grease
4	Gearbox and final drive	Castrol Hypoy B
5	Rear wheel bearings	Castrol LM Grease
6	Engine	Castrol GTX
7	Water pump bearings	Castrol Water Pump
8	Clutch bearings	Castrol GTX
9	Gear change bracket	Castrol LM Grease
10	Alternator	Castrol LM Grease
	Braking system	Castrol Girling Universal Brake and Clutch Fluid
	Locks, hinges, catches, cables etc.	Castrol Everyman

Please note that the above are general recommendations only. Different operating conditions require different lubricants. Consult the handbook supplied with the car.

Tools and working facilities

Introduction

A selection of good tools is a fundamental requirement for anyone contemplating the maintenance and repair of a motor vehicle. For the owner who does not possess any, their purchase will prove a considerable expense, offsetting some of the savings made by doing-it-yourself. However, provided that the tools purchased are of good quality, they will last for many years and prove an extremely worthwhile investment.

To help the average owner to decide which tools are needed to carry out the various tasks detailed in this manual, we have compiled three lists of tools under the following headings: Maintenance and minor repair, Repair and overhaul, and Special. The newcomer to practical mechanics should start off with the 'Maintenance and minor repair' tool kit and confine himself to the simpler jobs around the vehicle. Then, as his confidence and experience grows, he can undertake more difficult tasks, buying extra tools as, and when, they are needed. In this way, a 'Maintenance and minor repair' tool kit can be built-up into a 'Repair and overhaul' tool kit over a considerable period of time without any major cash outlays. The experienced do-it-yourselfer will have a tool kit good enough for most repair and overhaul procedures and will add tools from the 'Special' category when he feels the expense is justified by the amount of use these tools will be put to.

It is obviously not possible to cover the subject of tools fully here. For those who wish to learn more about tools and their use there is a book entitled 'How to Choose and Use Car Tools' available from the publishers of this manual.

Maintenance and minor repair tool kit

The tools given in this list should be considered as a minimum requirement if routine maintenance, servicing and minor repair operations are to be undertaken. We recommend the purchase of combination spanners (ring one end, open-ended the other); although more expensive than open-ended ones, they do give the advantages of both types of spanner.

Combination spanners - 10, 11, 13, 14, 17 mm
Adjustable spanner - 9 inch
Engine sump/gearbox/rear axle drain plug key (where applicable)
Spark plug spanner (with rubber insert)
Spark plug gap adjustment tool
Set of feeler gauges
Brake adjuster spanner (where applicable)
Brake bleed nipple spanner
Screwdriver - 4 in. long x ¼ in. dia. (plain)
Screwdriver - 4 in. long x ¼ in. dia. (crosshead)
Combination pliers - 6 inch
Hacksaw, junior
Tyre pump
Tyre pressure gauge
Grease gun (where applicable)
Oil can
Fine emery cloth (1 sheet)
Wire brush (small)
Funnel (medium size)

Repair and overhaul tool kit

These tools are virtually essential for anyone undertaking any major repairs to a motor vehicle, and are additional to those given in the Basic list. Included in this list is a comprehensive set of sockets. Although these are expensive they will be found invaluable as they are so versatile - particularly if various drives are included in the set. We recommend the ½ square-drive type, as this can be used with most proprietary torque wrenches. If you cannot afford a socket set, even bought piecemeal, then inexpensive tubular box spanners are a useful alternative.

The tools in this list will occasionally need to be supplemented by tools from the Special list.

Sockets (or box spanners) to cover range 6 to 27 mm
Reversible ratchet drive (for use with sockets)
Extension piece, 10 inch (for use with sockets)
Universal joint (for use with sockets)
Torque wrench (for use with sockets)
'Mole' wrench - 8 inch
Ball pein hammer
Soft-faced hammer, plastic or rubber
Screwdriver - 6 in. long x 5/16 in. dia. (plain)
Screwdriver - 2 in. long x 5/16 in. square (plain)
Screwdriver - 1½ in. long x ¼ in. dia. (crosshead)
Screwdriver - 3 in. long x 1/8 in. dia. (electricians)
Pliers - electricians side cutters
Pliers - needle nosed
Pliers - circlip (internal and external)
Cold chisel - ½ inch
Scriber (this can be made by grinding the end of a broken hacksaw blade)
Scraper (this can be made by flattening and sharpening one end of a piece of copper pipe)
Centre punch
Pin punch
Hacksaw
Valve grinding tool
Steel rule/straight edge
Allen keys
Selection of files
Wire brush (large)
Axle stands
Jack (strong scissor or hydraulic type)

Special tools

The tools in this list are those which are not used regularly, are expensive to buy, or which need to be used in accordance with their manufacturers instructions. Unless relatively difficult mechanical jobs are undertaken frequently, it will not be economic to buy many of these tools. Where this is the case, you could consider clubbing together with friends (or a motorists club) to make a joint purchase, or borrowing the tools against a deposit from a local garage or tool hire specialist.

The following list contains only those tools and instruments freely available to the public, and not those special tools produced by the vehicle manufacturer specifically for its dealer network. You will find occasional references to these manufacturers special tools in the text of this manual. Generally, an alternative method of doing the job without the vehicle manufacturers special tool is given. However, sometimes, there is no alternative to using them. Where this is the case and the relevant tool cannot be bought or borrowed you will have to entrust the work to a franchised garage.

> Valve spring compressor
> Piston ring compressor
> Ball joint separator
> Universal hub/bearing puller
> Impact screwdriver
> Micrometer and/or vernier gauge
> Carburettor flow balancing device (where applicable)
> Dial gauge
> Stroboscopic timing light
> Dwell angle meter/tachometer
> Universal electrical multi-meter
> Cylinder compression gauge
> Lifting tackle
> Trolley jack
> Light with extension lead

Buying tools

For practically all tools, a tool factor is the best source since he will have a very comprehensive range compared with the average garage or accessory shop. Having said that, accessory shops often offer excellent quality tools at discount prices, so it pays to shop around.

Remember, you don't have to buy the most expensive items on the shelf, but it is always advisable to steer clear of the very cheap tools. There are plenty of good tools around, at reasonable prices, so ask the proprietor or manager of the shop for advice before making a purchase.

Care and maintenance of tools

Having purchased a reasonable tool kit, it is necessary to keep the tools in a clean and serviceable condition. After use, always wipe off any dirt, grease and metal particles using a clean, dry cloth, before putting the tools away. Never leave them lying around after they have been used. A simple tool rack on the garage or workshop wall, for items such as screwdrivers and pliers is a good idea. Store all normal spanners and sockets in a metal box. Any measuring instruments, gauges, meters, etc., must be carefully stored where they cannot be damaged or become rusty.

Take a little care when the tools are used. Hammer heads inevitably become marked and screwdrivers lose the keen edge on their blades from time-to-time. A little timely attention with emery cloth or a file will soon restore items like this to a good serviceable finish.

Working facilities

Not to be forgotten when discussing tools, is the workshop itself. If anything more than routine maintenance is to be carried out, some form of suitable working area becomes essential.

It is appreciated that many an owner mechanic is forced by circumstance to remove an engine or similar item, without the benefit of a garage or workshop. Having done this, any repairs should always be done under the cover of a roof.

Wherever possible, any dismantling should be done on a clean flat workbench or table at a suitable working height.

Any workbench needs a vice: one with a jaw opening of 4 in. (100 mm) is suitable for most jobs. As mentioned previously, some clean dry storage space is also required for tools, as well as the lubricants, cleaning fluids, touch-up paints and so on which soon become necessary.

Another item which may be required, and which has a much more

general usage, is an electric drill with a chuck capacity of at least 5/16 in. (8 mm). This, together with a good range of twist drills, is virtually essential for fitting accessories such as wing mirrors and reversing lights.

Last, but not least, always keep a supply of old newspapers and clean, lint-free rags available, and try to keep any working area as clean as possible.

Spanner jaw gap comparison table

Jaw gap (in.)	Spanner size
0.250	¼ in. AF
0.275	7 mm AF
0.312	5/16 in. AF
0.315	8 mm AF
0.340	11/32 in. AF/1/8 in. Whitworth
0.354	9 mm AF
0.375	3/8 in. AF
0.393	10 mm AF
0.433	11 mm AF
0.437	7/16 in. AF
0.445	3/16 in. Whitworth/¼ in. BSF
0.472	12 mm AF
0.500	½ in. AF
0.512	13 mm AF
0.525	¼ in. Whitworth/5/16 in. BSF
0.551	14 mm AF
0.562	9/16 in. AF
0.590	15 mm AF
0.600	5/16 in. Whitworth/3/8 in. BSF
0.625	5/8 in. AF
0.629	16 mm AF
0.669	17 mm AF
0.687	11/16 in. AF
0.708	18 mm AF
0.710	3/8 in. Whitworth/7/16 in. BSF
0.748	19 mm AF
0.750	¾ in. AF
0.812	13/16 in. AF
0.820	7/16 in. Whitworth/½ in. BSF
0.866	22 mm AF
0.875	7/8 in. AF
0.920	½ in. Whitworth/9/16 in. BSF
0.937	15/16 in. AF
0.944	24 mm AF
1.000	1 in. AF
1.010	9/16 in. Whitworth/5/8 in. BSF
1.023	26 mm AF
1.062	1 1/16 in. AF/27 mm AF
1.100	5/8 in. Whitworth/11/16 in. BSF
1.125	1 1/8 in. AF
1.181	30 mm AF
1.200	11/16 in. Whitworth/¾ in. BSF
1.250	1 ¼ in. AF
1.259	32 mm AF
1.300	¾ in. Whitworth/7/8 in. BSF
1.312	1 5/16 in. AF
1.390	13/16 in. Whitworth/15/16 in. BSF
1.417	36 mm AF
1.437	1 7/16 in. AF
1.480	7/8 in. Whitworth/1 in. BSF
1.500	1½ in. AF
1.574	40 mm AF/15/16 in. Whitworth
1.614	41 mm AF
1.625	1 5/8 in. AF
1.670	1 in. Whitworth/1 1/8 in. BSF
1.687	1 11/16 in. AF
1.811	46 mm AF
1.812	1 13/16 in. AF
1.860	1 1/8 in. Whitworth/1¼ in. BSF
1.875	1 7/8 in. AF
1.968	50 mm AF
2.000	2 in. AF
2.050	1¼ in. Whitworth/1 3/8 in. BSF
2.165	55 mm AF
2.362	60 mm AF

Chapter 1 Engine

Contents

Specifications

Engine (general)

	100	100L	110L	110LS
Type	4 cylinder, 4 stroke, in-line, overhead valves			
Cubic capacity (cc)	988	988	1107	1107
Bore	68	68	72	72
Stroke	68	68	68	68
Compression ratio	8.3	8.3	8.8	9.5
Petrol octane required (minimum)	85	85	85	95

Oil pressure (minimum) ... ... 29 psi or 2 bar kg/sq. cm to 2000 rpm

Brake horse power (bhp):
 1000 MB ... ... 42 @ 4650 rpm (SAE)
 100 and 100L ... ... 48 @ 4750 rpm (SAE)
 110L ... ... 53 @ 5000 rpm (SAE)
 110LS and R ... ... 62 @ 5500 rpm (SAE)

Dry weight:
 1000 MB ... ... 182 lb (83 kg)
 100 and 100L ... ... 185 lb (84 kg)
 110L ... ... 187 lb (85 kg)
 110LS and R ... ... 189 lb (86 kg)

Oil capacity:
 1000 MB ... ... 6½ Imp pints (3.7 litres)
 100, 100L, 110L ... ... 7 Imp pints (3.97 litres)
 110LS and coupe ... ... 8 Imp pints (4.5 litres)

Cylinder liners*

Cylinder liners overlap in bores:

100, 100L	0.15 to 0.20 mm
110, 110LS	0.10 to 0.15 mm

Grading of cylinder liners according to diameters and tolerance classes (Skoda 100 and 100L):

Nominal diameter (mm)	Tolerance and rebore class	Diameter (mm)	Diameter tolerance (mm)
68 (Standard)	A	68.00	
	B	68.01	
	C	68.02	
68.25 (Rebore 1)	1A	68.25	
	1B	68.26	+0.01
	1C	68.27	
68.50 (Rebore 2)	2A	68.50	
	2B	68.51	
	2C	68.52	

Grading of cylinder liners according to diameters and tolerance classes (Skoda 110L):

Nominal diameter (mm)	Tolerance and rebore class	Diameter (mm)	Diameter tolerance (mm)
	A	72.00	
72	B	72.01	+0.01
	C	72.02	

Pistons*

Grading of pistons according to diameters and tolerance classes (Skoda 100 and 100L):

Nominal diameter (mm)	Tolerance and oversize class	Diameter 'D' as per Fig. 1.6 (mm)	Tolerance limits of 'D' (mm)
68 (Standard)	A	67.95	
	B	67.96	
	C	67.97	
68.25 (For rebore 1)	1A	68.20	
	1B	68.21	−0.01
	1C	68.22	
68.50 (For rebore 2)	2A	68.45	
	2B	68.46	
	2C	68.47	

Grading of pistons according to tolerance classes (Skoda 110L):

Nominal diameter (mm)	Tolerance class	Diameter 'D' as per Fig. 1.6 (mm)	Tolerance limits of 'D' (mm)
	A	71.93	
72	B	71.94	−0.01
	C	71.95	

Grading of pistons according to tolerance classes (Skoda 110LS):

Nominal diameter (mm)	Tolerance class	Diameter 'D' as per Fig. 1.6 (mm)	Tolerance limits of 'D' (mm)
	A	71.95	
72	B	71.96	−0.01
	C	71.97	

Gudgeon pins*

Table of matching gudgeon pins to pistons and con-rod small-end bushes:

Nominal diameter (mm)	Gudgeon pin diameter (mm)		Bore in con-rod small-end bush, diameter (mm)		Pin bore in piston, diameter (mm)	
20	20	−0.003	20	−0.004 −0.010	20	+0.005 −0.001
20.05	20.05	−0.003	20.05	−0.004 −0.010	20.05	+0.005 −0.001

Crankshaft*

Fitting crankshaft main bearings to journals:

Nominal crankshaft journal diameter (mm)	Bearing shell wall thickness, (mm)	Tolerance limits of wall thickness (mm)
55 Standard	1.497	
54.75 Regrind 1	1.622	
54.50 Regrind 2	1.747	
54.25 Regrind 3	1.872	−0.007
54 Regrind 4	1.997	

Crankshaft regrinding tolerances:

	Journal width (mm)	Journal width tolerance (mm)	Big-end journal dia (mm)	Big-end journal dia tolerance (mm)	Main bearing journal dia (mm)	Main bearing journal dia tolerance (mm)
Standard	31.5		45		55	
Regrind 1	31.625		44.75		54.75	
Regrind 2	31.75	+0.025	44.50	−0.009	54.50	−0.010
Regrind 3	31.875	−0.000	44.25	−0.025	54.25	−0.029
Regrind 4	32		44		54	

Correlation of journal width and guide rings:

Nominal crankshaft journal diameter (mm)		Journal width (mm)	Guide ring thickness (mm)	Tolerance (mm)
Standard	55	31.5	1.490	
Regrind 1	54.75	31.625	1.615	
Regrind 2	54.50	31.75	1.740	−0.01
Regrind 3	54.25	31.875	1.865	
Regrind 4	54	32	1.990	

Oil pump*

Type		Gear driven, force feed	
Clearances:		Standard (mm)	Maximum due to wear (mm)
Between driveshaft and its bearing		0.06 to 0.02	0.15
Between pin and driven gear		0.050 to 0.014	0.10
Axial between pump gears and cap		0.168 to 0.045	0.2

Camshaft*

Standard camshaft dimensions:

Bearing no.	Diameter of bearing in cylinder block (mm)		Diameter of camshaft journals (mm)	
1	39	+0.025	39	−0.050 −0.025
2	38.5		38.5	−0.041
3	30	+0.021	30	−0.020

Oversize camshaft dimensions:

Bearing no.	Diameter of bearing in cylinder block (mm)		Diameter of camshaft journals (mm)	
1	39.2		39.2	
2	38.7	+0.025	38.7	−0.050 −0.025
3	30.2		30.2	

Valves and valve gear*

Valve and valve guide dimensions:

	Standard		Oversize	
Inlet valve diameter (mm)	7.5	−0.013 −0.028	7.75	−0.013 −0.028
Exhaust valve diameter (mm)	7.5	−0.025 −0.040	7.75	−0.025 −0.040
Guide (inlet and exhaust) diameter (mm)	7.5	+0.022	7.75	+0.022

Tappet (cam follower) dimensions:

Valve tappet	Diameter of bearing in cylinder block (mm)		Tappet diameter (mm)	
Standard	21	+0.021	21	−0.020
Oversize	21.2		21.2	−0.007

Valve springs - free length:

Inner (mm)	43.6
Outer (mm)	45.85

Valve timing (inlet):

	Opens before TDC	Closes after TDC
S100 and S100L	14° 30'	45° 30'
S110L	14° 30'	45° 30'
S110LS	18°	49°

Valve timing (exhaust):

	Opens before TDC	Closes after TDC
S100 and S100L	40° 10'	13° 10'
S110L	49° 30'	10° 30'
S110LS	53°	14°

Valve clearances (cold):

Exhaust	0.20 mm (0.008 in)	
Inlet	0.15 mm (0.006 in)	

* Note: All engine components are fabricated to metric dimensions which cannot accurately be translated into imperial measurements. Therefore all critical dimensions in this Specifications Section are metric.

Torque wrench settings:

	lb f ft	kg f m
Cylinder head nut (10 mm)...	36	5
Cylinder head bolt (8 mm)	18 to 20	2.5 to 2.8
Connecting rod nut (8 x 1 mm)	18 to 20	2.5 to 2.8
Crankshaft bearing bolt nut (10 mm)	28 to 33	4 to 4.5
Rocker shaft support nut or bolt	18 to 21	2.5 to 3
Camshaft timing gear bolt (10 mm)	21 to 25	3 to 3.5
Flywheel bolt (10 x 1)	40 to 47	5.5 to 6.5
Crankshaft pulley bolt (20 x 15 mm)	72 to 86	10 to 12
Cylinder head bolt (10 mm)	36 to 40	5 to 5.5
Crankcase bolt nut (8 mm)	16 to 20	2.2 to 2.7
Drain plug (tapered) (22 x 1.5 mm)	18 to 21	2.5 to 3

1 Engine - general description, modifications and maintenance

The Skoda engine is a four cylinder in line unit incorporating an overhead valve layout.

It has a three main bearing crankshaft, which drives the camshaft via sprockets and twin chain.

A helical gear on the camshaft, directly in front of the chain sprocket, drives the distributor which is mounted on top of the timing case.

The gear type oil pump is located in the base of the timing chest and is driven by a vertical connecting shaft, attached to one of the two gears at the bottom and slotted into the distributor shaft at the top.

The block and sump are cast in aluminium, whilst the head is iron.

The cooling system incorporates a water pump, thermostat, radiator and a nine bladed fan.

The fuel system consists of a Jikov mechanically operated pump and a Jikov carburettor, of which there are different types to suit the various models.

Although basically the same layout, two engine capacities are currently in production, these being of 988 cc for the 1000 MB series, the current '100' and '100 L' models and 1107 cc unit which powers the '110 L', and '110 LS' and '110 R' coupe.

The MB series was first introduced in 1964 with the 988 cc unit and in 1968 the 1100 engine was introduced in the same bodyshell.

In 1970 the MB series was discontinued and the 'S' series introduced. Although basically the same in appearance, the power output had increased throughout the range due to various minor modifications.

Engine modifications
Cylinder head valves - all series: In 1974, the valve safety ring and its retaining groove in the valve stem were discontinued. The latest type of valve is fully interchangeable with the earlier type, for both the inlet and exhaust.

Cylinder head - all series: In September 1975 a modified cylinder head was fitted to all models; it is recognised by the Skoda emblem positioned between number 3 and 4 cylinders.

Although interchangeable with the earlier type, the respective valve rocker assemblies must be changed also, due to valve spacing differences. If fitting the early type head and rocker assembly, remove the shim spacers (part No. 112 - 029660) which are located between the pedestals and rocker arms on all types except the Coupe and LS models.

The new and old type valves are fully interchangeable.

LS series - piston rings: Modified piston rings were fitted from September 1975. These have an expander incorporated in the oil control ring and the ring groove is therefore deeper in section.

This type of ring cannot be fitted to the earlier type pistons without modifying the ring groove to suit.

S110 R series models: In November 1972 (engine No. 597996 onwards), the oil pressure gauge union at the engine was relocated from the timing chest to the rear of the engine, where the electrical oil switch is situated.

Engine - maintenance
The engine is the heart of the car and, as such, should be treated with respect. Weekly checks should be made on the oil and coolant levels, and they should be topped-up if required. As detailed in the Maintenance Section at the front of this book, engine oil should, periodically, be drained and replenished.

Look for coolant and oil leaks around the engine and, if found, repair as required.

All the electrical connections should be clean and secure, and cables and pipes should be kept clear of 'hot spots' and not allowed to chafe.

Careful and regular maintenance will ensure a long and reliable life for your engine.

2 Engine and transaxle removal - general notes

Before commencing removal of the engine and transaxle, the following points should be observed:

The engine may be removed with, or without, the transmission assembly as required. The following text covers the complete engine/ transaxle removal.

If the engine only is to be removed, follow paragraphs 1 - 22 of Section 3 (with the exception of paragraph 4), and for the final engine or transaxle removal, Sections 4 and 5.

Prior to removal of the engine or transaxle the rear of the car should be jacked-up, the wheels removed, and blocks or axle-stands placed securely under the body, the best point being the outside of the forward point thrust arm anchorage.

If axle-stands are being used a piece of suitable flat wood should be placed between the stand and car floor, to prevent distortion. The ground should be level and blocks should be placed each side of both the front wheels, to prevent car movement.

If a pit is available, it will not be necessary to block the car up until paragraph 30.

The engine transaxle assembly is quite heavy and awkward. It therefore follows that adequate lifting tackle is essential, in particular the reader should have means of raising the rear of the car at least 2½ feet clear of the ground, as well as means of supporting the engine/ transaxle unit during removal and installation.

It is also useful to have containers (e.g. egg boxes) in which the various nuts and bolts can be kept clean and safe.

An assistant will be necessary during the actual removal and installation and may also be useful during certain other operations. Extra care must be taken when transporting or moving the engine/ transaxle assembly as the cylinder block, transaxle housings, and fan mounting bracket are all cast aluminium, and therefore more fragile than the conventional cast iron.

3 Engine and transaxle - removal preparation procedure

1 Disconnect the battery terminals. The battery is situated behind the rear seats and access to it is gained by removing the seat backs, lifting the rear storage compartment floor covering and folding forwards out of the way. Remove the battery cover and disconnect the terminals.

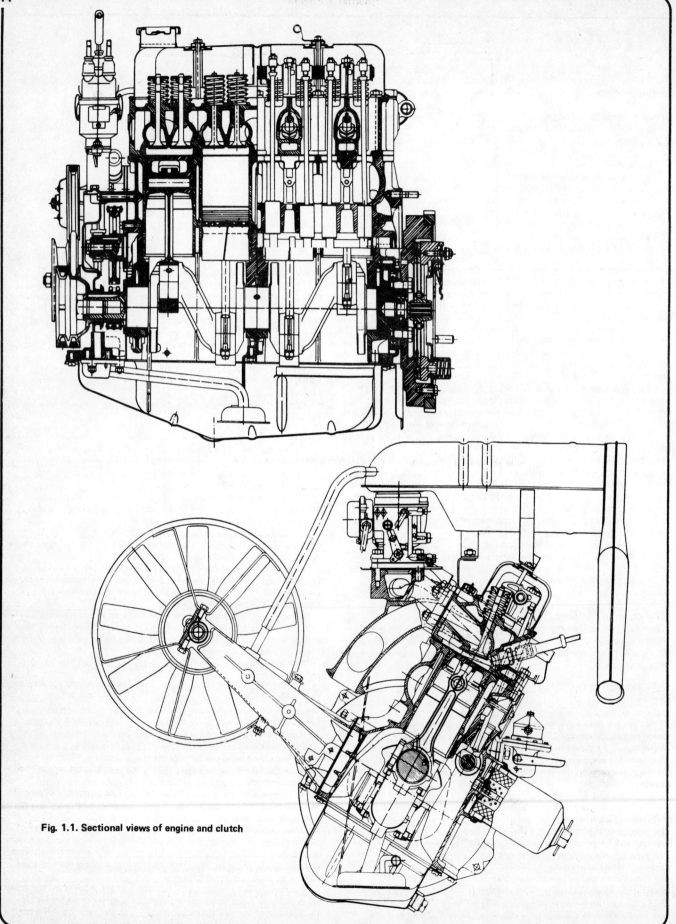

Fig. 1.1. Sectional views of engine and clutch

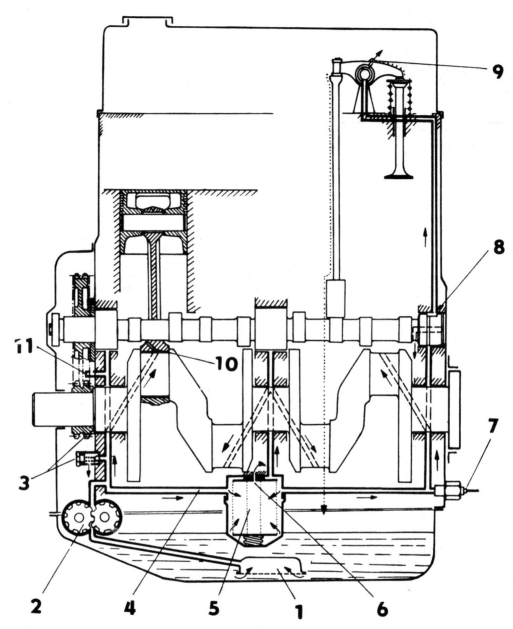

Fig. 1.2. Engine lubrication system

1 Suction strainer	4 Oil passage	7 Oil pressure switch	10 Connecting rod splash hole
2 Pump	5 Oil filter	8 Pulse chamber	11 Chain splash bolt
3 Pressure control valve	6 By-pass hole	9 Rockers	

2 Open and then remove, the rear bonnet, by unscrewing the four hinge nuts and freeing from retaining clip. Store out of the way to avoid damaging the paintwork.

3 Drain the engine oil into a container having at least 1 Imp. gallon (4.6 litres) capacity. Replace the drain plug afterwards to ensure it does not get mislaid.

4 If the transaxle assembly is also being removed this should also be drained. The gearbox and axle housing capacity on all models is 4.5 Imp. pints (2.5 litres).

5 Drain the cooling system. Place a container of at least 1½ Imp. gallons (6.8 litres) capacity at the rear of the nearside wheel and under the wing, in line with the drain pipe outlet. The radiator tap is at the base of the radiator on the left-hand side.

6 Disconnect the carburettor air cleaner by removing its three retaining nuts and rubber sealing ring clamp screw (photo).

7 Undo the fan cowling retaining clamp screw, so that the rubber ring can be pulled clear of the fan rim (photo).

8 Remove the choke cable by undoing its clamp nut and outer cable

clamp screw.

9 Remove the throttle cable by undoing the clamping screw in its location tube and 'C' clip.

10 Remove the engine dirt protector plate from its position on the inside of the right-hand rear wing. There are two nuts on top and four bolts underneath.

11 Remove the oil pressure switch cable from its terminal (located in front of the oil filter), and remove the oil pressure switch and oil cooler pipe (photo).

12 Disconnect the oil cooler pipe outlet, from the right-hand side of the block near the timing case. The ends of the three oil pipes can now be wrapped in a polythene bag or piece of rag, to prevent any spillage, and tied out of the way. The respective sealing washers may be used again if in good condition (photo).

13 Remove the distributor cap, rotor arm and HT leads from the spark plugs and coil. Place a piece of rag over the distributor to protect it.

14 Disconnect the two alternator leads — yellow from top, blue engine side — and tack the cables out of the way behind the coil.

3.6 Removing the air cleaner

3.7 Unscrewing fan cowling rubber clamp

3.11 Removing the oil pressure switch, cooler pipe and gauge pipe connection

3.12 Removing the oil cooler pipe

3.16 Radiator top hose connection

3.18 Removal of thermostat housing

3.21 Removing exhaust guard shield

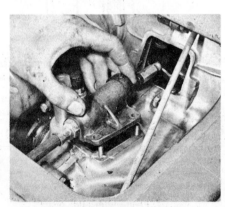
3.23 Removing the clutch slave cylinder

3.25 Undoing the telescopic shock absorber retaining nut

3.28 Gear selector rod locating bolt

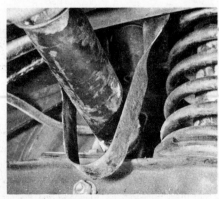
3.30 Driveshaft yoke limiting strap

3.31a Sling taking weight of engine/transaxle

15 Remove the water temperature cable from its terminal near the thermostat housing.
16 Disconnect the radiator top hose at the radiator end (photo). Original Skoda hose clips are somewhat awkward to undo and can get distorted. It is therefore suggested that these be changed for Jubilee clips during reassembly.
17 Undo and remove the heater hose clip and remove from the thermostat.
18 It is not necessary, but advisable, to remove the thermostat and housing complete at this stage to protect it from damage (photo).
19 Remove the radiator bottom hose from the intake pipe of the water pump and leave connected to the radiator.
20 Remove the returns pipe hose from the water pump housing, by undoing the rubber connecting hose clip at the bottom and where the heater hose goes into the rear bulkhead, and also the 'T' section pipe into the cylinder block water jacket.
21 Remove the exhaust guard shield by undoing the two fixing bolts (photo).
22 Undo the three bolts securing the nearside dirt shield to the under-body above the exhaust silencer, and remove.
23 Remove the central inspection cover in the rear storage compartment to gain access to the clutch slave cylinder. This in turn is protected by a cover retained by a spring: cover and spring must be removed, together with the slave cylinder retaining bolts. Unhook the two clutch release fork springs. The slave cylinder can now be disconnected (photo), and tucked out of the way, being still connected to the hydraulic hose.
24 Disconnect the handbrake by removing the two cable adjusting nuts on the handbrake link. Access to this assembly is gained by folding forward the floor carpet and removing the inspection cover at the rear end of the central drive tunnel, in front of the rear seats. The cables should then be pulled through the guide holes in the body and left to hang free under the car.
25 Disconnect the telescopic shock absorbers. To prevent the shock absorber turning, insert a 17 mm open-jawed spanner through the spring and locate on the nut on the base of the shock absorber body, whilst undoing the retaining nut (photo). If wheels are removed, place a jack under brake drum to support.
26 From underneath remove the two cables from the reversing light switch - located on the forward end of the gearbox on the right-hand side.
27 Disconnect the rear brake hydraulic pipes. To prevent spillage through the breather hole of the brake fluid reservoir, remove the filler cap, place a piece of polythene over the filler neck and replace cap. Disconnect each of the two rear brake hydraulic connections from the respective backplates. These are 'banjo' type connectors, and the copper sealing washers should always be renewed on replacement.
28 Gear selector rod disconnection: Select 1st or 3rd gear then release the gear selector rod from underneath, by undoing the locknut and loosening off the selector rod locking bolt (photo). Push the selector shaft forward to disconnect. Should the shaft fail to move, check that the locking bolt is slackened off sufficiently and move the gear selector lever to the rear to obtain more leverage.
29 Next remove the bolt through the speedo cable clamp. Withdraw it from its driveshaft and pull the cable clear.
30 With the rear of the body on blocks and the wheels removed, place

a jack under a brake drum and *just* support the weight. Remove the yoke limiting strap (photo), for the driveshaft. Undo the four nuts retaining the 'thrust arm' at the forward end and gently lower and remove the jack. Remove the coil springs and repeat the operation on the opposite side.
31 Place a sling firmly round the engine and attach it to the hoist, which should be raised to *just* take the weight (photo). Place the jack in position under the gearbox and support. Then remove the four bolts (two each side), retaining the gearbox forward mounting plate (photo) to the underbody, being careful not to damage the brake pipes.
32 Undo the four bolts, two each side, retaining the rear crossmember on the right and left-hand *under* body panel (photo).

---

4 Engine and transaxle - removal (with rear body panel in position)

1 Ensure that all the surrounding attachments are free and disconnected.
2 Place a flat piece of wood or, ideally, a low trolley on the floor under the engine to protect the sump and silencer.
3 Lower the hoist and jack in unison so that the sump rests on the wood or trolley. Ensure that the fan pulley does not foul the rear body panel.
4 The engine/transaxle may now be removed from underneath the car. Take care not to foul the air cleaner stud on the lower edge of the rear body panel, and also the distributor vacuum diaphragm.
5 If the car has to be moved, remove the rear engine mounting crossmember from the engine assembly. Unless being renewed the engine mounting rubbers can remain attached to their respective mounting plates. Re-attach the crossmember to the car and this now provides a secure jacking or hoist point, with which to move the car.

---

5 Engine or engine and transaxle - removal (with rear body panel removed)

If facilities do not allow safely lifting the rear bodywork at least 2½ feet (0.76 metre) clear of the ground, the engine/transaxle may alternatively be withdrawn through the back of the car by removing the rear body panel as follows:
1 Disconnect all wiring to the rear lights, indicators and reversing lights, taking note of the various colour codings, and pull the cables clear of the retaining hooks.
2 Disconnect the bonnet cable.
3 Remove the rear bumper (two bolts each side).
4 Remove the rear panel bolts and nuts (photo) and slide the panel out - taking care not to damage the paintwork. The engine may now be removed.

---

6 Engine (only) - removal

If the engine only is being removed from the car, follow the instructions given in the general notes and paragraphs 1 - 22 of Section 3 (with the exception of paragraph 4), and then continue as follows:
1 With the lifting sling securely in place round the block and the

3.31b Gearbox mounting brackets and bolts

3.32 Engine mounting bar location bolts

5.4 Rear panel retaining bolts

tension just taken up, place a jack under the gearbox to provide support.
2 Now remove the clutch housing to transmission housing flange nuts and also the lower exhaust silencer bracket nut.
3 Check that all fittings are now free between the car and engine.
4 The engine may now be withdrawn from the transmission taking care not to damage surrounding fittings.

7 Engine - dismantling (general)

Having decided to complete your own reconditioning, a few hints:
1 Owners who have dismantled engines will know the need for a strong workbench and the many tools and pieces of equipment, which make their life much easier when going through the process of dismantling an engine. For those who are doing a dismantling job for the first time, there are a few 'musts' in the way of preparation which, if not done, will only cause frustration and long delays in the job.

It is essential to have sufficient space in which to work. Dismantling and reassembly is not going to be completed all in one go and it is therefore absolutely essential that you have sufficient area to leave things as they are, when necessary. A strong workbench is also necessary together with a good engineer's vice, and lastly but by no means least, your work area, bench and tools must be clean; if any dirt is conveyed into the engine during dismantling or reassembly, your work will be wasted completely.
2 The necessity for cleanliness also applies to the engine and transaxle assembly; therefore once the assembly is clear of the car thoroughly clean the outside of the units. Remove all traces of oil and congealed dirt. A good grease solvent such as 'Gunk' will make the job easier, as, after the solvent has been applied and allowed to stand for a time, the grease and dirt may be washed off with a jet of water. Finally the engine/transaxle unit may be wiped dry and clean in preparation for dismantling.
3 Once the ancillary components together with the transaxle unit have been removed from the engine, it may be lifted onto a clean bench for the main dismantling task.
4 During dismantling, clean the components in a solvent such as paraffin and carefully store them in clean containers - in readiness for assembly.
5 Never clean components with oilways (e.g. crankshaft) in petrol or paraffin, but wipe down carefully with a petrol dampened rag. Nylon pipe cleaners or compressed air may be used to clear and clean the oilways.
6 It is false economy to re-use old gaskets. New gasket kits are available and with correct assembly, ensure first rate joints. The old gaskets may be useful as templates for new gaskets, if a replacement is not immediately available from a Skoda dealer.

8 Engine - ancillary components removal

The next stage of engine dismantling is the removal of the components in the following list. Details will be found in the following Sections. It is possible to remove all the following ancillary components (except the clutch assembly), with the engine in place in the car - if it is individual items that require attention.

    1   Fan/belt assembly
    2   Carburettor and inlet manifold
    3   Exhaust system and manifold
    4   Dynamo or alternator
    5   Distributor
    6   Water pump
    7   Fuel pump
    8   Clutch assembly
    9   Thermostat
    10 Cylinder head assembly

9 Fan unit - removal

1 Remove the fan blade guard (photo). Grip the fan to prevent it turning and undo the pulley nut. Split the pulley and remove the fanbelt. Relocate the pulley on its spindle to retain the spacer shims.
2 Remove the fan support bracket support tie-rod.

3 Undo the four nuts retaining the fan support bracket to the cylinder block, and remove complete with gaskets and metal spacer.

See special note for dismantling the fan assembly in place in car (Chapter 2, Section 11).

10 Carburettor and inlet manifold - removal

1 Disconnect the fuel line from the fuel pump.
2 Disconnect the distributor timing vacuum tube from the carburettor.
3 Remove the four carburettor to manifold nuts, and unclip the throttle connecting rod balljoint linkage, and release (photo).
4 Lift the carburettor off the manifold (photo).
5 Undo the four nuts and remove the inlet manifold, complete with the carburettor throttle return spring and bracket (photo).

11 Exhaust system and manifold - removal

1 The exhaust manifold can be removed complete with the downpipe/s and silencer by undoing the manifold nuts, the silencer support bracket bolts, complete with the tie-rods at the clutch belly cover plate.
2 Alternatively, if the head only is being removed, or a new manifold gasket being fitted, it can be parted at the manifold and downpipe flange by undoing the three clamping bolts and nuts.

12 Dynamo/alternator - removal

To disconnect the dynamo or alternator, remove the adjustment strap bolt at the top and the hinge bolt from the mounting bracket.
If the engine is being stripped, the adjustment strap and mounting bracket should also be removed.

13 Distributor - removal

1 Scratch mark the relative positions of the distributor timing with the crankshaft on TDC - see Chapter 4, Section 7.
2 Remove the two distributor extension tube flange bolts to the timing chest and withdraw the distributor (photo). Avoid moving the preset clamp plate if possible.

14 Water pump - removal

Undo the retaining nuts and remove the water pump complete with pulley and gasket from its position on the front of the block (photo).

15 Fuel pump - removal

Undo the fixing nuts and remove the fuel pump/insulating washer and gaskets (photo).

16 Clutch unit - removal

If the transaxle unit is still attached to the engine, remove the starter motor and bellhousing bolts and separate the engine from the gearbox by pulling apart.
1 Prior to clutch removal, mark the adjacent positions of the flywheel and clutch cover, assuming they are to be refitted. This is because the clutch, flywheel and crankshaft were fully balanced as a unit, and should therefore be kept in unison on reassembly.
2 Undo the six clutch retaining bolts half a turn at a time, in diagonal fashion. This method will relieve the spring pressure without distorting the cover or putting excessive strain on individual bolts. Remove clutch complete.
3 Mark the flywheel to crankshaft relative position, and bend flat the four lock tabs of the washer and undo the four bolts (photo), to remove.
4 Remove the pilot bearing from its recess in the crankshaft end flange.

9.1 Fan blade guard

10.3 Retaining the throttle connecting linkage

10.4 Lifting the carburettor off the inlet manifold

10.5 Inlet manifold and throttle return spring bracket

13.2 Distributor removal

14.1 Water pump removal

15.1 Fuel pump removal

16.3 Flywheel/retaining bolts and locking washer

17.3a Removing rocker assembly with pedestals

5   The engine is now stripped of all ancillary equipment and is ready for the final dismantling.

17 Cylinder head - removal

1   Remove the rocker cover complete with gasket and washers.
2   Disconnect the rocker shaft pedestals, there are four bolts for the pedestals (earlier engines had studs and nuts). Note that at each end the pedestals are retained by two long Allen screws, which also double as cylinder head bolts.
3   Carefully lift clear the rocker assembly (photo) and dismantle for inspection. Note the oil feed hold in one of the pedestals, and keep all parts in the order of original assembly. To dismantle the rockers, remove the circlip (photo) from the end of the shaft and slide off the rockers, pedestals, etc.

4   Remove the pushrods, keeping them in the relative order in which they were removed. The easiest way to do this is to push them through a sheet of thick paper or thin card in the correct sequence.
5   Undo the four head nuts in front of the spark plug holes and the nine head bolts. These should be undone in the reverse order to the tightening sequence as shown in Fig. 1.13.
6   Remove the water temperature gauge unit.
7   The cylinder head may now be lifted off (photo). If the head is jammed, try to rock it to break the seal. Under no circumstances try to prise it apart from the cylinder block with a screwdriver or cold chisel as damage may be done to the faces of the head and/or block. If the head will not readily free, turn the engine over by the flywheel as the compression in the cylinders will often break the cylinder head joint. If this fails to work, strike the head sharply with a plastic or wooden headed hammer, at the same time pulling upwards. This action should free the head. Under no circumstances should you strike the cylinder head directly with a metal hammer.

17.3b Removing circlip from rocker shaft

17.7 Removing the cylinder head

18.2 Cam follower removal

18.4 Right-hand engine mounting bracket and earth strap

18.8 Removing the timing chest

18.11 Withdrawing the camshaft

18 Cylinder block - dismantling

1   Remove the tappet side cover by removing the four nuts and flat washers. Withdraw complete with gasket. It may help to prise if off with a screwdriver but be careful not to damage the cover, as oil leakage will occur on reassembly if distorted.
2   Lift and remove to the bench the cam followers, keeping in order of removal (photo).
3   Remove the oil filter. Place a container under the oil filter and remove the complete filter with element and sealing ring by undoing the centre stud bolt.
4   Remove the right-hand engine mounting bracket, complete with earth strap (photo), and rubber shock absorbers.
5   Remove the clutch belly plate cover, two bolts with flat and shakeproof washers (which should be replaced if worn flat).
6   Undo the sump bolts and remove the sump. If stuck, lightly tap the protruding tabs on the sump casting with a soft-headed mallet.
7   Remove the oil suction tube and filter, by undoing the four bolts to the base of the timing case, and the support stay bolt located on the middle main bearing cap.
8   Now remove the timing chest by undoing the seven screws (photo). If tight, place a screwdriver in the screw slot and lightly tap with a hammer, directly in line with the screw, then try unscrewing.
9   Bend the lock washer tab flat and undo the camshaft gear retaining nut. To stop the crankshaft and camshaft revolving, place a block of wood between the cylinder wall and the crankshaft.
10 Now withdraw the distributor driving gear, from the camshaft, followed by the crankshaft and camshaft sprockets, complete with timing chain. The sprockets are a sliding fit on their respective shafts, being located by Woodruff keys and thrust washers, which are also removed at this stage.
11 Undo the three setscrews and remove the camshaft thrust plate (29) and withdraw the camshaft (photo).
12 Remove the rear oilseal and housing complete, by undoing the five screws.
13 Remove the respective connecting-rod bearing caps by flattening

the lockwasher tabs and undoing the nuts. Note that the connecting-rods and caps are marked on the right-hand side. With the shells removed, push hammer handle against the rod and withdraw the piston and rod through the top of the cylinder bores. Lay out the connecting-rod assemblies and shells on a worktop, in sequence, ready for cleaning and careful inspection.

14 Now remove the three main bearing caps and note their markings. If unmarked, mark them yourself to ensure correct refitment. Care should be taken to keep the shells with their respective caps if it is intended to re-use them. Note, as with the big-end shells, it is probably false economy to re-use old main bearing shells unless they are virtually as new.
15 Lift the crankshaft clear of the crankcase. Clean ready for inspection.
16 Remove the oil pressure relief valve assembly.
17 The cylinder block should now be fully cleaned inside, and out, prior to inspection.

19 Engine - component examination and renovation (general)

With the engine stripped down and the various components cleaned, they can be thoroughly examined for wear or other damage.
At this stage it can be decided whether only a partial engine overhaul is required, or a complete reconditioning. If the latter is the case, an exchange reconditioned unit is often the best solution. If an exchange 'short-engine' is to be purchased, the main components in the existing short block (i.e. pistons, connecting-rods, crankshaft) should be loosely reassembled prior to exchanging the unit.
The items covered in the following Sections must be checked, and where necessary, renewed or renovated before the engine can be rebuilt.

20 Crankshaft - examination and renovation

1   Examine the crankpin and main journal surfaces for signs of scoring or scratches, check the ovality of the crankpins at different positions

with a micrometer. If more than 0.001 inch (0.025 mm) out of round, the crankpins will have to be reground. They will also have to be reground if there are any scores or scratches. Check the big-end journals in the same fashion.

2   If it is necessary to regrind the crankshaft and fit new bearings, your local Skoda garage or engine reconditioning specialist will be able to decide on how much metal needs to be ground off and also the size of replacement bearing shells.

21 Big-end and main bearings - examination and renovation

Big-end bearing failure is recognised by a noisy knocking from the crankcase and a slight drop in oil pressure. Main bearing failure is accompanied by vibration, which can be quite severe as the engine speed rises and falls, and a drop in oil pressure.

Bearings which have not broken up, but are badly worn, will give rise to low oil pressure and some vibration. Inspect the big-ends and main bearing shells and the crankshaft thrust washers for signs of general wear, scoring, pitting and scratches. The bearings should be matt grey in colour. With lead bronze bearings should a trace of copper colour be noticed the bearings are badly worn as the lead bearing material has worn away to expose the indium underlay. Renew the bearings if they are in this condition or if there is any sign of scoring or pitting. We recommend that bearing shells and thrust washers are renewed as a matter of course - regardless of their condition.

The undersizes available are designed to correspond with the regrind sizes (i.e. 0.10 in. bearings are correct for a crankshaft reground 0.010 in. undersize). The bearings are in fact slightly more than the stated undersize as running clearances have been allowed for during their manufacture.

Very long engine life can be achieved by changing big-end bearings at intervals of 30,000 miles and main bearings at intervals of 50,000 miles, irrespective of bearing wear. Normally, crankshaft wear is infinitesimal and a change of bearings will ensure mileages of 80,000 to 100,000 miles before crankshafts normally have to be reground because of scoring due to bearing failure.

22 Cylinder bores - examination and renovation

1   Cylinder bores must be examined for taper, ovality, scoring and scratches. Start by carefully examing the top of the cylinder bores, if they are at all worn, a very slight ridge will be found on the thrust side. This marks the top of the bore travel. The owner will have a good indication of the bore wear prior to dismantling the engine or removing the cylinder head. Excessive oil consumption accompanied by blue smoke from the exhaust, is a sure sign of worn cylinder bores and piston rings.

2   Measure the bore diameter just under the ridge with a micrometer and compare it with the diameter at the bottom of the bore which is not subject to wear. If the difference between the two measurements is more than 0.003 in. (0.1 mm), then it will be necessary to fit special piston rings or to have the cylinders rebored and fit oversize piston and rings. If no micrometer is available, remove the rings from the pistons and place the piston in each bore in turn about ¾ inch (19 mm) below the top of the bore. If an 0.010 inch (0.25 mm) feeler gauge can be slid between the piston and the cylinder wall on the thrust side of the bore, then remedial action must be taken. Oversize pistons are available.

3   These are accurately machined to just below their specified measurements, so as to provide correct running clearances in bores bored out to the exact oversize dimensions.

4   If the bores are slightly worn, but not so badly worn as to justify reboring them, special oil control rings can be fitted to the existing pistons, which will restore the compression and stop the engine burning excessive quantities of oil. Several different types are available and the manufacturer's instructions concerning their fitting must be followed closely.

5   To ensure that new rings fitted to a worn bore bed-in correctly the bores must be deglazed, and if possible, the top ridge in the bore removed. If a de-ridging tool or deglazing hone are not available, suitable results can be obtained by rubbing the interior of the bore with a fine grade emery paper in a criss-cross fashion on the horizontal. Never deglaze in a vertical line down the bore! If deglazing with a hone powered by a drill, take care not to foul the cylinder block casing which protrudes just below the base of the bores.

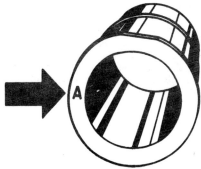

Fig. 1.3. Cylinder tolerance class marking (Sec. 22)

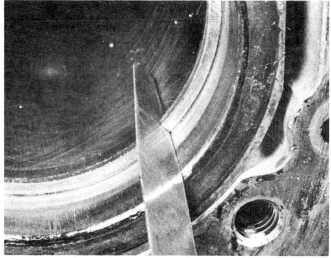

23.2 Measuring the ring gap in the cylinder bore

6   Each cylinder liner is marked, on its top face (Fig. 1.3) with an A, B or C - this denotes the cylinder tolerance class (these are given in the Specifications Section). Check each cylinder prior to ordering any pistons and/or rings to ensure the correct replacements are specified.

23 Pistons and rings - examination and renovation

1   If the existing pistons are to be refitted, carefully remove the piston rings and then thoroughly clean them. Take particular care to clean out the piston ring grooves. At the same time do not scratch the aluminium in any way. If new rings are to be fitted to the old pistons, then the top ring should be stepped so as to clear the ridge left above the previous top ring. If a normal but oversize new ring is to be fitted it will hit this ridge in the cylinder bore and break, this is because the new ring will not have worn in the same way as the old - which will have worn in unison with the ridge.

2   Before fitting the rings on the pistons each should be inserted part way down the cylinder bore and the gap in the ring measured with a feeler gauge. This should be between 0.009 in. and 0.015 in. (0.22 mm and 0.38 mm) (photo). It is essential that the gap is measured at the bottom of the ring travel. Also, if it is measured at the top of the worn bore only and gives a perfect fit, it could easily seize at the bottom. If the ring gap is too small rub down the ends of the ring with a very fine file until the gap when fitted, is correct. To keep the rings square in the bore for measurement, line each up in turn with an old piston. Use the piston, upside-down, to push the ring down. Remove the piston and measure the piston ring gap.

3   When fitting new pistons and rings to a rebored engine the ring-gap can be measured at the top of the bore, as the bore will not taper. When fitting new oil control piston rings it may be necessary to have the grooves widened, by machining, to accept new wider rings. In this instance the manufacturer's representative will make this quite clear and will supply the address to which the pistons must be sent for

machining.

4 When new pistons are fitted take great care to fit the exact size best suited to the particular bore of your engine. Skoda go one stage further than merely specifying one size of piston for all standard bores. Because of very slight differences in cylinder machining during production, it is necessary to select just the right piston for the bore. A range of different sizes are available either from the piston manufacturers or the Skoda dealer.

5 The tolerance class, for standard sized pistons, is stamped on top of the piston. The relevant tolerance classes are given in the Specifications.

24 Gudgeon pin and small-end - examination and renovation

1 If the existing pistons are to be used again it is advisable to check the gudgeon pin and small-end bush. The gudgeon pin is removed by removing the circlips from the grooves in the pistons and pressing or drifting the gudgeon pins out. They should be an interference fit in the piston (photo) and a sliding fit in the small-end bush.

2 Providing the gudgeon pin is not badly worn, it is re-usable but it is

well worthwhile fitting new small-end bushes to the connecting rods, considering the relatively small cost involved. The bush size required is obtained by measuring the gudgeon with a micrometer, and then referring to Specifications.

3 Fit the bush with the oil hole in line with the corresponding oil hole in the small-end boss in the connecting rod. Ream the bush to suit. This task is best undertaken by your Skoda agent, or an engine rebuilding specialist, as they are not only better equipped, but can also check the piston and rod alignment at the same time.

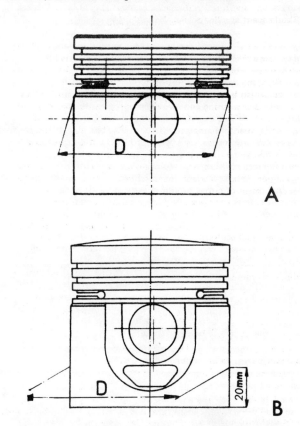

Fig. 1.6. Measuring points for checking piston diameter (see Specifications and Sec. 23). Diameter should be measured at 90° to gudgeon pin centre line. Note different measuring points for 100 and 110L (A) and 110LS (B).

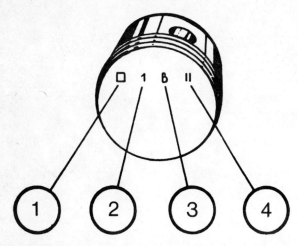

Fig. 1.4. Piston crown markings (100 and 110L). (Sec. 23)

1 Manufacturer's mark
2 Piston diameter (68 mm - no mark. 68.25 mm = 1. 68.50 = 2).
3 Tolerance class
4 Weight group

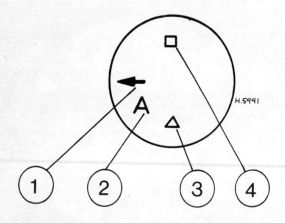

Fig. 1.5. Piston crown markings (110 LS). (Sec. 23)

1 Piston direction arrow   3 Weight group
2 Tolerance class   4 Manufacturer's mark

24.1 Checking gudgeon pin in piston

25 Camshaft and camshaft bearings - examination and renovation

1   Carefully examine the camshaft for wear. Slight scoring of the cams may be removed by gently rubbing down with a fine emery cloth or oilstone. The greatest care should be taken to keep the cam profiles smooth.

2   Carefully examine the camshaft bearings in the cylinder block. If they are badly worn, an oversize camshaft will have to be fitted and the existing bearing apertures in the block reamed out. This is a job for your Skoda agent as a line reamer is required.

26 Oil pressure relief valve - removal, inspection and reassembly

1   To prevent excessive oil pressure, for example when the engine is cold, an oil pressure relief valve is built into the oilway system and briefly consists of a spring and ball valve which opens according to pressure.

2   Very little wear takes place in this assembly but in order to clean the oilway out or to check for a suspected faulty oil pressure reading, remove, as follows, from its location at the front right-hand block face.

3   Undo the retaining bolt and remove complete with spring ball and sealing washer. Should the ball not come out, insert a small magnet or a rod with a smear of grease on the end to extract it.

4   Clean and inspect the parts for signs of deterioration and renew as necessary.

5   Reassemble in the reverse sequence and be sure to fit a new sealing washer under the bolt head.

27 Oil pump - removal, inspection and assembly

1   The oil pump is located in the base of the timing case and is driven by a shaft from one of the gears which is located in the driving mechanism of the distributor, see Fig. 1.7.

2   To examine the gears of the pump with the engine assembled, it is necessary to remove the sump (see Section 18) and the oil suction strainer assembly (photo).

3   Inspect the gears and pump body for signs of wear and ensure clearances are as given in Specifications (photo). Renew pump assembly if in any doubt.

4   Prior to assembly, the gears of the pump and the driving shaft must be lubricated with engine oil.

5   Reassembly is the reverse sequence of removal but always be sure to fit a new suction strainer gasket. If a manufacturer's replacement is not available, it can be made from a suitable gasket paper of 0.003 in. (0.1 mm) thickness. **This thickness is critical.**

28 Flywheel and starter ring - removal and replacement

1   If the teeth on the flywheel starter ring are badly worn or some are missing, then it will be necessary to remove the ring and fit a new one.

2   To remove, either split the ring with a cold chisel after initially making a cut with a hacksaw blade between two teeth, or use a copper headed mallet to knock the ring off, striking it evenly and alternately at equally spaced points. Take great care not to damage the flywheel in any way during this process.

3   Clean and polish with emery cloth four evenly spaced areas on the outside face of the new starter ring.

4   Heat the ring evenly with an oxy-acetylene flame until the polished portions turn dark blue (356° to 392°F/180° to 200°C).

5   Keep the ring at this temperature for a few minutes and then quickly but carefully fit it to the flywheel. **Do not overheat the ring.**

6   The ring should be tapped evenly onto its location and left to cool naturally. The contraction of the metal during cooling, ensures a tight and permanent fit.

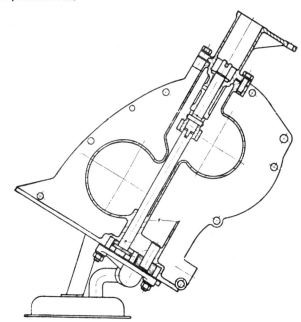

Fig. 1.7. Sectional view of timing chest showing oil pump drive (Sec. 27)

27.2 Removing the oil pump suction pipe and strainer

27.3 Checking oil pump gears end float with feeler gauge

29 Timing gears and chain - examination and renovation

1 Examine the teeth on both the crankshaft sprocket and the camshaft sprocket for wear. Each tooth forms an inverted 'V' with the gearwheel periphery and if worn the side of each tooth under tension will be slightly concave in shape when compared with the other side of the tooth. If any sign of wear is present the gearwheels must be renewed.
2 Examine the links of the chain for side slackness by bending the chain sideways. If excessive slackness is noticeable the chain should be renewed. It is a sensible precaution to renew the chain at about 30,000 miles and at lesser mileage if the engine is stripped down for a major overhaul. The actual rollers on a very badly worn chain may be slightly grooved.
3 Examine the distributor driving gear and the locating Woodruff keys. Any sign of excessive wear necessitates renewal.

30 Oil filter - removal and replacement

1 The oil filter is of the cylinder type and is located on the right-hand side of the engine. To remove, place a receptacle underneath (to catch any oil left inside), unscrew the centre bolt, and withdraw the filter body from the block.
2 Withdraw the element and discard.
3 Wash the filter bowl out with petrol.
4 Install the new element over the centre bolt (photo) and against the retaining spring, and smear some oil around the sealing washer under the bolt head - this will ensure ease of removal at a later date. Always fit a new sealing washer and sealing ring for the filter bowl as a matter of course (photo).
5 Never overtighten the centre bolt.
6 Having refitted the filter, a check should be made for leaks around the sealing ring and washer areas as soon as the engine is restarted. If leakage does occur it is probably due to distortion of the seals and the bowl will have to be reseated.

31 Sump - renovation

1 It is most essential that the oil sump should be thoroughly cleaned inside with petrol, ensuring that all signs of old oil and any metal particles are removed.
2 Scrape all traces of the old sump gasket from the mating flange and clean out the external cooling fins.

32 Oil cooler - removal, inspection and replacement

1 The oil cooler is situated directly in front of the radiator within the air intake channel of the body (photo). Removal of the cooler can be achieved by removing the radiator assembly, as described in the Cooling System Chapter, or if you have a long enough reach, by removing the intake vent in the nearside bodywork.
2 Removal is as follows: With the intake vent or radiator removed, place a suitable container under the oil cooler feed pipe in the lower right-hand side of the timing chest and remove the pipe to drain the cooler of oil.
3 Undo the intake and return pipes from the cooler.
4 Undo the two cooler retaining bolts from the bodywork and remove.
5 Clean the core of the cooler out by blowing through with compressed air from an airline, and inspect for any leakage points.
6 Replacement is the reverse sequence to removal.

33 Cylinder head, pistons and bores - decarbonisation

This can be carried out with the engine in or out of the car. With the cylinder head off (see Section 17), carefully remove with a wire brush and blunt scraper all traces of carbon deposits from the combustion spaces and ports. The valve head stems and valve guides should also be freed of any carbon deposits. Wash the combustion spaces and ports down with petrol and scrape the cylinder head surface free of any foreign matter with a brass scraper, or one made of a similar soft metal.

Clean the pistons and top of the cylinder bores. If the pistons are still in the block then it is essential that great care is taken to ensure that no carbon falls down the side of the pistons as this could scratch the cylinder walls or cause damage to the piston and rings. To ensure this does not happen, first turn the crankshaft so that two of the pistons are at the top of their bores. Stuff rag into the other two bores or seal them off with paper and masking tape. The waterways should also be covered with small pieces of masking tape to prevent particles of carbon entering the cooling system and damaging the water pump.

There are two schools of thought as to how much carbon should be removed from the piston crown. One school recommends that a ring of carbon should be left round the edge of the piston and on the cylinder bore wall as an aid to low oil consumption. Although this is probably true for early engines with worn bores, on modern type engines the thought of the second school can be applied, which is that for effective decarbonisation all traces of carbon should be removed.

If all traces of carbon are to be removed, press a little grease into the gap between the cylinder walls and the two pistons which are to be worked on. With a blunt scraper carefully scrape away the carbon from the piston crown, taking great care not to scratch the aluminium. Also scrape away the carbon from the surrounding lip of the cylinder wall. When all carbon has been removed, scrape away the grease which will now be contaminated with carbon particles, taking care not to press any into the bores. To assist prevention of carbon build-up the piston crown can be polished with a metal polish. Remove the rags or masking tape from the other two cylinders and turn the crankshaft so that the two pistons which were at the bottom are now at the top. Place rag or masking tape in the cylinders which have been decarbonised and proceed as just described.

34 Valves - removal

1 The valves can be removed from the cylinder head by compressing each spring in turn with a valve spring compressor, until the two halves

30.4a Inserting new element into oil filter bowl

30.4b Fitting oil filter unit into position on cylinder block

32.1 Position of oil cooler with radiator removed

of the collets can be removed (photo). Then slowly release the compressor and remove the spring retainer, springs, and on the earlier models, the valve 'C' ring from the stem.

2   If, when the valve spring compressor is screwed down, the valve spring retaining cap refuses to free to expose the split collet, do not continue to screw down on the compressor as there is a likelihood of damaging it.

3   Gently tap the top of the tool directly over the cap with a light hammer. This will free the cap. To avoid the compressor jumping off the valve spring retaining cap when it is tapped, hold the compressor firmly in position with one hand.

4   It is essential that the valves are kept in their correct sequence unless they are so badly worn that they are to be renewed. If they are going to be kept and used again, place them in a sheet of card having eight holes numbered 1 to 8 corresponding with the relative positions the valves were in when originally installed. Also keep the valve springs, washers and collets in their original sequence.

35 Valves and valve seats - examination and renovation

1   Examine the heads of the valves for pitting and burning, especially the exhaust valves. The valve seats should also be examined at the same time. If pitting is only slight on valves and seats they may be renovated by grinding.

2   Valve grinding is carried out as follows: Smear a trace of coarse carborundum paste on the seat face and apply a suction grinder tool to the valve head. With a semi-rotary motion, grind the valve head to its seat, lifting the valve occasionally to redistribute the grinding paste. When a dull matt even surface finish is produced on both the valve seat and the valve, then wipe off the paste and repeat the process with fine carborundum paste, lifting and turning the valve to redistribute the paste as before. A light spring placed under the valve head will greatly ease this operation. When a smooth, unbroken ring of light grey matt finish is produced, on both valve and valve seat faces, the grinding operation is complete. This can be further checked with the use of 'Engineer's Blue', if available.

3   Scrape away all carbon from the valve head and the valve stem. Carefully clean away every trace of grinding compound, taking great care to leave none in the ports or in the valve guides. Clean the valves and valve seats with a paraffin soaked rag then with a clean rag, and finally, if an airline is available, blow the valves, valve guides and valve ports clean.

4   Where bad pitting has occurred to the valve seats, it will be necessary to recut them and fit new valves. If the valve seats are so worn that they cannot be recut, then it will be necessary to fit new valve seat inserts. These latter two jobs should be entrusted to the local Skoda agent or engineering works. In practice it is very seldom that the seats are so badly worn that they require renewal. Normally, it is the valve that is too badly worn for re-use, and the owner can easily

purchase a new set of valves and match them to the seats by valve grinding.

36 Valve guides - examination

The valve guides are formed within the cylinder head casting itself - there are no separate guide sleeves. It therefore follows that if a guide bore is badly worn and the valves are a loose fit, the bores will have to be reamed and valves with oversize stems fitted. This is a job for your Skoda dealer as he is equipped for this operation.

The valve guide port dimensions are given in the Specifications.

37 Rockers and rocker shaft - dismantling and inspection

With the rocker shaft assembly removed from the cylinder head, dismantle as follows:

1   Release the circlips from the end of the shaft and remove the rockers, pedestals, springs and washers, keeping in order of removal.

2   Clean the individual components for inspection.

3   Check the rocker shaft for straightness by rolling it on a perfectly flat surface, a sheet of plate glass is ideal. A slightly bent shaft should be straightened if possible; if not, a replacement shaft is required. This is also the case if the shaft has signs of excessive wear, such as ridges worn by the rocker arms.

4   Slide the rocker arms onto their respective locations on the shaft and inspect for excess wear. No sloppiness should be apparent.

5   Inspect the wear face of the rocker arms, and the ball-end of the adjusting screws, which locate in the pushrods. If there are any signs of cracking or wear through the case-hardening of these components, they must be renewed.

6   Check the pushrods correspondingly, and also roll them on a flat surface to check for straightness. Any defective ones should be renewed (photo).

38 Tappets (cam followers) - examination and renovation

1   Clean and inspect the tappet wear faces, which bear on the camshaft lobes. Any indentations or cracks in the surface indicate serious wear, and therefore, the need for renewal.

2   Check each tappet in its respective bore: if any are loose and can readily be rocked, they should be renewed. It is most unusual to have badly worn tappet side faces.

39 Engine - reassembly (general)

1   To ensure maximum life with minimum trouble from a rebuilt

34.1 Compressing the valve spring retaining shroud to release the locking collets

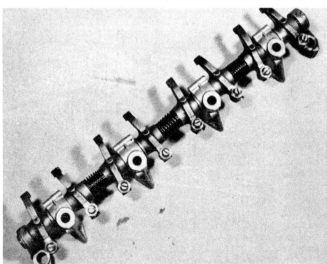

37.6 Rocker shaft unit cleaned and ready for reassembly to cylinder head

engine, not only must everything be correctly assembled, but all the parts must be spotlessly clean. All the oilways must be clear, locking washers and spring washers must always be fitted where indicated and all bearing and other working surfaces must be thoroughly lubricated during assembly. Before assembly begins renew any bolts or studs, the threads of which are in any way damaged, and whenever possible use new spring washers.

2   Apart from your normal tools, a supply of clean rag, an oil can filled with engine oil (an empty plastic detergent bottle thoroughly cleaned and washed out will invariably do just as well), a new supply of assorted spring washers and a set of new gaskets should be gathered together. A torque wrench is essential as the engine is largely made from aluminium. If a torque wrench cannot be bought then one must be borrowed as if one is not used, then it is almost a certainty that trouble will be experienced after a few thousand miles through aluminium components distorting.

40 Crankshaft - replacement

See Figs. 1.8 and 1.9.
Ensure that the crankcase is thoroughly clean and that all oilways are clear. A thin-twist drill or a pipe cleaner is useful for cleaning them out. If possible, blow them out with compressed air.
Treat the crankshaft in the same fashion and then inject engine oil

into the crankshaft oilways.
Commence work on rebuilding the engine by replacing the crankshaft and main bearings.

1   Note that at the back of each bearing is a tab which engages in locating grooves in either the crankcase or the main bearing cap housings.

2   If new bearings are being fitted, carefully clean away all traces of the protective grease with which they are coated.

3   If the old main bearing shells are to be re-used (a false economy, unless they are virtually new), fit the three upper halves (i.e. those in the actual cylinder block casting) of the main bearing shells to their location in the crankcase (photo), after wiping the locations clean.

4   With the three upper bearing shells securely in place, wipe the lower bearing cap housings and fit the three lower shell bearings to their caps ensuring that the right shell goes into the right cap, if the old bearings are being refitted.

5   Fit the thrust washer onto the front main bearing journal of the crankshaft (photo), and lubricate. The lubrication grooves on the washer must face the crankshaft web.

6   Generously lubricate the crankshaft journals and the upper and lower main bearing shells and carefully lower the crankshaft into place (photo).

7   The next task is to fit the rear main bearing caps. The seal strips in the side joints of the rear main bearing caps must be fitted as shown in photo. This done, jointing compound should be very sparingly applied

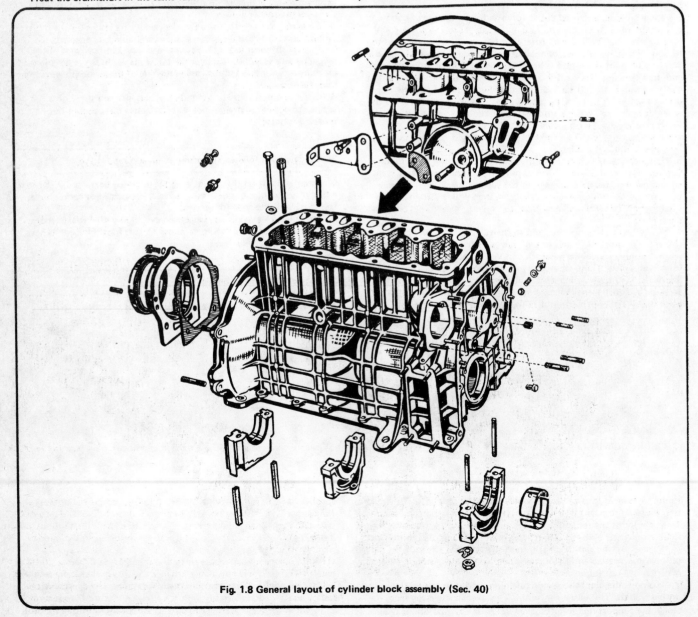

Fig. 1.8 General layout of cylinder block assembly (Sec. 40)

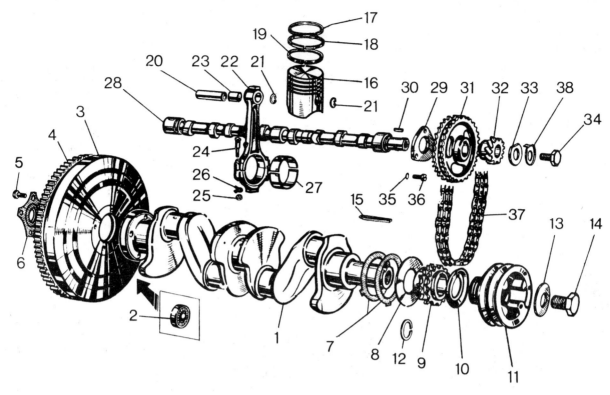

Fig. 1.9. General layout of crankshaft and camshaft assemblies (Sec. 40)

1 Crankshaft	11 Crankshaft pulley	20 Gudgeon pin	29 Thrust plate
2 Bearing	12 Compensating washer	21 Circlip	30 Woodruff key
3 Flywheel	13 Washer	22 Connecting rod assembly	31 Sprocket
4 Ring gear	14 Fixing screw	23 Bush	32 Worm wheel
5 Flywheel screw	15 Woodruff key	24 Connecting rod bolt	33 Washer
6 Bearing cover	16 Piston	25 Connecting rod nut	34 Bolt
7 Thrust ring	17 Top piston ring (chromium)	26 Tab washer	35 Spring washer
8 Support ring	18 Stepped piston ring	27 Big-end bearing shell	36 Screw cheesehead
9 Sprocket	19 Oil control piston ring	28 Camshaft	37 Timing chain (Duplex)
10 Oil thrower			38 Lock washer

40.3 Fitting main bearing shells to block

40.5 Thrust washer on front journal of crankshaft

40.6 Lowering crankshaft into position in block

to the joint faces, and also to the block location recess. Place the main bearing cap into position and tap it home with a non-metallic hammer. Temporarily fit the retaining nuts and washers (photo), clamping just tight enough to retain the cap in position. Fit the middle (photo) and front main bearing caps and shells in similar fashion, the location tag of the thrust washer to face upwards and locate in the slot of the front main bearing cap (photo).

8   To check the crankshaft endfloat, temporarily fit the following onto the crankshaft: The thrust ring with oil grooves facing away from the block, the support ring (photo), the Woodruff key, the timing chain

sprocket, the dished washer, the driving pulley, compensating washer, flat washer and retaining bolt. Tighten the bolt to the specified torque pressure. Rotate the crankshaft to ensure it freely rotates, without any binding or tight-spots. Now insert a screwdriver between the middle main bearing and the crankshaft web and lever backwards and forwards. The endfloat should be between 0.001 and 0.003 in. (0.04 and 0.10 mm). If it is not, then exchange the thrust washer for one of a suitable thickness. When the correct endfloat is achieved, remove the pulley and sprocket assembly with the exception of the 'support ring'.

9   Tighten the main bearing cap nuts to the specified torque (photo),

40.7a Oil seal strips located in rear main bearing cap

40.7b Rear main bearing caps in position with seals prior to tightening the nuts and locking with tab washers

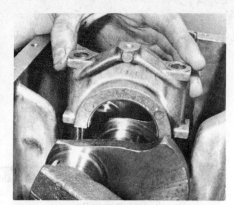
40.7c Fitting the middle main bearing cap. Note that the oil strainer strut location bolt hole is offset to the front

40.7d Thrust washer tag in location slot in front main bearing cap

40.8 Fitting the thrust washer (note oil grooves) and support ring to the crankshaft

40.9 Tightening the main bearing cap nuts to the specified torque

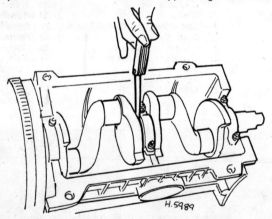
Fig. 1.10. Method of checking the crankshaft endfloat (Sec. 40)

41.4 Model 110LS piston crown showing arrow marking

43.4 Piston with ring compressor in position

44.5 Connecting rod and cap number marking

44.6 Tightening the connecting rod bearing cap nuts to the specified torque

and lock in position by bending the lock washer tags against the nuts on the bearing cap faces.

10 Test the crankshaft for freedom of rotation; should it be stiff to turn or possess high-spots a careful inspection must be made of the crankshaft journals and main bearings, preferably by a qualified mechanic with a micrometer, to get to the root of the problem. However, this problem is seldom experienced.

41 Pistons and connecting rods - assembly

1 If the existing pistons are being re-used, then they must be mated to the same connecting rod with the same gudgeon pin. If new pistons are being fitted it does not matter with which connecting rod or gudgeon pin they are used.
2 Lay the correct piston adjacent to each connecting rod and remember that the same rod and piston must go back into the same bore. If new pistons are being used it is only necessary to ensure that the right connecting rod is placed in each bore.
3 Fit a gudgeon pin circlip in position at one end of the gudgeon pin hole in the piston.
4 Place one piston in boiling water for a few minutes. Remove it from the water and quickly wipe away any excess oil or water with a non-fluffy rag. Take care not to burn yourself during this process. **Note:** It is essential that the piston is assembled to the connecting rod as follows:

Models 100, 100L and — Splash hole in connecting rod big-end
110L   faces the split piston skirt
Model 110LS   — Splash hole in big-end to point opposite
*   the arrow on piston crown (photo)*

5 Hold the connecting rod in position inside the piston. Push the gudgeon pin through the piston and connecting rod small-end until it contacts the fitted circlip. Fit the remaining circlip in its groove. Repeat this process with the other three pistons and connecting rods.
6 When all four pistons are assembled to their connecting rods, the following items should be checked:
   a) *When the piston and connecting rod assembly is held horizontal, the connecting rod should be free to fall by its own weight.*
   b) *Gripping the piston firmly with one hand and the connecting rod with the other, ensure that the connecting rod cannot be rocked from side to side on the gudgeon pin. It is normal for there to be a sliding movement from one side to the other.*
   c) *Check that all the gudgeon pin retaining circlips are firmly seated in their grooves. It is essential that new circlips are used.*

42 Piston rings - replacement

1 Check that the piston ring grooves and oilways are thoroughly clean and unblocked. Piston rings must always be fitted over the head of the piston and never from the bottom.
2 The easiest method to use when fitting rings is to wrap a 0.020 in. (0.50 mm) feeler gauge, round the top of the piston and place the rings one at a time, starting with the bottom oil control ring, over the feeler gauge.
3 The feeler gauge, complete with ring, can then be slid down the piston over the other piston ring grooves until the correct groove is reached. The piston ring is then slid gently off the feeler gauge into the groove.
4 An alternative method is to fit the rings by holding them slightly open with the thumbs and both of your index fingers. This method requires a steady hand and great care as it is easy to open the ring too much and break it. When fitting the top ring ensure the chamfered edge faces up or if fitting a set of replacement rings into a worn bore, the top ring may be stepped and this step should face upwards. This acts as a safeguard to avoid the ring fouling the wear ridge at the top of the cylinder bore. Always gap check the new rings in their respective bores (see Section 23). Always follow the manufacturer's instructions most carefully when fitting a replacement ring set to used pistons.

43 Pistons and connecting rods - replacement

1 Clean and lubricate each cylinder bore with a good quality engine oil.

2 It is essential that each piston and connecting rod assembly is replaced in the bore from which it was originally removed.
3 Locate the piston rings on each piston so that the ring gaps are staggered in relation to each other by 90°, with the oil scraper ring at 45° offset from the gudgeon pin. On 110LS series engines there are only three piston rings and the ring gaps should therefore be staggered through 120°.
4 Lubricate the pistons and rings and install them into their respective cylinders. The piston rings should be compressed with a ring compressor. Ensure when clamped round the piston that it is 'squarely' located and is compressing all of the rings (photo).
5 The pistons must be inserted down the bores with the expansion split in the skirt facing to the camshaft side, or on the 110LS series which does not have a split skirt piston, the marking arrow to the camshaft.

44 Connecting rods to crankshaft - reassembly

During the following procedures it is essential that the utmost cleanliness is observed as any dirt caught between the crankpins and bearings will score the crankshaft journals and will thus lead to early bearing failure.
1 Wipe the connecting rod half of the big-end bearing cap and the underside of the shell bearing clean, and fit the shell bearing in position with its locating tongue groove engaged with the corresponding rod.
2 If the old bearings are nearly new and are being refitted, then ensure they are replaced in their correct locations on the correct rods.
3 Generously lubricate the crankpin journals with engine oil and turn the crankshaft so that the crankpin is in the most advantageous position for the connecting rod to be drawn onto it.
4 Wipe the connecting rod bearing cap and back of the shell bearing clean and fit the shell bearing in position ensuring that the locating tongue at the back of the bearing engages with the locating groove in the connecting rod cap.
5 Generously lubricate the shell bearing and offer up the connecting rod bearing cap to the connecting rod. Note that each rod and cap are numbered as a pair according to their respective bore. Therefore always fit the cap and rod numbers opposite each other (photo).
6 Fit the connecting rod bolt self-locking nuts and tighten to the specified torque (photo).
7 When all the connecting rods have been fitted, rotate the crankshaft to check that everything is free, and that there are no high-spots causing binding.

45 Crankshaft oilseal (rear) - replacement

1 To fit the new oilseal into its housing, place the housing onto a flat surface on the workbench.
2 Insert the seal into its housing recess so that the coil spring side faces inwards (the serrated lip and direction arrow facing out) (photo).
3 Before fitting to the engine, smear some sealing compound lightly over the inner face of the housing and fit the gasket over the two location pegs, then lightly smear the gasket with some sealant.
4 Fit the seal carefully over the crankshaft rear flange and insert and tighten the five retaining screws and spring washers (photo), to the torque specified.

46 Camshaft - replacement

1 Insert the camshaft into position in the block, having first lubricated the location apertures.
2 Oil and refit the camshaft thrust plate, and retain with the three bolts and spring washers (photo).
3 Rotate the camshaft to ensure it turns freely.

47 Timing gear, chain and cover - replacement

1 If not already fitted, slide the compensating washer onto the crankshaft.
2 Fit the camshaft and crankshaft keys to their respective keyways.
3 Locate the camshaft and crankshaft chain sprockets into the chain so that there are twelve link hinge pins between the respective marking

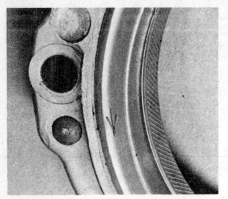

45.2 Position of rear oil seal in its housing

45.4 Rear oil seal fitted into position

46.2 Camshaft thrust plate in position

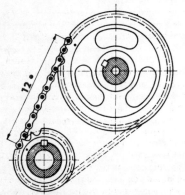

Fig. 1.11 Camshaft and crankshaft positions for correct timing (Sec. 47)

47.4 Crankshaft and camshaft sprockets and timing chain in position

47.5 The distributor driving pinion in position on the camshaft

47.6 Dished oil thrower washer in position against the crankshaft sprocket

48.2 Oil pump suction tube unit in position

48.3 Fitting the sump

49.1 Crankshaft pulley in position

49.3 The clutch belly plate in position

49.4 The flywheel in position on the crankshaft with the locking bolts being torqued to the specified reading

dots on the sprocket outer faces (see Fig. 1.11).

4 Turn the two shafts so that the keys line up with the sprocket keyways, and fit the chain and sprockets as a single assembly, to the shafts (photo).

5 Now fit the distributor driving pinion with the boss facing towards the camshaft sprocket. Fit the retaining washers and bolt (photo). Tighten to the specified torque and lock by bending over the tab washer.

6 Fit the dished oil thrower washer to the crankshaft and locate over the Woodruff key, so that the concave side faces away from the crankshaft sprocket (photo).

7 Apply some jointing compound to the timing chest and block flanges and locate the gasket in position on the block. Lubricate the chain and sprockets, then carefully fit the timing cover into position, complete with the oil pump gears. Secure the timing chest with the setscrews, but do not over-tighten.

48 Oil pump suction unit and sump - assembly

1 Lubricate the gears and then smear the location flanges of the pump suction tube and timing chest with sealing compound and place the gasket in position.

2 Carefully fit the suction tube unit and retain with the bolts and spring washers, over the pump, and the tube filter to the middle main bearing cap (photo).

3 Ensure that the sump and block facing flanges are clean, smear them with jointing compound and fit together complete with the gasket (photo). Insert the retaining bolts and washers and tighten to the specified torque.

49 Crankshaft pulley and flywheel - assembly

1 Slide the pulley over the crankshaft and locate the keyway over the Woodruff key (photo).

2 Fit the compensating washer and flat washer, over the bolt and screw into crankshaft. Tighten to the specified torque pressure.

3 Fit to the clutch housing the belly plate cover (photo).

4 Now fit the flywheel so that the crankshaft and flywheel markings are in line and retain with the locking washer plate and bolts. Tighten the bolts to the specified torque and bend over the ears of the locking tabs to retain in position (photo).

5 With the flywheel fully bolted in position the clutch unit may now be fitted. The assembly procedure is fully described in the Clutch Chapter.

50 Valves and valve springs - replacement

1 Fit each valve in turn, wiping down and lubricating each valve stem as it is inserted into the same valve guide from which it was removed (photo).

2 Build up each valve assembly by first fitting the valve springs and then the valve spring shroud (photo), (and on the earlier models the

safety stop rings to their grooves).

3 With the base of the valve compressor on the valve head, compress the valve spring until the cotters can be slipped into place in the cotter grooves (photo). Gently release the compressor. **Note:** Great care should be taken not to compress the inlet valve springs any more than is necessary to replace the cotters, otherwise valve seals (if fitted) will be damaged.

4 Repeat this procedure until all eight valves and valve springs are fitted.

51 Rocker shaft - assembly

1 Oil the rocker shaft and reassemble the pedestals, springs, washers, etc., in the reverse sequence to that used for dismantling.

2 When the retaining circlips are in position, check that the individual rockers and pedestals turn freely (except for the spring tension) on the shaft.

52 Cylinder head - assembly to block

After checking that both the cylinders/block and cylinder head mating surfaces are perfectly clean, lubricate each cylinder with engine oil.

1 Always use a new head gasket as the old one will be compressed and incapable of giving a good seal.

2 Two types of head gasket are currently available and these are as follows:

S100 — Semex and Czechoslovakian gaskets
S110 — Semex gasket only

Be sure to fit the correct type if it is for an S110 Series. The Semex gasket is recognisable by its grey fire rings, whilst the Czechoslovakian type has copper coloured fire rings.

3 Fit the gasket to the cylinder block face - the gasket only fits correctly in one position with the mark 'Donit' facing up as confirmation (photo).

4 Place the cylinder head in position over the gasket, locating over the four head studs.

5 Fit the number 2 and 3 head bolts in position (see tightening sequence, Fig. 1.13), complete with the air cleaner bracket, and finger tighten.

6 Replace the remaining bolts (10 mm) and stud nuts (8 mm) finger-tight. The dynamo/alternator bracket fits under the number '14' stud nut (photo).

7 Lubricate and insert the tappets into their respective apertures.

8 Insert the pushrods through the head and locate in the tappets (photo).

9 Refit the rocker assembly to the cylinder head, carefully locating the rocker arms to pushrods and insert the location bolts and flat washers and at the ends, the two Allen screws.

10 Tighten the bolts, nuts and Allen screws gradually in the tightening sequence shown in Fig. 1.13, and finally tighten the sequence to the torque pressure quoted in the Specifications.

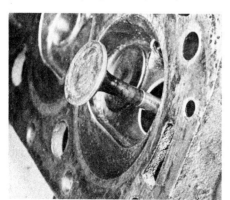

50.1 Fitting valve to its guide

50.2 Fitting valve springs over the valve stem

50.3 Fitting the cotters in position between the shroud and valve stem groove with the aid of a compressor

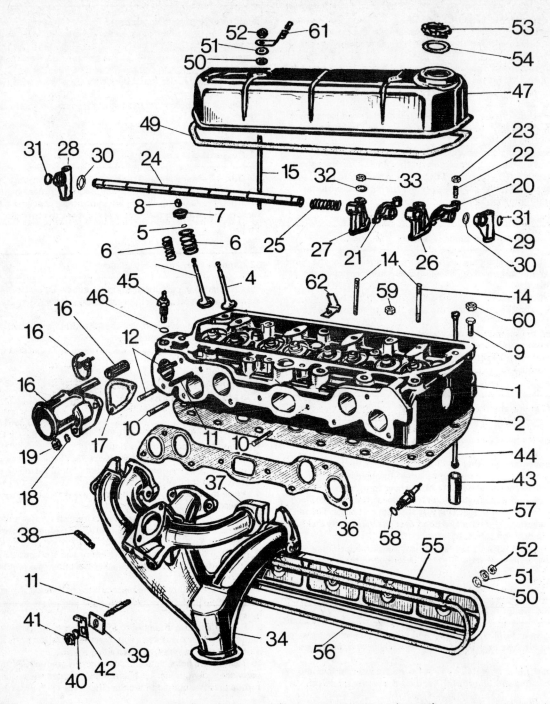

Fig. 1.12. General layout of cylinder head unit, and manifolds (Sec. 52)

1 Cylinder head	15 Stud cylinder head cover	29 Support rocker shaft - front	44 Push rod
2 Cylinder head gasket	16 Thermostat housing	30 Spring washer	45 Thermometer transmitter
3 Inlet valve	16a Hose	31 Circlip	46 Sealing washer
4 Exhaust valve	16b Clip	32 Washer	47 Rocker cover
5 Valve circlip	17 Gasket thermostat housing	33 Nut	49 Cover gasket
6 Valve spring outer	18 Spring washer	34 Exhaust manifold	50 Sealing washer
6a Valve spring inner	19 Nut	36 Flange gasket	51 Washer
7 Spring pan	20 Front rocker arm	37 Induction manifold	52 Nut
8 Cotters/Two parts	21 Rear rocker arm	38 Carburettor stud	53 Oil filler cap
9 Screw generator strut	22 Adjuster rocker arm	39 Adaptor	54 Gasket
10 Manifold studs	23 Nut	40 Washer/spring washer	55 Push rod cover
11 Manifold studs	24 Rocker shaft	41 Nut	56 Gasket, push rod cover
12 Stud	25 Spring rocker arm	42 Pipe clip	57 Spark plugs
14 Stud/screw for rocker arm	26 Support rocker shaft	42a Stud manifold	58 Spark plug washer
	27 Support rocker shaft	43 Valve tappet	60 Cover nut
	28 Support rocker shaft - rear		61 Fuel feed pipe support
			62 Connecting pipe support

52.3 Cylinder head gasket in position over cylinder block studs

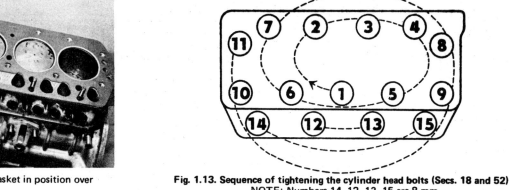

Fig. 1.13. Sequence of tightening the cylinder head bolts (Secs. 18 and 52)
NOTE: Numbers 14, 12, 13, 15 are 8 mm
All others are 10 mm

52.6 The dynamo/alternator bracket position

52.8 Inserting the pushrods

52.12a Fitting the tappet side cover

52.12b The tappet side cover retaining nut and washers

53.5 Adjusting the valve clearances

11 Tighten the rocker pedestal bolts to the specified torque.
12 Fit the tappet side cover (photo) and gasket - which should be smeared with a sealing solution. Retain with the four nuts, rubber washers and dished washers (photo). Do not overtighten.

53 Valve clearance (tappet) - adjustment

1 The valve adjustments should be made with the engine cold. The importance of correct rocker arm/valve stem clearances cannot be overstressed as they vitally affect the performance of the engine.
2 If the clearances are set too open, the efficiency of the engine is reduced as the valves open later and close earlier than was intended. If, on the other hand, the clearances are set too close there is a danger that the stem and pushrods will expand upon heating and not allow the valves to close properly which will cause burning of the valve head and possible warping.
3 If the engine is in the car, to gain access to the rockers, undo and remove the rocker cover bolts and washers. Carefully lift away the

rocker cover.
4 It is important that the clearance is set when the tappet of the valve being adjusted is on the heel of the cam (i.e. opposite the peak). This can be done by carrying out the adjustments in the following order, which also avoids turning the crankshaft more than necessary:

Valve fully open	Check and adjust
Valve No. 8	*Valve No. 1*
Valve No. 6	*Valve No. 3*
Valve No. 4	*Valve No. 5*
Valve No. 7	*Valve No. 2*
Valve No. 1	*Valve No. 8*
Valve No. 3	*Valve No. 6*
Valve No. 5	*Valve No. 4*
Valve No. 2	*Valve No. 7*

5 The correct valve clearance is given in technical data at the beginning of this Chapter. It is obtained by slackening the hexagonal locknut with a spanner while holding the ball pin against rotation with an adjustable spanner as shown in this photograph. Then still pressing

down with the adjustable spanner, insert a feeler gauge of the required thickness between the valve stem head and the rocker arm and adjust the ball pin until the feeler gauge will just move in and out without nipping. Then, still holding the ball pin in the correct position, tighten the locknut.

6 Smear the rocker cover gasket with sealant and replace complete with cover over the rockers, securing with bolts and washers.

54 Engine - final assembly

1 The following items in this Section can now be refitted to the engine. Although they can be fitted at this stage, the thermostat, carburettor, and distributor are best left off the engine assembly during refitting to the car, thus avoiding the possibility of damage. We therefore suggest that they are eventually fitted when the engine is fully positioned in the car.

2 Fit the fuel pump complete with gaskets and insulating washer.

3 Refit the oil filter bowl complete with new filter and sealing washers. Do not overtighten the bowl retaining bolt.

4 Assemble the water pump and gasket which should be smeared with a sealing compound. Slide the pump and gasket over the four retaining studs and retain with the nuts and spring washers.

5 Refit the fan and support arm assembly, to its position on the block, over the four studs, ensuring that the gaskets and plate are fitted (photo). The fan pulley can also be fitted at this stage. The correct belt tension is established by the number of shims used, between the fan pulley halves. The correct lateral play in the middle of the belt run is approximately 2 in (50 mm). **Note:** The fan belt runs in the outer crankshaft pulley channel.

6 Fit the fan blade guard rim in position and also the strut between the mounting bracket and water pump stud (photo).

7 Attach the right-hand rear engine mounting bracket in correct relative position to the protruding flange face with the two bolts. The upper bolt also retains the alternator/dynamo bracket.

8 Refit the alternator/dynamo and drivebelt (photo). Tension the belt by hinging the alternator/dynamo as required so that there is approximately 0.5 in (12.7 mm) lateral play in the middle of the belt run. Tighten the bolts to secure.

9 Fit the left-hand engine mounting bracket to the fan mounting bracket.

10 Fit the feed pipe to the water pump from the heater and attach the bypass hose into the 'T' section junction from the cylinder block.

11 Place the manifold gasket over the studs and refit the exhaust manifold (photo) and inlet manifold. It is vitally important that the manifold mating faces are cleaned of any previous gasket pieces that may have stuck in position, if the manifolds are to seal correctly. The manifolds fit over the studs and are retained by nuts and washers. Note the special square section washers that are bridged over the studs between the inlet and exhaust manifolds. Also fit the vacuum tube retaining clip between the nut and square washer of the inlet/exhaust retaining stud (photo). If they are not already fitted, the downpipe/s and silencer assembly can be fitted to the exhaust manifold pipe flange, complete with gasket. Again, check that the flange faces are clean. At this stage the exhaust silencer mounting bracket is also fitted together with the stay rod. The bracket is fitted round the silencer and bolted to the mounting lugs and the top of the curved bracket is located in its upper and lower sections by the gearbox/engine mounting bolts (photo). Note that the lower section is spaced by a small bush between the bracket and the belly plate, fitted over the bolt.

12 Refit the engine mounting bar to the mounting brackets, slot into position with the rubbers and tighten the nuts to secure (photo).

55 Engine and transaxle - assembly

1 The engine and transaxle can now be reassembled (photo). Proceed carefully when inserting the mainshaft of the gearbox into the clutch disc and crankshaft bearing. Do not force the gearbox in any way. If difficulties are encountered, check that the clutch disc is centralised. When in place, replace the nuts and bolts and tighten to the recommended torque setting.

56 Half-axles - refitting

1 Refit the half-axle assemblies complete with wheel hubs and struts. This procedure is the reverse of the dismantling sequence, but be sure to refit the exact number and thickness of bearing preload shims (photo), to each side as were originally extracted. Always fit a new gasket with the bearing cover and ensure that the breather hole is at the top, as in the axle flange on the gearbox. If on assembly the half-axle radial movement is stiff, fit another or thicker gasket as required. If a new crownwheel and pinion assembly has been fitted, the correct number and thickness of preload shims has to be fitted to ensure the correct meshing of the crownwheel and pinion (see Gearbox Chapter).

2 An assistant will be required to support the brake drum end of the half-axle assembly when fitting to the transaxle.

3 Smear some sealant solution over the respective flange faces and fit the gasket over the studs.

4 Then offer the half-axle to the transaxle. Rotate the brake drum to align the knuckle joint with the slot in the differential. When in place, slide home the outer cover and fit the six nuts and spring washers. Check when in place that the half-axles swivel freely. **Note:** When fitting (or removing) the right-hand half-axle unit, it is not essential, but easier, if the starter motor is removed.

5 Refit the starter motor.

57 Engine and transaxle - replacement in car

Reposition the engine and transaxle assembly under the car and then proceed as follows:

1 Attach the hoist around the engine securely, to give a centrally balanced lift; then raise the assembly slightly.

2 Place a jack under the gearbox.

3 Raise slightly the engine/transaxle assembly. **Note:** If the distributor is in position on the engine, ensure when lifting that the diaphragm does not foul the rear panel, if this is also in position. At the forward end, the thermostat housing, if fitted, should clear the rear body bulkhead panel.

4 Insert the rear suspension coil springs into their location channels, and over the telescopic shock absorbers.

5 Now continue raising the engine and transaxle in unison and locate the coil springs into their recess channels in the body at the top. The shock absorber studs at the bottom are located through their respective holes in the radius struts. This can be made easier if a further jack is available to raise the brake drum and outer axle, so that the nut, spring washers and rubber bushes can be fitted to retain the shock absorber, and spring in position.

6 Align the gearbox mountings and fit the four retaining bolts, flat and spring washers.

7 Align the engine bearer bar each side under the body and retain with the bolts, springs and flat washers.

8 Locate the thrust arms over their location studs and retain with nuts and spring washers.

9 Now tighten the engine, gearbox mounting, shock absorber, strut arm retaining nuts and bolts, to their respective torque pressures as given in the Specifications Section.

10 Remove the hoist and jack, and refit the axle safety limiting straps and the right and left-hand splash plates.

11 Refit the brake pipes and cables. The system will have to be bled and the brakes checked for adjustment (see Braking System Chapter).

12 Reconnect the speedometer cable.

13 Reconnect the gear selector rod. An assistant is useful to operate the gearlever in the car: select 1st or 3rd gear and then locate the locking bolt into the recess in the rod and retain in position by tightening the nut.

14 Refit the carburettor and its attachments.

15 Refit the thermostat to its housing and fit the rubber connecting pipe and clips. Fit the housing to the studs in the cylinder head, and retain with nuts and washers. Connect the rubber pipe to the radiator top hose connection, and secure with the clip.

16 Connect the radiator bottom hose to the water pump..

17 Reconnect the oil pipes. The longer pipe is the oil feed from the timing chest connection to the base of the oil cooler. The top hose from the oil cooler is located in connection with the oil pressure switch and gauge pipe at the rear of the block (photo). Ensure that all connecting pipes are in good condition before fitting. Always use new

54.5 Fan bracket support arm flange to cylinder block gaskets and plate in position

54.6 The fan bracket support arm strut in position

54.8 The alternator in position

54.11a Fitting the exhaust manifold

54.11b Vacuum tube location clip

54.11c Exhaust silencer mounting

54.12 Engine mounting bar to mounting bracket (LH)

55.1 Transaxle to engine assembly

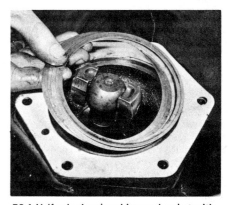

56.1 Half-axle showing shims and gasket with breather hole at the top

57.17 View showing oil gauge sender unit, oil pipe to gauge, and oil cooler pipe in position

57.21 Filling the engine with oil

sealing washers when refitting the pipes. Then refit the splash guard.

18 Reconnect the petrol pipe connection from the carburettor to the fuel pump.

19 Refit the distributor. This will have to be timed. (See Ignition Chapter).

20 Refit the spark plugs, after checking that their gaps are correctly set. Then refit the plug leads, distributor cap and the vacuum tube from the carburettor.

21 Refill the engine (photo) and gearbox with the recommended lubricants (ensure the drain plugs and level plug in the gearbox are in place and tightened to the correct torque).

22 Refit the clutch slave cylinder to the top of the gearbox and reconnect the hydraulic pipe. Adjust the clearance of the operating rod, as described in the Clutch Chapter, and replace the protection cover and spring clamp.

23 Refill the cooling system and check for leaks.

24 Remake all electrical connections (except battery). Check that all the fittings and attachments are securely in position and then reconnect the battery (negative terminal last).

25 Replace the air filter unit.

26 The car is now ready for starting (see following Section).

58 Engine - initial start-up after overhaul or major repair

1 Make sure that the battery is fully charged and that all lubricants, coolant and fuel are replenished.

2 If the fuel system has been dismantled it will require several revolutions of the engine on the starter motor to pump the petrol up the carburettor.

3 As soon as the engine fires and runs, keep it going at a fast tickover only (no faster) and bring it up to normal working temperature.

4 As the engine warms-up there will be odd smells and some smoke from parts getting hot and burning off oil deposits. The signs to look for are leaks of water or oil which will be obvious, if serious. Check also the exhaust pipe and manifold connections as these do not always 'find' their exact gas tight position until the warmth and vibration have acted on them and it is almost certain that they will need tightening further. This should be done, of course, with the engine stopped.

5 When normal running temperature has been reached, adjust the engine idle speed as described in Chapter 3.

6 Stop the engine and wait a few minutes to see if any lubricant or coolant is dripping out when the engine is stationary.

7 Recheck the fan and alternator belt tensions and adjust if necessary.

8 Road test the car to check that the timing is correct and that the engine is giving the necessary smoothness and power. Do not race the engine - if new bearings and/or pistons have been fitted it should be treated as a new engine and run in at a reduced speed for, at least, the first 300 miles (500 km).

59 Fault diagnosis - engine

Symptom	Reason/s	Remedy
Engine fails to turn over when starter control operated		
No current at starter motor	Flat or defective battery	Charge or replace battery. Push start car.
	Loose battery leads	Tighten both terminals and earth ends of earth leads.
	Defective starter solenoid or switch or broken wiring	Run a wire direct from the battery to the starter motor or by-pass the solenoid.
	Engine earth strap disconnected	Check and retighten strap.
Current at starter motor	Jammed starter motor drive pinion	Place car in gear and rock to and fro.
	Defective starter motor	Remove and recondition.
Engine turns over but will not start		
No spark at spark plug	Ignition damp or wet	Wipe dry the distributor cap and ignition leads.
	Ignition leads to spark plugs loose	Check and tighten at both spark plug and distributor cap ends.
	Shorted or disconnected low tension leads	Check the wiring on the CB and SW terminals of the coil and to the distributor.
	Dirty, incorrectly set, or pitted contact breaker points	Clean, file smooth and adjust.
	Faulty condenser	Check contact breaker points for arcing, remove and fit new.
	Defective ignition switch	By-pass switch with wire.
	Ignition leads connected wrong way round	Remove and replace leads to spark plugs in correct order.
	Faulty coil	Remove and fit new coil.
	Contact breaker point spring earthed or broken	Check spring is not touching metal part of distributor. Check insulator washers are correctly placed. Renew points if the spring is broken.
No fuel at carburettor float chamber or at jets	No petrol in petrol tank	Refill tank!
	Vapour lock in fuel line (in hot conditions or at high altitude)	Blow into petrol tank, allow engine to cool, or apply a cold wet rag to the fuel line.
	Blocked float chamber needle valve	Remove, clean and replace.
	Fuel pump filter blocked	Remove, clean and replace.
	Choked or blocked carburettor jets	Dismantle and clean.
	Faulty fuel pump	Remove, overhaul and replace.
Engine stalls and will not start		
Excess of petrol in cylinder or carburettor	Too much choke allowing too rich a mixture to wet plugs	Remove and dry spark plugs or with wide open throttle, push start the car.
	Float damaged or leaking or needle not seating	Remove, examine, clean and replace float and needle valve as necessary.
	Float lever incorrectly adjusted	Remove and adjust correctly.
No spark at spark plug	Ignition failure - sudden	Check over low and high tension circuits for breaks in wiring.
	Ignition failure - misfiring precludes total stoppage	Check contact breaker points, clean and adjust. Renew condenser if faulty.
	Ignition failure - in severe rain or after traversing water splash	Dry out ignition leads and distributor cap.
No fuel at jets	No petrol in petrol tank	Refill tank!
	Petrol tank breather choked	Remove petrol cap and clean out breather hole or pipe.
	Sudden obstruction in carburettor(s)	Check jets, filter, and needle valve in float chamber for blockage.
	Water in fuel system	Drain tank and blow out fuel lines.
Engine misfires or idles unevenly		
Intermittent spark at spark plug	Ignition leads loose	Check and tighten as necessary at spark plug and distributor cap ends.
	Battery leads loose on terminals	Check and tighten terminal leads.
	Battery earth strap loose on body attachment point	Check and tighten earth lead to body attachment point.
Intermittent sparking at spark plug	Engine earth lead loose	Tighten lead.
	Low tension leads to terminals on coil loose	Check and tighten leads if found loose.
	Low tension lead from CB terminal side to distributor loose	Check and tighten if found loose.
	Dirty, or incorrectly gapped plugs	Remove, clean and regap.
	Dirty, incorrectly set, or pitted contact breaker points	Clean, file smooth, and adjust.
	Tracking across inside of distributor cover	Remove and fit new cover.
	Ignition too retarded	Check and adjust ignition timing.
	Faulty coil	Remove and fit new coil.

Symptom	Reason/s	Remedy
Fuel shortage at engine	Mixture too weak	Check jets, float chamber needle valve, and filters for obstruction. Clean as necessary. Carburettors incorrectly adjusted.
	Air leak in carburettor	Remove and overhaul carburettor.
	Air leak at inlet manifold to cylinder head, or inlet manifold to carburettor	Test by pouring oil along joints. Bubbles indicate leak. Renew manifold gasket as appropriate.
Lack of power and poor compression		
Mechanical wear	Incorrect valve clearances	Adjust rocker arms to take up wear.
	Burnt out exhaust valves	Remove cylinder head and renew defective valves.
	Sticking or leaking valves	Remove cylinder head, clean, check and renew valves as necessary.
	Weak or broken valve springs	Check and renew as necessary.
	Worn valve guides or stems	Renew valve guides and valves.
	Worn pistons and piston rings	Dismantle engine, renew pistons and rings.
Fuel/air mixture leaking from cylinder	Burnt out exhaust valves	Remove cylinder head, renew defective valves.
	Sticking or leaking valves	Remove cylinder head, clean, check, and renew valves as necessary.
	Worn valve guides and stems	Remove cylinder head and renew valves and valve guides.
	Weak or broken valve springs	Remove cylinder head, renew defective springs.
	Blown cylinder head gasket (accompanied by increase in noise)	Remove cylinder head and fit new gasket.
	Worn pistons and piston rings	Dismantle engine, renew pistons and rings.
	Worn or scored cylinder bores	Dismantle engine, rebore, renew pistons and rings.
Incorrect adjustments	Ignition timing wrongly set. Too advanced or retarded	Check and reset ignition timing.
	Contact breaker points incorrectly gapped	Check and reset contact breaker points.
	Incorrect valve clearances	Check and reset rocker arm to valve stem gap.
	Incorrectly set spark plugs	Remove, clean and regap.
	Carburation too rich or too weak	Tune carburettor for optimum performance.
Carburation and ignition faults	Dirty contact breaker points	Remove, clean and replace.
	Fuel filters blocked causing poor top end performance through fuel starvation	Dismantle, inspect, clean, and replace all fuel filters.
	Distributor automatic balance weights or vacuum advance and retard mechanisms not functioning correctly	Overhaul distributor.
	Faulty fuel pump giving top end fuel starvation	Remove, overhaul, or fit exchange reconditioned fuel pump.
Excessive oil consumption		
Oil being burnt by engine	Excessively worn valve stems and valve guides	Remove cylinder head and fit new valves and valve guides.
	Worn piston rings	Fit oil control rings to existing pistons or purchase new pistons.
	Worn pistons and cylinder bores	Fit new pistons and rings, rebore cylinders.
	Excessive piston ring gap allowing blow-up	Fit new piston rings and set gap correctly.
	Piston oil return holes choked	Decarbonise engine and pistons.
Oil being lost due to leaks	Leaking oil filter gasket	Inspect and fit new gasket as necessary.
	Leaking rocker cover gasket	Inspect and fit new gasket as necessary.
	Leaking timing gear cover gasket	Inspect and fit new gasket as necessary.
	Leaking sump gasket	Inspect and fit new gasket as necessary.
	Loose sump plug	Tighten, fit new gasket if necessary.
Unusual noises from engine		
Excessive clearances due to mechanical wear	Worn valve gear (noisy tapping from rocker box)	Inspect and renew rocker shaft, rocker arms, and ball pins as necessary.
	Worn big-end bearing (regular heavy knocking)	Drop sump, if bearings broken up clean out oil pump and oilways, fit new bearings. If bearings not broken but worn fit bearing shells.
	Worn timing chain and gears (rattling from front of engine)	Remove timing cover, fit new timing wheels and timing chain.
	Worn main bearings (rumbling and vibration)	Drop sump, remove crankshaft, if bearing worn but not broken up, renew. If broken up strip oil pump and clean out oilways.
	Worn crankshaft (knocking, rumbling and vibration)	Regrind crankshaft, fit new main and big end bearings.

Chapter 2 Cooling system

Contents

Specifications

Type of system	Pressurised, centrifugal pump, fan assisted. Thermostatic temperature control
Radiator cap pressure	4 lb/sq in (0.28 kg/sq cm)

Fan

Number of blades	9
Fan diameter	12 in (304.8 mm)
Fanbelt tension	2 in (50 mm) free-play between water pump and dynamo/alternator

Water pump

Type	Centrifugal
Water pump drive	Belt from crankshaft pulley

Thermostat

Type	Bellows - opens at 82°C (180°F)
	- fully open at 90°C (194°F)

Drain tap location

Radiator	Bottom water compartment
Heater unit	Heater radiator control valve under rear passenger seat

Capacity of cooling system	12 Imp. pints (7 litres)

Torque wrench setting

	lb f ft	kg fm
Water pump pulley nut	11	1.5

1 General description and maintenance

The engine cooling water is circulated by a thermo-siphon, water pump assisted system. The cooling system is pressurised, this increases the temperature that the water can attain before boiling. If the water reaches boiling point it will increase the pressure in the cooling system to more than 4 lb/sq in. (0.28 kg/sq cm). This pressure will lift the internal part of the radiator cap off its seat, thus exposing the overflow pipe down which the steam from the boiling water escapes. In this way the cap acts as a safety valve and relieves excess pressure in the cooling system.

It is, therefore, important to check that the radiator cap is in good condition and that the spring behind the sealing washer has not weakened. Most garages have a special machine in which radiator caps can be tested.

The cooling system comprises the radiator, top, bottom and intermediate hoses and heater hoses.

There is also a nine bladed cooling fan, driven by belt from the crankshaft pulley, mounted on a support arm from the cylinder block.

The system functions in the following fashion. Cold water in the bottom of the radiator circulates up the lower radiator hose to the water pump, where it is pushed round the water passages in the cylinder block, helping to keep the cylinder bore and pistons cool.

The water then travels up into the cylinder head and circulates round the combustion spaces and valve seats absorbing more heat, and then, when the engine is at its optimum operating temperature, travels out of the cylinder head, past the open thermostat into the upper radiator hose and so into the radiator header tank.

The water travels down the radiator where it is rapidly cooled by the in-rush of cold air through the radiator core, which is created by both the fan and the motion of the car. The water, now cold, reaches the bottom of the radiator, whereupon the cycle is repeated.

When the engine is cold, the thermostat (a valve which opens and closes according to the temperature of the water), maintains the circulation of the same water in the engine.

Only when the correct minimum operating temperature has been reached (see Specifications), does the thermostat begin to open, allowing water to return to the radiator.

A bypass hose from the thermostat housing circulates hot water to the heater unit and from there it is recirculated back to the water pump. (See Fig. 2.1 for diagram of system).

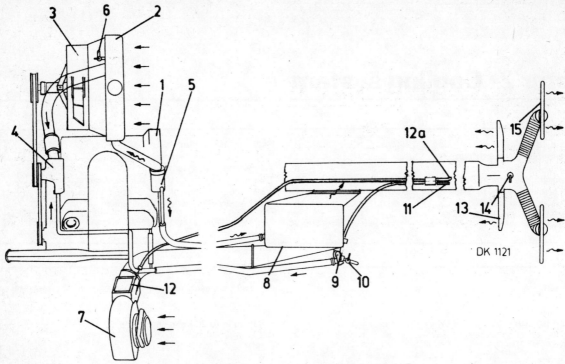

Fig. 2.1. Engine cooling and car heating diagram (Sec. 1)

1 *Engine*	5 *Thermostat*	10 *Heater drain tap*	13 *Heater vents in car*
2 *Radiator*	6 *Radiator drain tap*	11 *Heater control valve lever*	14 *Windscreen demister control*
3 *Cooling fan*	7 *Fan*	12 *Heater fan flap valve*	15 *Windscreen demist vents*
4 *Water pump*	8 *Heater*	12a *Heater fan flap control lever*	
	9 *Heater control valve*		

Routine maintenance

1   Once a week check the level of coolant in the radiator and top-up as necessary. Every 3,000 miles (5,000 km) check the fanbelt tension, and adjust if required.

2   Periodically, check the exterior of the radiator core, and remove any debris that may have gathered.

3   Check the hose connections for chafing, cracking and leakage. Renew as required.

4   Every 12,500 miles (20,000 km), remove the fan guard retaining bolt (8 mm) on the top face of the fan shaft housing (Fig. 2.2) and lubricate the bearings with grease.

---

2   Cooling system - draining

When draining the cooling system, the car should be level or with the front facing downhill if on a slope.

1   If the engine is hot, having just been run, it is preferable to leave it to cool off before draining. This is because removal of the filler cap causes a sudden drop in pressure, which can result in the coolant boiling and pouring out of the radiator filler neck at high pressure, possibly, with dangerous and painful results. A water temperature gauge should not be used as a guideline, as they are often inaccurate. When the radiator header tank is warm to the touch, turn the filler cap very slightly until the pressure in the system has had time to disperse. Use a rag over the cap to protect the hand from any escaping steam before finally removing the cap.

2   If an antifreeze solution is in the radiator, drain it into a clean bucket or bowl for re-use.

3   The radiator drain tap is located in the base of the bottom tank (photo), and the outlet pipe is situated in the splash panel by the nearside rear wing. Therefore, place the drainage receptacle directly behind the rear wheel.

4   If the heater is to be drained also, it is located under the right-hand seat cushion and a drain tap is provided (photo).

Fig. 2.2. Fan blade guard retaining bolt which doubles as a greasing point for the fan bearings (Sec. 2)

---

3   Cooling system - flushing

1   Over a period of time the radiator will gradually lose its efficiency as the inner tubes become chocked with rust scales, lime deposits and other sediment. To clean out the system, remove the radiator cap and the drain tap and leave a hose running in the radiator cap orifice for 10 to 15 minutes.

2   In severe cases, the radiator should be reverse flushed. This can best be done with the radiator removed, as it must be inverted to enable the hose entry into the drain tap orifice, or over the drain tap in the open position. Again run the tap for 10 to 15 minutes. The bottom

2.3 Radiator drain taps

2.4 Heater control and drain tap

4.3 Modified radiator locations showing tab in slot

4.5 Removing the radiator

hose outlet pipe can be temporarily blocked off with some masking tape, or similar, the water will then circulate through the radiator in the reverse direction, removing deposits and emerging from the filler cap orifice.

4 Radiator - removal and replacement

1 Drain the coolant, as described in Section 2.
2 Disconnect the top and bottom hoses.
3 Slacken the spring clip retaining the fan guard (photo), and rubber strip, and lever over towards the fan rim.
4 Unscrew the radiator retaining bolts and lift clear.
5 Refit the radiator (photo) in the reverse sequence.
6 Always stand the radiator in an upright position when removed from the car, to prevent sediment in the lower section blocking the tubes.
7 Never reconnect perished, worn, or split hoses. Carefully inspect, and renew as necessary.

5 Radiator - inspection

1 With the radiator out of the car any leaks can be soldered up or

repaired with a compound such as Cataloy. Clean out the radiator by flushing, as described in Section 3. It should be mentioned that solder repairs are best completed professionally. It is too easy to damage other parts of the radiator by excessive heating.
2 When the radiator is out of the car, it is advantageous to turn it upside down for reverse flushing. Clean the exterior of the radiator by hosing down the radiator matrix with a strong jet of water to clean away road dirt, dead flies etc.
3 Inspect the radiator hoses for cracks, internal and external, perishing and damage caused by over-tightening of the hose clips. Renew the hoses as necessary.
4 Examine the hose clips and renew them if they are rusted or distorted. The drain plugs and washers should be renewed if leaking.

6 Cooling system - filling and antifreeze

1 If removed, refit hoses and drain tap - which should be turned to the closed position.
2 If the heating system has been drained, open the heater inlet valve.
3 If the bottom hose has been removed it should be reconnected.
4 Fill the system slowly to ensure that no air locks develop. Check that the valve on the heating and ventilation unit is open (hot) otherwise an airlock may form in the heater. The water used in the

cooling system ideally ought to be soft; if the local supply is hard then it may be boiled to remove the temporary hardness.
5   The coolant level should be approximately ¾ inch (19 mm) above the tubes in the radiator.
6   Start the engine and run for several minutes, enough time for minor air pockets to clear. Once the engine has been run re-check the level of coolant in the radiator.
7   If the engine has overheated due to lack of water, **do not top-up immediately with cold water!** Wait for the engine to cool naturally. Alternatively, refill with hot water with the engine ticking over.
8   If an antifreeze solution is to be used, and this is obviously essential during the winter months, be sure to use a good quality type, having a mixture that is non-corrosive to aluminium. It should have a glycol or ethylene base. The amount of dilution with water varies, but strictly follow the antifreeze manufacturer's instructions, bearing in mind the temperature variations which may be encountered.

7   Thermostat - removal, testing and replacement

1   To remove the thermostat, drain the cooling system, as described in Section 2.
2   The thermostat is located at the rear of the cylinder head, attached to a flange on the left-hand side. To remove, disconnect the hoses and undo the thermostat housing flange nuts. Remove the housing. If it sticks in position, try soaking the studs and joint area with penetrating oil.
3   Extract the thermostat from its housing and the top hose (photo), and inspect as follows:
   a) *Examine the thermostat and ensure that no riveted or soldered joints are broken or loose.*
   b) *Check that the jiggle pin is in position and free to float.*
4   To test for correct opening, hang the thermostat and a thermometer by separate pieces of string in a saucepan of cold water. Neither items should touch the side or bottom of the saucepan or an incorrect reading will result.
5   Heat the water gently stirring with the thermometer. The temperature should be taken at the precise moment the thermostat begins to open. The thermostat should start to open at approximately 82°C (180°F).
6   As a further guide at a temperature of 90°C (194°F) the thermostat should be fully open. Whilst the valve is open ensure there is no dirt or foreign matter around its seat.
7   Remove the thermostat from the hot water and immerse it in cold water, it should close itself within 15 to 20 seconds. If the thermostat fails any of these tests discard it, and replace it with a new unit.
8   Replacement is a straightforward reversal of the removal procedure. However, do not forget to renew the gasket. If the two joint faces have minor corrosion smear the gasket with jointing compound such as

Hermetite. If the water outlet/thermostat housing unit is badly corroded it will be necessary to renew it.

8   Water pump - removal and replacement

1   To remove the pump, drain the cooling system as described in Section 2.
2   Undo the fan pulley nut and split the pulley to remove the drivebelt. Replace the 'half pulley' temporarily, together with the shims.
3   Loosen the dynamo/alternator tension clamping bolts and remove the drivebelt.
4   Disconnect the hoses from the pump body.
5   Undo the pump body flange fixing nuts and remove the pump assembly complete (photo). If the pump body should be stuck, apply some penetrating oil to the studs and flange fixings. Never hit the pump body with a steel hammer or lever the flange face.
6   Replacement of the pump is the reverse of above, but ensure the flange faces are free of old gasket material and gasket cement. Always refit with a new gasket.

9   Water pump - dismantling, inspection and reassembly

1   If the water pump bearings or seals are defective, they can be replaced but it should be borne in mind, prior to dismantling, that considering the time and marginal cost involved, it will probably be more practical to obtain a new or exchange pump unit complete. It is also unlikely that pump spares will be readily available. However, if the pump is to be dismantled proceed as follows (refer to Figs. 2.3 and 2.4).
2   Undo and remove the pulley nut and washer.
3   Withdraw the pulley from the shaft. A puller may be required, and care should be taken not to distort the pulley.
4   Remove the Woodruff key from the shaft keyway and press, or drive out, the pump shaft.
5   Remove the bearing retaining ring and drive out the bearings and spacer tube from opposing ends with a suitable drift.
6   Remove the rubber sealing ring from the pump body.
7   Clean and inspect all the parts, in particular the bearings and rubber seal. Renew as required if showing signs of wear.
8   Reassembly is the reverse sequence of dismantling, but be sure to grease the bearings and ensure the rubber seal is located correctly. Tighten the pulley nut to the specified torque.

10   Fanbelt - removal, replacement and adjustment

1   Should the fanbelt be over-stretched, or worn, it should be renewed.

7.3 Removing the thermostat from its housing

8.5 Removing the water pump

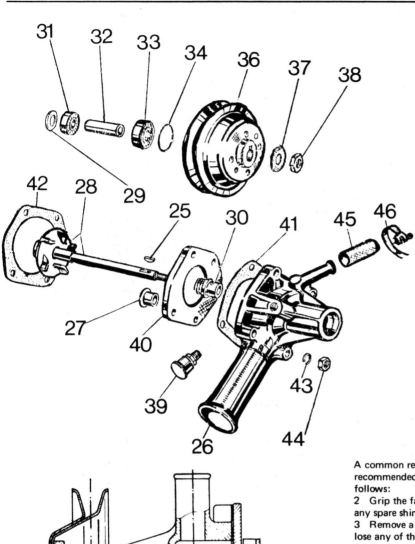

Fig. 2.3. The component parts of the water pump (Sec. 9)

26 Water pump body
27 Bush
28 Pump shaft
29 Rubber ring
30 Water seal for shaft
31 Ball bearing
32 Spacer
33 Sealed bearing
34 Safety ring
35 Woodruff key
36 Pulley
37 Washer
38 Nut
39 Grease lubrication plug
40 Body plate
41 Gasket
42 Gasket
43 Washer
44 Nut
45 Hose
46 Hose clip

A common reason for fanbelt replacement is breakage. It is therefore recommended that a spare belt is always carried in the car. Remove as follows:

2   Grip the fan and undo the fan pulley retaining nut, and remove with any spare shim washers.

3   Remove a 'half-pulley' and the fanbelt (if still attached). **Do not** lose any of the pulley dividing shim washers.

4   Replacement is the reverse sequence but the correct belt tension of 2 inches (50 mm) lateral movement, midway between the pulleys, is acquired by shimming between the pulleys, with the washers as required. Any spare shim washers are located over the spindle on the outside of the pulley prior to refitting the retaining nut.

11 Fan unit and bracket - removal, dismantling and refitting

The fan, and the bracket on which it is mounted, can be removed with the engine in, or out, of the car. If removing with the engine in the car it is essential to support the engine from underneath, as the engine mounting bracket and support strut are also attached to the fan bracket. Remove as follows, referring to Figs. 2.5 and 2.6.

1   Undo the fan pulley retaining nut (photo) and remove the 'half-pulley' complete with adjustment shims, to release the drivebelt.

2   Unscrew the fan guard rubber sealing strip securing clip.

3   Undo the engine mounting nuts to the fan bracket at the front, and also the support strut bolt to the fan bracket.

4   Undo the bracket securing nuts to the cylinder block and remove complete with fan and guard.

5   Undo the fan guard bolts and remove the guard over the fan.

6   Remove the inner 'half pulley' from the shaft, and prise the Woodruff key from its groove (photo).

7   Remove the retaining ring from its groove in the bracket bearing housing and drive, or press, the shaft through the bearings in the housing.

8   If the fan is to be removed from the shaft (and this can be achieved without extracting the shaft from the housing), undo the locknut and tab washer (photo), or withdraw the fan from the shaft. To do this, support the fan securely by the inner flange (not the blades) and drift

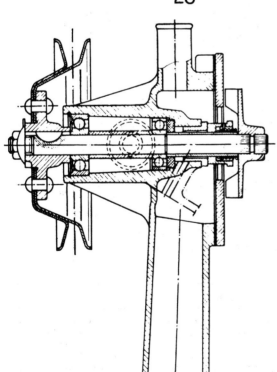

Fig. 2.4. Sectional view of water pump (Sec. 9)

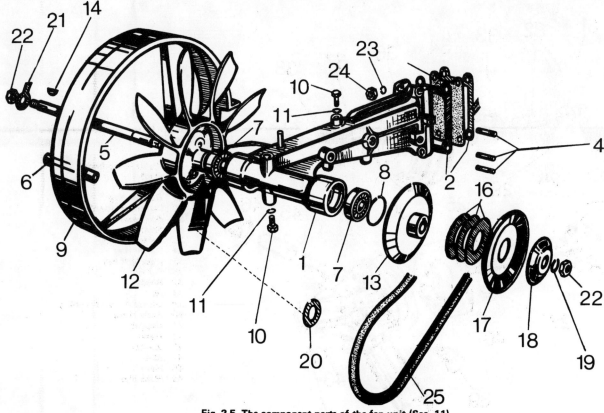

Fig. 2.5. The component parts of the fan unit (Sec. 11)

1	Fan bracket	7	Ball bearing	13	Pulley half disc	20	Washer
2	Gasket	8	Safety ring	14	Woodruff key	21	Securing washer
3	Partition plate	9	Fan rim	16	Pulley shims	22	Nut
4	Engine mounting studs	10	Bolt	17	Pulley half disc	23	Spring washer
5	Shaft	11	Spring washer	18	Support cup washer	24	Nut
6	Distance tube	12	Fan	19	Spring washer	25	'V' belt

Fig. 2.6. Sectional view of fan (Sec. 11)

the shaft through, or use a suitable puller. Remove the Woodruff key from its slot.

9   Clean all the parts thoroughly and blow the bearing dry with compressed air. If the components show signs of wear (do not run smoothly or are loose in the housing), they will have to be removed and renewed.

10 Reassembly is the reversal of dismantling, but be sure to grease the bearings and shaft well. Fit new gaskets to the bracket to cylinder block flange, and carefully adjust the drivebelt by altering the number of shims fitted between the pulley halves (photo). Any spare shims are placed over the shaft, between the outer pulley half and retaining nut/washer. Belt tension is correct when there is approximately 2 inches (50 mm) of lateral play in the belt at the middle of its run between the pulleys.

12 Temperature gauge sensor unit

1   A water temperature warning sensor unit is fitted, and is located in the top of the cylinder head at the side of the thermostat housing (photo). Removal of this unit is only required if the temperature gauge fails to work, and the gauge and wiring are known to be in good order. It is not possible to repair either the gauge or sensor unit and they must therefore be renewed if at fault. Prior to removal of the gauge or sensor unit, check the wiring for breaks using an ohmmeter or continuity tester. The sensor and gauge can be tested by substitution.

2   The sensor unit is removed from the head after draining half of the coolant from the system, and disconnecting the electrical terminal. Unscrew the unit with a spanner of the correct size.

3   Replacement is a reversal of the above procedure.

4   For details of removing the temperature gauge, see Chapter 10.

11.1 Fan pulley and retaining nut

11.6 Fan shaft Woodruff key removal

11.8 Fan and retaining nut

11.10 Fan half pulley and shims

12.1 Water temperature warning sender unit in
position in cylinder head unit

13 Fault diagnosis - cooling system

Symptom	Reason/s	Remedy
Heat generated in cylinder not being successfully disposed of by radiator	Insufficient water in cooling system	Top-up radiator.
	Drive belt slipping (accompanied by a shrieking noise on rapid engine acceleration)	Tighten drive belt to recommended tension or replace if worn.
	Radiator core blocked or radiator grille restricted	Reverse flush radiator, remove obstructions.
	Bottom water hose collapsed, impeding flow	Remove and fit new hose.
	Thermostat not opening properly	Remove and fit new thermostat.
	Ignition advance and retard incorrectly set (accompanied by loss of power and perhaps, misfiring)	Check and reset ignition timing.
	Carburettor incorrectly adjusted (mixture too weak)	Tune carburettor/s.
	Exhaust system partially blocked	Check exhaust pipe for constrictive dents and blockages.
	Oil level in sump too low	Top up sump to full mark on dipstick.
	Blown cylinder head gasket (water/steam being forced down the radiator overflow pipe under pressure)	Remove cylinder head, fit new gasket.
	Engine not yet run in	Run in slowly and carefully.
	Brakes binding	Check and adjust brakes if necessary.
Too much heat being dispersed by radiator	Thermostat jammed open	Remove and renew thermostat.
	Incorrect grade of thermostat fitted allowing premature opening of valve	Remove and replace with new thermostat which opens at a higher temperature.
	Thermostat missing	Check and fit correct thermostat.
Leaks in system	Loose clips on water hoses	Check and tighten clips if necessary.
	Top, bottom, or by-pass water hoses perished and leaking	Check and replace any faulty hoses.
	Radiator core leaking	Remove radiator and repair.
	Thermostat gasket leaking	Inspect and renew gasket.
	Radiator pressure cap spring worn or seal ineffective	Renew radiator pressure cap.
	Blown cylinder head gasket (pressure in system forcing water/steam down overflow pipe)	Remove cylinder head and fit new gasket.
	Cylinder wall or head cracked	Dismantle engine, dispatch to engineering works for repair.

Chapter 3 Carburation; fuel and exhaust systems

Contents

Specifications

Carburettor (1000 MB)

Type	Jikov 32 BST 13, single choke, downdraught, automatic choke

Settings:

Choke tube (diameter)	23 mm
Main jet	120
Main air bleed	200
Idling jet	50
Idling air bleed	150
Booster jet	42
Acceleration pump jet	50
Pump bypass jet	42
Starter jet	80
Starter air bleed (diameter)	6 mm
Needle valve (diameter)	1.5 mm

Carburettor (100, 100L and 110L)

Type (100 and 100L)	Jikov 32 BST 3120, single choke, automatic choke. (early models: 32 BST 18)
Type (110L)	Jikov 32 BST 3140, single choke, automatic choke. (early models: 32 BST 21)

Settings:

	100 and 100L	110L
Choke tube (diameter)	23 mm	24 mm
Main jet	120	125
Main air bleed	200	190
Idling jet	50	50
Idling air bleed	150	150
Booster jet	42	55
Accelerator pump jet injector	50	50
Pump bypass jet	0.8 mm	0.8 mm
Starter jet	80	80
Starter air bleed (diameter)	6 mm	4.5 mm
Needle valve (diameter)	1.5 mm	2 mm

Carburettor (100, 100L and 110L)

Type (100 and 100L)	Jikov 32 BS 3170, single choke, mechanical choke
Type (110L)	Jikov 32 BS 3171, single choke, mechanical choke

Settings:

	100 and 100L	110L
Choke tube (diameter)	23 mm	24 mm
Main jet	118	122
Main air bleed	200	200
Idling jet	50	50
Idling air bleed	130	130
Booster jet	50	55

	100 and 100L	110L
Acceleration pump jet injector	50	50
Pump bypass jet (diameter)	0.8 mm	0.8 mm
Starter jet	90	90
Starter air bleed (diameter)	4.5 mm	4.5 mm
Needle valve (diameter)	1.5 mm	2.0 mm
Vacuum control connector	120 + 5	120 + 5

Carburettor (110LS and R)

Type ... ... Jikov 32 DDSR 5139, twin choke

Settings:	Stage I	Stage II	Stage I and II
Choke tube (diameter)	22 mm	24 mm	
Main jet	110	125	
Main air bleed	170	180	
Idling jet	50	80	
Idling air bleed	150	100	
Boosting jet	—	—	65
Booster air bleed	—	—	6 mm (diameter)
Pump bypass jet (diameter)	0.5 mm	—	
Injector	50	—	
Stage II regulator air bleed	160	90	
Needle valve (diameter)	—	—	2 mm
Venting connector	—	—	120 + 5

Fuel tank capacity ... ... 7 Imp. gallons (32 litres)

Fuel pump

Type ... ... Jikov HF51 - 6517 OORS, diaphragm type, camshaft operated

1 General description and modifications

The fuel tank is located under the floor panel of the front luggage compartment and is filled through a pipe connection in the right-hand front wing panel.

Fuel from the tank is delivered to the carburettor by a fuel pump, which is mechanically operated, and located on the cylinder block in line with the camshaft. A lever from the pump is actuated by the camshaft.

The carburettors and fuel pumps of all models are of Jikov manufacture.

A fuel gauge is fitted to all models.

Fuel system modifications

Models S100 and 110L - from July 1973: The carburettor float was changed from the above date, in that the original brass floats are now manufactured in plastic. Although interchangeable, the fuel level will have to be changed to suit, if fitting a plastic type to an earlier model carburettor. The correct fuel level with a plastic float is 0.75 in (19 mm), from the top face. Adjustment can be made by bending the lip of the float mounting to suit.

Models S100, S100L and S110 - from September 1975: Modified carburettors were fitted from the above date. The principal modifications included a reduction in the number of progression jets from two to one; also the main and emulsion jet tube dimensions were altered. The modified later carburettors are fully interchangeable with those used on earlier models as follows. S100 and 1000 MB models: Type 32 BS 2903 to be used in place of 32 BS 3170; S110 and MB 1100 models: Type 32 BS 2904 to be used in place of 32 BS 3171.

2 Routine maintenance

Every 6,250 miles (10,000 km) remove and clean the air filter, as described in Section 11.

If required, adjust the carburettor slow running as described in Sections 7 and 10.

Check and clean, if necessary, the fuel pump filter by undoing the central bolt in the pump cap and lifting the cover clear. Inspect the filter gauze for sediment; if necessary, carefully lift it out and clean it with petrol and a soft brush. Take care not to distort the filter.

Replace in the reverse sequence, but always fit a new sealing washer under the cap retaining bolt head. Renew the cap seal if it shows signs of cracks or has distorted. Do not overtighten the cap retaining bolt,

the pressure should be just enough to seal the joints.

Every 12,500 miles (20,000 km) check the manifold and carburettor retaining bolts for tightness.

Renew the air cleaner filter, as described in Section 11.

Lubricate the accelerator linkage with a light oil. Check the fuel supply pipes and connections and renew, as necessary, if distortion, cracking or leaks are apparent.

3 Carburettors - description of operation

The carburettor as fitted to all Skoda models is of Jikov manufacture. There are basically two types, these being (a) carburettors with an automatic choke control, or (b) carburettors with a mechanically operated choke system.

Basically, the carburettor has four stages of operation, according to requirements.

Stage one is for cold starting. In carburettors with the automatic choke control, the mixture of air and fuel is regulated by a thermo-choke system, in which a bimetallic spring opens or closes the choke slide valve according to the ambient temperature. When the engine is cold the spring is contracted, and the slide valve is open. As the temperature increases, the spring expands and the choke is progressively closed, until the engine reaches its normal running temperature. The choke automatically opens again when the engine is stopped and cools. In the mechanically operated choke type carburettors the mixture control is regulated by the driver, who operates the choke control connection in the car, according to requirements.

Stage two of the carburettor requirements is to govern the fuel/air mixture when the engine is idling. Smooth idling is obtained via the idling jet and the air bleed adjustment of the fast idling screw and throttle control screw.

On acceleration the air/mixture throttle opens and increases the flow of fuel through the idling jet, until the engine is under load.

Stage three is when the carburettor is working under a normal load, when the increased opening of the throttle operates the principal carburettor system, which comprises the main jet and main air bleed.

The quantity of air relative to fuel intake is controlled via the air bleed from where it enters the emulsion tube, is mixed with fuel, regulated by the main jet, and is then sucked through the atomizer and choke tube into the engine.

Stage four is when the engine is under a high or full load, and an additional fuel mixture is required.

In the 32 BST model carburettors, the increased fuel mixture is supplied when the throttle butterfly opens to 35° at which point a

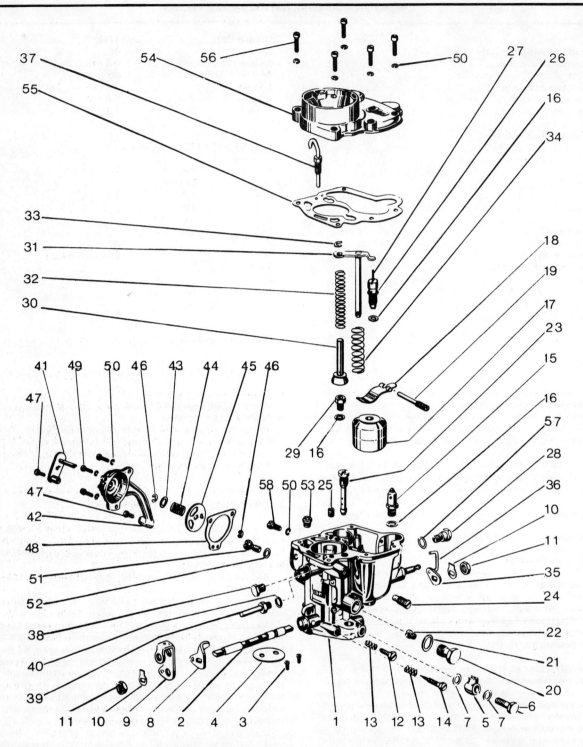

Fig. 3.1. Jikov 32 BS 3170 and 32 BS 3171 single choke carburettor (mechanical choke type) (Sec. 4)

1 Carburettor body	16 Sealing washer	30 Plunger	45 Choke slide valve
2 Spindle	17 Float	31 Pump drive	46 Ring
3 Valve plate	18 Float toggle	32 Pump spring	47 Screw
4 Screws	19 Toggle retaining screw	33 C-clip	48 Choke gasket
5 Banjo union	20 Main jet carrier bolt	34 Drive spring	49 Screw
6 Banjo bolt	21 Fibre washer	35 Lever	50 Washer
7 Fibre washer	22 Main jet 118	36 Clip rod	51 Choke jet
8 Swivel plate	22 Main jet 122	37 Injector	52 Sealing washer
9 Lever	23 Emulsion tube 200	38 Screw plug	53 Choke air bleed
10 Lock washer	24 Pilot jet 50	39 Banjo union 120 + 5	54 Cover
11 Nut	25 Pilot air bleed 130	40 Fibre washer	55 Cover gasket
12 Throttle screw	26 Booster valve	41 Slide valve drive	56 Screw
13 Safety spring	27 Pin	42 Cover of choke	57 Sealing washer
14 Volume control screw	28 Booster pilot 50	43 Washer	58 Screw
15 Needle valve assembly	29 Suction valve	44 Spring	

booster valve opens. The extra fuel then flows through the booster jet to the atomizer direct.

Each carburettor is fitted with a piston type accelerator pump, which, when the throttle is opened quickly, supplies fuel through an injector to the atomizer. The piston is operated by leverage and is governed by the throttle opening in the carburettor. With the throttle opened, the piston descends and fuel is pumped into the injector and through to the atomizer. Any excess fuel is returned to the float chamber through the bypass port. The faster the movement of the accelerator, the greater the fuel supply to the injector.

On closing the carburettor throttle, the piston rises in the float chamber and the pump draws fuel through the non-return valve.

Twin choke carburettors

The Jikov 32 DDSR - 5139 carburettor, as fitted to sportier models, differs from the above type of carburettor, in that it is of twin choke type. Briefly explained, it is a two stage carburettor. The first stage is mechanically operated by the interconnecting rods and cable from the accelerator pedal and the second stage comes into use when the accelerator is operated beyond a certain point. This causes a diaphragm to open (governed by the vacuum in the respective choke tubes); fuel is then supplied to the second choke chamber as well as the first.

4 Carburettor (single choke) - removal

1 The carburettor can be removed with the engine in, or out, of the car. However, ensure the relevant gaskets are available before removing the carburettor.
2 Remove the air cleaner unit by undoing the three retaining nuts and the rubber sealing ring clamp screw.
3 Disconnect the choke/thermo-choke and throttle connections.
4 Disconnect the distributor vacuum timing tube and the fuel line from the fuel pump.
5 Remove the carburettor to manifold nuts and remove the carburettor.

5 Carburettor (single choke) - dismantling, inspection, reassembly and refitting

Although various types of Jikov carburettors have been used (see Specifications), all single choke types have been basically similar. The main differences are in the jet dimensions. Therefore, if replacing jets, always quote the type of carburettor you have and if possible, take the carburettor along to your dealer so that he may be sure of supplying you with the correct replacement part. Dismantle as follows, referring to Fig. 3.1.

1 Clean down the exterior of the carburettor body and remove to bench, where it should be dismantled on a sheet of clean newspaper and the parts kept in order of removal.
2 Remove the cover by unscrewing the four retaining screws and washers. Carefully lift the cover clear - try not to damage the gasket, as it may be useful for a pattern if you have to make a replacement.
3 Unscrew the main air bleed screw and also the idling air bleed screw.
4 Unscrew the float toggle retaining screw and withdraw to release the toggle, and then remove the float.
5 Unscrew the fuel injection nozzle.
6 Remove the needle valve from its aperture beneath the float toggle.
7 Remove, from the outside of the carburettor body, the starter jet, power jet, idling jet, main jet and the fast idling screw.
8 Clean all parts thoroughly in clean petrol and blow dry with an airline.
9 Inspect all parts thoroughly for signs of wear, renewing as necessary.
10 Refitting and reassembly to the car is a direct reversal of the dismantling procedure. Always use new gaskets when assembling. Do not over-tighten the retaining screws, and do not use any form of sealing compound.

6 Thermo-choke

If the thermo-choke is suspected of incorrect operation, there is no set procedure for checking the bimetal spring unit, as this can only be

achieved with specialized equipment. Therefore, if the unit is suspect, check that the choke slide valve operates smoothly. If the slide operates correctly the thermo-choke unit will have to be renewed. On reassembly ensure that the bimetallic spring locates correctly with the throttle lever recess.

7 Carburettor (single choke) - adjustments

Before adjusting the carburettor, ensure that the engine and ignition system are in good condition. The carburettor should be adjusted with the engine at normal operating temperature.

Idling adjustment (refer to Fig. 3.2)

The air cleaner should be fitted and the engine at its normal operating temperature.
1 With the engine running, turn the throttle screw to increase the engine speed slightly, above normal idling speed.
2 The idling mixture screw is now screwed outwards until the engine shows signs of stalling, at which point it should be gradually screwed in until the engine just runs smoothly.
3 The throttle screw is now turned to adjust the engine speed to normal idling level. As a guide, the ignition warning light will just go out when the correct adjustment is made.
4 When the throttle is opened and closed at a slow and fast rate the engine should increase or decrease its speed smoothly. If backfiring occurs, the idling mixture screw will have to be screwed out and the throttle screw correspondingly tightened.

8 Carburettor (twin choke) - removal

1 The carburettor may be removed easily with the engine in the car, but ensure that a new replacement gasket set is available prior to removal and dismantling.
2 Remove the air cleaner unit by undoing the three retaining nuts, and the rubber sealing ring clamp screw.
3 Remove the choke cable, by undoing its clamp nut and outer cable clamp screw.
4 Remove the throttle cable by undoing the clamping screw in the location sleeve, and 'C' clip.
5 Disconnect the fuel line from the fuel pump.
6 Unscrew the distributor timing vacuum tube retaining bolt from its position adjacent to the air cleaner bracket, and slide the pipe clear of the carburettor along its guide.
7 Remove the four carburettor to manifold nuts.
8 Disconnect the throttle control rod ball joint connection.
9 Now lift the carburettor clear of the manifold.

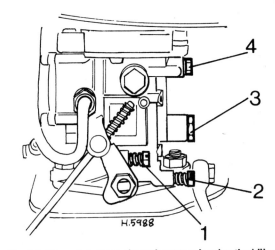

Fig. 3.2. View of single choke carburettor showing the idling adjustments (Sec. 7)

1   Throttle stop screw
2   Fast idling screw
3   Main jet holder
4   Idling jet

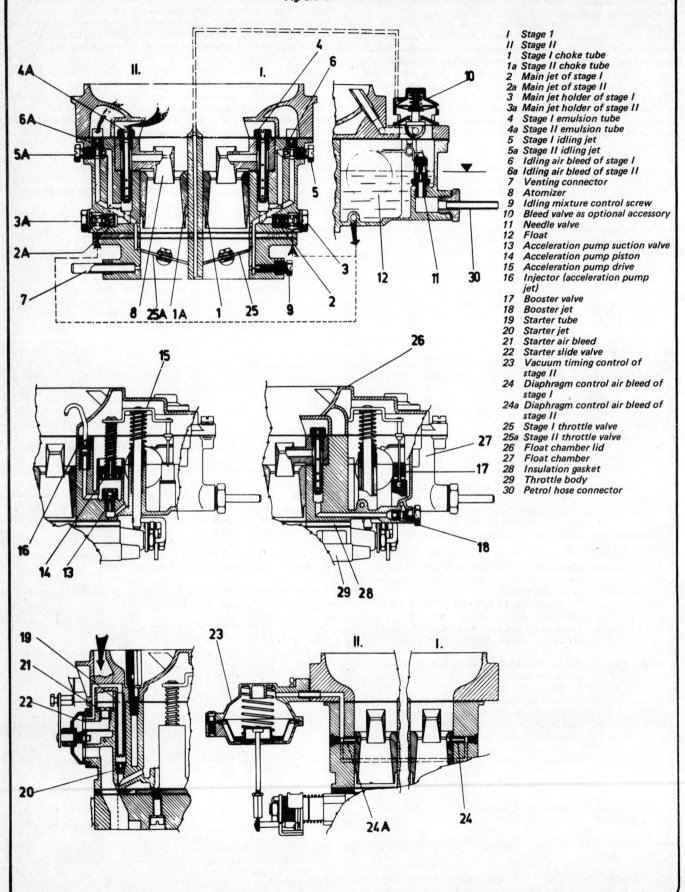

I Stage 1
II Stage II
1 Stage I choke tube
1a Stage II choke tube
2 Main jet of stage I
2a Main jet of stage II
3 Main jet holder of stage I
3a Main jet holder of stage II
4 Stage I emulsion tube
4a Stage II emulsion tube
5 Stage I idling jet
5a Stage II idling jet
6 Idling air bleed of stage I
6a Idling air bleed of stage II
7 Venting connector
8 Atomizer
9 Idling mixture control screw
10 Bleed valve as optional accessory
11 Needle valve
12 Float
13 Acceleration pump suction valve
14 Acceleration pump piston
15 Acceleration pump drive
16 Injector (acceleration pump jet)
17 Booster valve
18 Booster jet
19 Starter tube
20 Starter jet
21 Starter air bleed
22 Starter slide valve
23 Vacuum timing control of stage II
24 Diaphragm control air bleed of stage I
24a Diaphragm control air bleed of stage II
25 Stage I throttle valve
25a Stage II throttle valve
26 Float chamber lid
27 Float chamber
28 Insulation gasket
29 Throttle body
30 Petrol hose connector

9 Carburettor (twin choke) - dismantling, inspection, reassembly and refitting

1 Refer to Fig. 3.3. Remove the carburettor to the workbench and clean off the exterior, prior to dismantling. Dismantle on a sheet of clean newspaper and lay the individual parts out, taking note of the removal sequence. **Do not clean the jets out with wire** - wash in petrol and blow through with compressed air.

2 There are three main body sections to this carburettor. To clean the float chambers and jets, it is only necessary to remove the top section. The lower section contains only the butterfly spindles and these should not be dismantled. The only reason for dismantling the middle and lower sections is to replace the gasket, but this item rarely needs attention.

3 To remove the top section, unscrew and remove the seven retaining screws and the diaphragm retaining rod from the lower operating shaft by unclipping the 'C' clip. Undo and remove the air cleaner stud (photos).

4 Lift the upper section clear, taking care not to damage the gasket - it may need to be used as a template if a new replacement is not available.

5 Drain any remaining fuel from the carburettor and remove the floats by undoing the two screws (photo), retaining the float **spindle.**

6 Pull out of its location the accelerator pump jet (photo).

7 Unscrew the 1st and 2nd emulsion tubes and remove (photo).

8 Remove the idling air bleed supply jet (photo) and the cold **start** mechanism, which is retained by four screws and the cold start air supply jet (photo).

9 Remove the remaining jets and wash the various components thoroughly in petrol, and blow dry with an airline.

10 Inspect the various components for signs of wear, or damage. Shake the floats to ensure that petrol has not leaked into them. Check the accelerator pump jet 'O' ring for distortion or signs of cracking. Renew if necessary. Check the cold start unit (photo). The seal valve should move smoothly and the spring should have adequate tension. Although it rarely needs attention, the vacuum timing control for the second stage can be unscrewed from its flange on the upper section. Its upper and lower body retaining screws are then removed and the unit split for inspection. Remove any traces of dirt and check the spring tension and diaphragm.

11 Reassembly and refitting are a reversal of dismantling and removal. When refitting the carburettor, be sure to fit the new gasket the correct way up or the starter air bleed will be blocked (photo). Do not over-tighten the retaining screws or nuts and ensure all sealing faces are perfectly clean.

9.3a 'C' clip retaining the diaphragm operating shaft

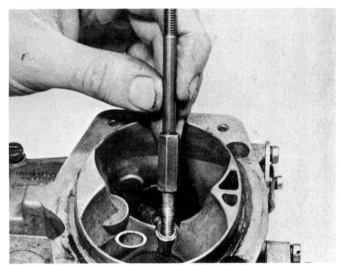
9.3b Removing the air cleaner retaining stud

9.5 Removing the float spindle retaining screws

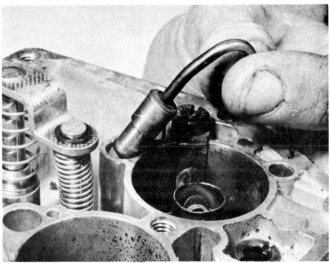
9.6 Removing the accelerator pump jet

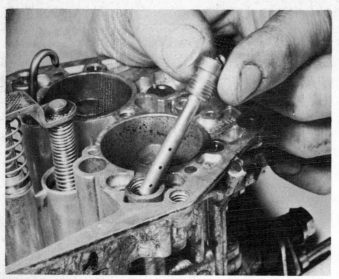

9.7 Removing the 2nd stage emulsion tube

9.8a Removing the idling air supply jet

9.8b Cold start air supply jet removed

9.10 Cold start unit removed

9.11 Top view of carburettor showing correct gasket position

10.1 and 10.2 Throttle adjustment screw 'A' and idling screw 'B'

10 Carburettor (twin choke) - adjustments

To adjust the carburettor it is essential that the engine be at its normal operating temperature, and the air cleaner in position. The idling mixture and speed should be set as follows (refer to Fig. 3.3).
1   With the engine running, tighten the throttle screw (A) slightly to increase the engine idling speed (photo).
2   The idling mixture screw (B) should now be screwed out until the engine shows signs of stalling. The fast idling mixture screw should then, gradually, be screwed back in until the engine just runs smoothly (photo).
3   Now turn the throttle screw to adjust to the correct idling speed for the engine. As an approximate guide, the ignition warning light will dim as the engine speed is increased until the light is just off, at which point the idling speed should be correct.
4   It should be remembered that if a smooth idle is to be achieved, not only does the carburettor have to be in good condition, but the general condition of the engine and ignition system must also be good.
5   To further check for correct adjustment and operation, the throttle should be opened quickly and the increase in engine speed should be accomplished smoothly. Turn the engine off and restart. This should be achieved without using the throttle and must be immediate.
6   If backfiring occurs then the idling mixture screw should be turned to correct the engine idling speed.

11 Air filter - servicing

1   The air entering the carburettor is filtered through a paper cartridge type filter. This should be periodically cleaned at 3,000 miles (5,000 km) intervals and renewed at 12,500 miles (20,000 km).
2   To extract the element from its casing, release the two intake tube retaining clips and remove the tube.
3   Extract the element and sealing ring from its case. Some air cleaner elements are additionally retained by a plate and spring. To remove an element of this type, simply push and twist the plate, release the tension and remove the element complete with plate and spring (photo).
4   Clean the element by tapping it against a solid object, followed by a light blow through with compressed air.
5   Replacement, or renewal of the element, is a reverse procedure to the above. For the removal of the air cleaner unit complete, from the carburettor, refer to the engine removal Section of Chapter 1.

12 Fuel pump - removal and refitting

1   Disconnect the fuel inlet and outlet pipes from the pump body. Plug the feed pipe from the tank.
2   Undo the two pump flange retaining nuts and remove the pump complete with gasket.
3   Refitting is a reversal of the above procedure. However, ensure that the pipe connections are secure (but not over-tightened - Jubilee clips are suggested as replacements for the original Skoda split pin type clips).
4   Always refit the pump with a new gasket of the same thickness as the one originally fitted.
5   It should be noted that the filter in the pump can be removed and cleaned without removing the pump from the car.

13 Fuel pump - dismantling, inspection and reassembly

1   The fuel pump filter gauze may be cleaned out without removing the pump from the engine. To do this, remove the cover retaining screw and carefully lift the cover clear. The gauze filter may then be removed. Take great care not to damage the filter, or cause any distortion. Wash it through in clean petrol or blow dry with compressed air. If on removal of the gauze filter there is a quantity of dirt or sludge within the filter body, then the pump should be completely removed and thoroughly cleaned as follows (refer to Fig. 3.4).
2   First clean the pump exterior thoroughly and mark the edges of the two halves of the body.
3   Undo the cover retaining screw and lift off the cover. The gasket and gauze filter may then be removed, if not already done.

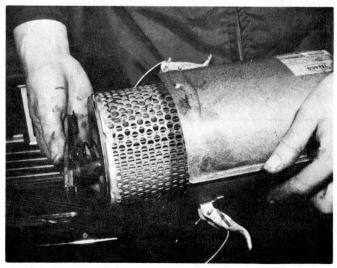
11.3 Removing the air filter element

4   Remove the eight screws and washers holding the two halves of the pump together and the top half may then be lifted off.
5   The diaphragm and pushrod should be removed next, but you will have to remove the pump lever and its spindle to release it. This will require removing the circlips which retain the spindle in the pump housing before drifting out the spindle. Once the spindle is out, retrieve the lever spring, and carefully lift out the diaphragm and its actuating rod.
6   If there are signs of wear in the pump lever pivot pin, and pump lever and link bushes then they should be renewed.
7   Examine the diaphragm for signs of cracking or perforation and renew if necessary.
8   Overhaul kits are available for the fuel pump.
9   To replace the diaphragm and lever arm it will be necessary to place the diaphragm spring in the body of the pump, then the diaphragm and its rod. Press the diaphragm spring down and fit the spring, push in the lever (the right way up) and connect over the top of the machined stop on the rod. Push in the lever arm pivot pin and push through the lever. Replace the circlip on the pivot pin. Always use a new circlip.
10 Fit the upper half of the pump body and line up the mating marks. In order to assemble the two halves and the diaphragm properly, push the rocker arm upwards so that the diaphragm is drawn level. Then place the eight screws in position lightly. It is best if the base of the pump is held in a vice whilst the lever arm is pushed right up to bring the diaphragm to the bottom of its stroke. A short piece of tube over the lever arm will provide easy leverage. In this position the eight screws should be tightened evenly and alternately.
11 Fit a new filter bowl gasket carefully in the groove of the upper body, making sure that it does not twist or buckle in the process. Replace the cover and screw it tight.
12 When the pump is reassembled the suction and delivery pressure can be felt at the inlet and outlet ports when the lever arm is operated. Be careful not to block the inlet port completely when testing suction. If the rocker arm were to be operated strongly and the inlet side was blocked the diaphragm could be damaged.

14 Fuel tank - removal and refitting

1   The fuel tank is mounted at the front of the car, beneath the spare wheel in the luggage compartment. A fuel gauge sender unit is fitted to the tank and this can be removed with the tank in-situ, once electrical leads have been disconnected.
2   The capacity of the fuel tank is 7 Imp. gallons (32 litres). If the fuel tank is to be removed it is advisable to remove any fuel within the tank, prior to dismantling; a drain plug is located in the base of the tank. Use a clean container to collect the petrol if it is to be re-used.
3   It must be emphasised that draining a fuel tank is a dangerous operation unless suitable precautions are taken. As soon as possible after draining, transfer the petrol to a sealable container.

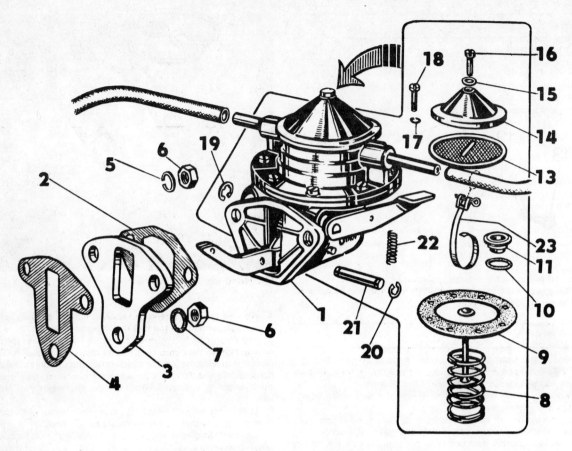

Fig. 3.4. The component parts of the fuel pump (Sec. 13)

1	Fuel pump	7	Washer	14	Cover	19	C-washer
2	Gasket	8	Diaphragm spring	15	Gasket	20	C-washer
3	Insulating washer	9	Diaphragm	16	Screw	21	Rocker arm pin dowel
4	Gasket	10	Gasket	17	Spring washer	22	Spring
5	Spring washer	11	Valve assembly	18	Screw	23	Hose clip
6	Nut	13	Filter				

4 Remove the tank as follows, referring to Fig. 3.5.

5 Unscrew the fuel gauge, sender unit cap and disconnect the electrical terminals. Then unscrew the five screws securing the sender unit to the tank and carefully lift the unit clear - taking care not to damage or distort the float mechanism.

6 Unscrew the rubber filler pipe clip and remove the pipe from the tank neck, and also the tank breather hose. Jack-up the car and support on axle stands. Then from underneath, remove the anti-roll bar brackets.

8 Undo the securing nuts from the tank undertray stiffener to front axle wishbone.

9 Undo and remove the main fuel line connection.

10 Support the tank and unscrew first the rear and then front bolts, securing the tank and undertray to its position in the underbody, and remove the tank from the car.

15 Fuel tank - cleaning and repair

1 With time, it is likely that sediment will collect in the bottom of the fuel tank. Condensation, resulting in rust and other impurities, will usually be found in the fuel tank of any vehicle more than three years old.

2 When the tank is removed it should be swilled out using several changes of clean paraffin and finally rinsed out with clean petrol. Remember that the float mechanism is delicate and the tank should not be shaken violently, or turned upside-down quickly, in case damage to the sender unit is incurred.

3 If the tank is leaking, it should be taken to a specialist firm for

repair. **Do not attempt to solder, braze or weld the tank yourself; it is most dangerous.** A temporary repair may be made with fibreglass or similar material, but a new tank should be fitted as soon as possible.

16 Fuel gauge sender unit - removal and refitting

1 Before removing the sender unit, disconnect the battery terminals.

2 Unscrew the fuel gauge sender unit connector cap and disconnect the electrical connections.

3 Unscrew the five screws retaining the sender unit to the tank, and carefully remove the unit. Take care not to damage the float mechanism.

4 Replacement is the reverse sequence of removal.

17 Fuel tank - filler neck assembly

1 Two types of fuel tank filler units have been fitted. On the earlier models, the filler neck rests on a gasket and is attached to the wing panel (right-hand front) with nuts and spring washers.

2 The filler cap has a rod attached, which carries a spring loaded guide and plug and which is locked in position by a spring loaded latch. The latch is released by operating a handle inside the car.

3 If the releasing handle action becomes stiff, or fails to return, it is a sign that the cable is in need of lubrication or the return spring is weak or broken. To remove the cable, unscrew the cable retaining nuts and guide to the filler neck.

4 The filler neck is attached to the body by four nuts and spring washers.

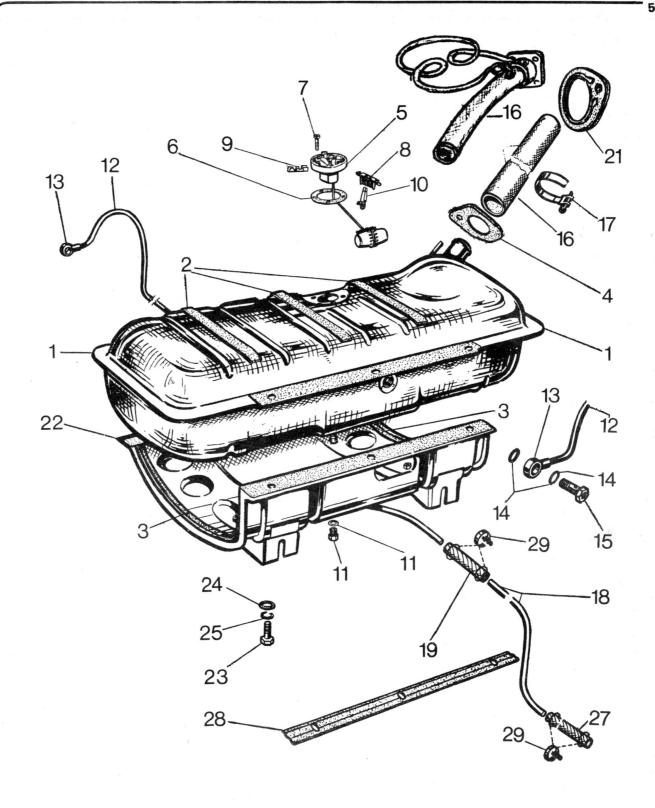

Fig. 3.5. The component parts of the fuel tank (Sec. 14)

1	Fuel tank assembly	8	Resistance band	14	Packing ring	22	Stiffener assembly

1 Fuel tank assembly
2 Top packing belt
3 Bottom packing belt
4 Filler neck gasket
5 Fuel gauge float
6 Float gasket
7 Screw

8 Resistance band
9 Cable union
10 Float equipment runner
11 Tapered plug
11 Packing ring
12 Fuel line
13 Banjo union

14 Packing ring
15 Banjo bolt
16 Connecting hose
17 Clip assembly
18 Fuel pipe
19 Connecting hose
21 Rubber gasket

22 Stiffener assembly
23 Hexagonal headed screw
24 Washer
25 Spring washer
27 Hose
28 Rubber gasket
29 Hose clip

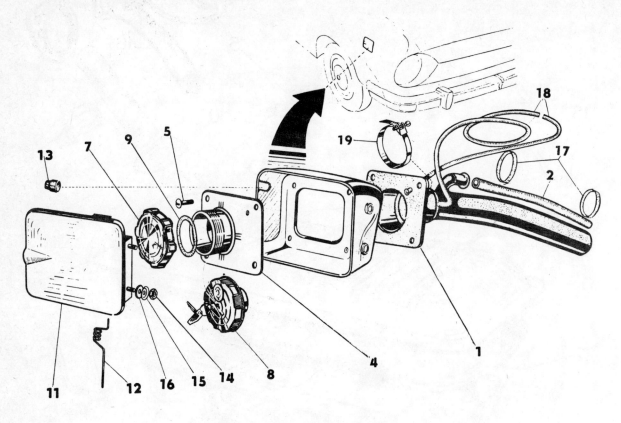

Fig. 3.6. Late type fuel filler unit (Sec. 17)

1 Connecting hose assembly	12 Hinge spring
2 Breather hose	13 Rubber buffer
4 Filler neck	14 Nut
5 Button head screw	15 Washer
7 Cover assembly	16 Rubber washer
8 Cap with lock	17 Rubber cup
9 Cover gasket	18 Air bleeding hose
11 Pocket cover	19 Hose clip

5   The later type filler (Fig. 3.6) is enclosed within a pocket, in the right-hand front wing panel, which is sealed by a spring loaded hinged 'door'. Two types of filler cap are fitted, one being a plain cap with retaining screw, the other a key lock type.

6   To remove the connecting hose assembly from the tank, remove the four button-head screws retaining the filler neck. Unscrew the two nuts retaining the door assembly. Unscrew the filler hose at the tank neck and withdraw the filler connecting unit, taking care not to damage the air bleed hoses.

18 Exhaust system - general

1   The exhaust system on the Skoda is simple and compact. It comprises a cast iron manifold and one or two pipes running from the manifold to the silencer which is mounted on the left-hand side of the engine. When repairing the system, it is wise only to use the original type of exhaust clamps and proprietary made systems.

2   When any one section of the exhaust system needs renewal it often follows that the whole lot is best replaced.

3   It is most important when fitting exhausts that the twists and contours are carefully followed and that each connecting joint overlaps the correct distance. Any stresses or strain imparted, in order to force the system to fit, will result in early fractures and failures.

4   When fitting a new part or a complete system, it is well worth removing the whole system from the car and cleaning up all the joints so that they fit together easily. The time spent struggling with obstinate joints whilst flat on your back under the car is eliminated and the likelihood of distorting or even breaking a section is greatly reduced. Do not waste a lot of time trying to undo rusted and corroded clamps and bolts. Cut them off. New ones will be required anyway if they are that bad.

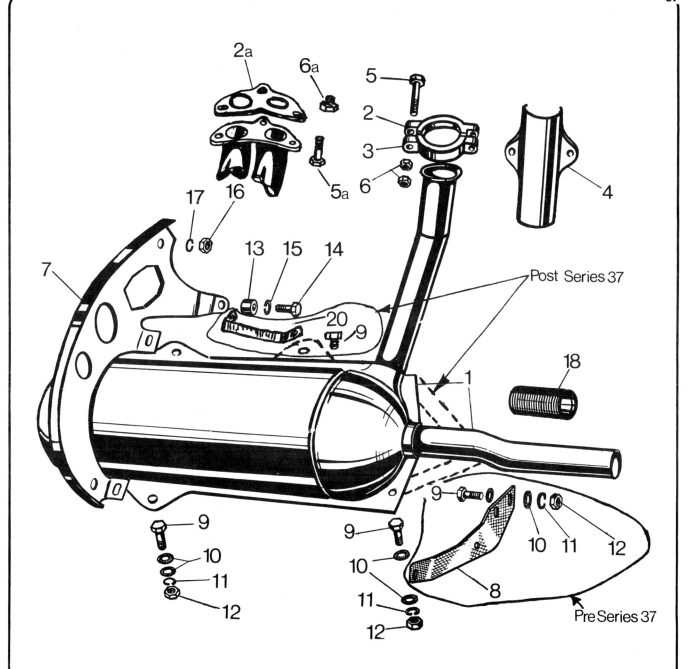

Fig. 3.7. The component parts of the exhaust system (Sec. 18)

1 Exhaust silencer
2 Exhaust clamp
2a Flange gasket
3 Exhaust clamp
4 Guard cover
5 Bolt
5a Bolt
6 Nut, brass plated
6a Nut
7 Front exhaust support
8 Rear exhaust support

9 Bolt
10 Washer
11 Spring washer
12 Nut
13 Spacer
14 Bolt
15 Spring washer
16 Nut
17 Washer
18 Silencer insertion
20 Bracket

19 Fault diagnosis - fuel system

Symptom	Reason/s	Remedy
Fuel consumption excessive, black deposits in exhaust pipe, difficult hot starting		
Carburation and ignition faults	Air cleaner choked and dirty giving rich mixture	Remove, clean and replace air cleaner.
	Fuel leaking from carburettor, fuel pumps, or fuel lines	Check for and eliminate all fuel leaks. Tighten fuel line union nuts.
	Float chamber flooding	Check and adjust float level.
	Generally worn carburettor	Remove, overhaul and replace.
	Distributor condenser faulty	Remove and fit new unit.
	Balance weights or vacuum advance mechanism in distributor faulty	Remove and overhaul distributor.
	Incorrect main jet fitted (calibre too large)	Check with Specifications and renew as necessary.
Incorrect adjustment	Carburettor incorrectly adjusted, mixture too rich	Tune and adjust carburettor.
	Idling speed too high	Adjust idling speed.
	Contact breaker gap incorrect	Check and reset gap.
	Valve clearances incorrect	Check rocker arm to valve stem clearances and adjust as necessary.
	Incorrectly set spark plugs	Remove, clean, and regap.
	Tyres under-inflated	Check tyre pressures and inflate if necessary.
	Wrong spark plugs fitted	Remove and replace with correct units.
	Brakes dragging	Check and adjust brakes.
Idling system problems		
Erratic idling	Idling jets/passages blocked	Remove and clean jets, and blow clean the internal passages.
	Idling screw loose or over-tightened	Adjust as required.
	Air leaks through flange gaskets	Check and renew as required.
	Engine stops when revs. drop	Re-adjust the idling speed.
Flat spots or hesitation on acceleration		
Incorrect adjustment	Fuel/air mixture incorrect	Re-adjust mixture control screws.
Fuel injection pump faulty	Faulty mechanism or blocked injector	Inspect pump unit and blow clean the injector nozzle. Renew or repair as required.
Mixture incorrect	Obstruction (weakness)	Clean and replace as required.
	Wear (richness)	Clean and replace as required.
Lack of power, overheating, white deposits in exhaust pipe or difficult cold starting		
Vacuum in fuel system	Petrol tank air vent restricted	Remove petrol cap, clean out air vent.
Dirt in system	Partially clogged filter in pump	Remove and clean filter.
	Dirt lodged in float chamber needle housing	Remove and clean out float chamber and needle valve assembly.
	Partially blocked jets	Remove jets, clear obstruction and replace.
Fuel pump faults	Debris preventing fuel pump valves from seating correctly	Remove, dismantle and clean out fuel pump.
	Fuel pump diaphragm leaking or damaged	Remove and overhaul fuel pump.
	Gasket in fuel pump damaged	Remove and overhaul fuel pump.
	Fuel pump valves sticking due to petrol gumming	Remove and thoroughly clean fuel pump.
Air entering system	Union joints on pipe connections loose	Tighten joints and check for air leaks.
	Split in fuel pipe on suction side of fuel pump	Examine, locate, and repair.
	Inlet manifold to block or inlet manifold to carburettor gasket leaking	Test by pouring oil along joints - bubbles indicate leak. Renew gasket as appropriate.
	Fuel tank empty	Refill.

Chapter 4 Ignition system

Contents

Specifications

Type ... ...   Coil and distributor

Spark plugs
Type ... ...   Champion L-10S, KLG F80 or AC42/43F
Spark plug gap ... ...   0.024 to 0.026 in (0.7 to 0.8 mm)

Firing order ... ...   1 — 3 — 4 — 2

Coil
Make ... ...   Pal Magneton
Type ... ...   443.212 - 214.101

Distributor
Make ... ...   Pal Magneton

Model	Distributor type	Spark advance (BTDC)
100, 100L	443, 213, 204, 432	$5^{\circ} \pm 1^{\circ}$
	443, 213, 204, 34	$4^{\circ} \pm 2^{\circ}$
110L	443, 213, 204, 432	$3^{\circ} \pm 2^{\circ}$ — 95 octane rating
		$0^{\circ} \pm 2^{\circ}$ — 90 octane rating
	443, 213, 204, 34	$3^{\circ} \pm 1^{\circ}$ — 90 octane rating
110R, 110LS	443, 213, 204, 38	$7^{\circ} \pm 1^{\circ}$

Contact breaker points gap ... ...   0.015 in (4 mm)

Automatic advance ... ...   Centrifugal and vacuum
Drive ... ...   Gear driven from front of camshaft

1 General description

In order that the engine can run correctly it is necessary for an electrical spark to ignite the fuel/air mixture in the combustion chamber at exactly the right moment in relation to engine speed and load. The ignition system is based on feeding low tension voltage from the battery to the coil where it is converted to high tension voltage. The high tension voltage is powerful enough to jump the spark plug gap in the cylinders many times a second under high compression pressures, providing that the system is in good condition and that all adjustments are correct.

The ignition system is divided into two circuits. The low tension circuit and the high tension circuit.

The low tension (sometimes known as the primary) circuit consists of the battery, lead to the control box, lead to the ignition switch, lead from the ignition switch to the low tension or primary coil windings, and the lead from the low tension coil windings to the contact breaker points and condenser in the distributor.

The high tension circuit consists of the high tension or secondary coil windings, the heavy ignition lead from the centre of the coil to the centre of the distributor cap, the rotor arm, and the spark plug leads and spark plugs.

The system functions in the following manner:

Low tension voltage is changed in the coil into high tension voltage by the opening and closing of the contact breaker points in the low tension circuit. High tension voltage is then fed via the carbon brush in the centre of the distributor cap to the rotor arm of the distributor. The rotor arm revolves inside the distributor cap, and each time it comes in line with one of the four metal segments in the cap, which are connected to the spark plug leads, the opening and closing of the contact breaker points causes the high tension voltage to build up, jump the gap from the rotor arm to the appropriate metal segment and so via the spark plug lead to the spark plug, where it finally jumps the spark plug gap before going to earth.

The ignition is advanced and retarded automatically, to ensure the spark occurs at just the right instant for the particular load at the prevailing engine speed.

The ignition advance is controlled both mechanically and by a vacuum operated system. The mechanical governor mechanism comprises two lead weights, which move out from the distributor shaft as the engine speed rises due to centrifugal force. As they move outwards they rotate the cam relative to the distributor shaft, and so advance the spark. The weights are held in position by two light springs and it is the tension of the springs which is largely responsible for correct spark advancement.

The vacuum control consists of a diaphragm, one side of which is connected via a small bore tube to the carburettor, and the other side to the contact breaker plate. Vacuum in the inlet manifold and carburettor, which varies with engine speed and throttle opening, causes the diaphragm to move, so moving the contact breaker plate, and advancing or retarding the spark. A fine degree of control is achieved by a spring in the vacuum assembly.

2 Routine maintenance

Spark plugs
Remove the plugs and thoroughly clean away all traces of carbon. Examine the porcelain insulation round the central electrode inside the plug and if damaged discard the plug. Reset the gap between the electrodes. Do not use a set of plugs for more than 12,500 miles (20,000 km). It is false economy.

Distributor
Every 3,000 miles (5,000 km), apply with an oil can, 20 drops of engine oil to the distributor shaft by unscrewing the grub screw in the distributor body and inserting the oil can nozzle. Pump the oil under pressure to ensure good penetration of the inner felt bush.

Every 6,250 miles (10,000 km), remove the distributor cap and rotor arm and put one or two drops of engine oil into the centre of the cam recess. Smear the surfaces of the cam itself with petroleum jelly. Do not over-lubricate as any excess could get onto the contact point surfaces and cause ignition difficulties.

Every 6,250 miles (10,000 km), examine the contact point surfaces. If there is a build-up of deposits on one face and a pit in the other, it will be impossible to set the gap correctly and they should be refaced or renewed. Set the gap when the contact surfaces are in order. Examine the distributor cam shaft and contact breaker support plate. It is essential that there should not be any radial movement of the shaft and contact breaker location plate. Any sloppiness in the distributor mechanism will introduce a random ignition timing, which will reduce engine efficiency.

General
Examine all leads and terminals for signs of broken or cracked insulation. Also check all terminal connections for slackness or signs of fracturing of some strands of wire. Partly broken wire should be renewed.

The HT leads are particularly important as any insulation faults will cause the high voltage to 'jump' to the nearest earth and this will prevent a spark at the plug. Check that no HT leads are loose or in a position where the insulation could wear due to rubbing against part of the engine.

3 Distributors - identification

There are three types of Pal Magneton distributors fitted, the most notable difference being the body diameters. From May 1975 all models were fitted with the larger diameter distributors.

For reference purposes, the types, and models to which they are fitted are listed in the Specifications at the start of this Chapter.

It should be noted that the large and small types have different fitted positions in the engine, although the location on the top of the timing chest remains the same (see Figs. 4.1 and 4.2).

4 Contact breaker points - adjustment

1 Release the two spring clips retaining the distributor cap to the

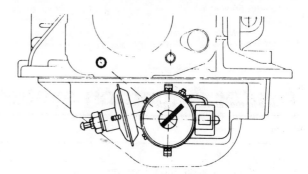

Fig. 4.1. Early (smaller body) type distributor installed position (Sec. 3)

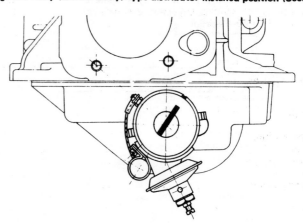

Fig. 4.2. Later (large body) type distributor installed position (Sec. 3)

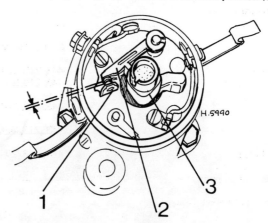

Fig. 4.3. The principle distributor adjustment components (Sec. 4)

1 Contact breaker fixed point
2 Contact breaker arm
3 Contact breaker cam

body and lift off the cap. Invert the cap so that the carbon brush and spring do not fall out.
2 With a dry cloth, clean the cap inside and out and examine the four 'brass' segments. If these are badly burned or scored the cap should be renewed, but a temporary improvement may be made by scraping the segments clean with a small penknife.
3 Check that the carbon brush is located correctly on its spring and that it has a free-movement within the cap.
4 Carefully prise the contact breaker points (Fig. 4.3) apart for inspection. If they are pitted or dirty, they will have to be removed for cleaning or replacement (see Section 5).
5 Assuming the points to be in satisfactory condition, adjust them as

follows:

a) *Remove the rotor arm, then turn the engine over until the contact breaker heel is on the very peak of one of the four cam lobes.*

b) *With a feeler gauge, measure the gap between the contact points, which will now be fully open (photo). The correct gap is 0.014 to 0.016 in (0.4 to 0.5 mm).*

c) *If the gap is incorrect it can be adjusted by loosening the contact plate screw slightly, inserting a screwdriver into the notched recess in the end of the plate (photo), and then moving the plate in the relevant direction to open or close the contact gap as required. The gap is correct when a feeler gauge of the correct size may be moved between the points without binding or slackness.*

d) *Tighten the contact plate screw, and re-check the gap.*

6   Replace the rotor arm and distributor cap and reclip the spring blade retainers into position.

5   Contact breaker points - removal and replacement

1   Unclip the retaining springs and remove the distributor cap complete with leads, then remove the rotor arm.
2   Release the C-clip on the points pivot shaft.
3   Remove the fibre washer.
4   Unscrew the pivot plate screw, and withdraw the contact breaker points from the distributor (photo). Unclip the low tension lead from behind the points spring. Be careful not to drop the small pivot plate screws down through the base plate holes.
5   Replacement is a reversal of the dismantling sequence, but the contact points will have to be 'gapped', as described in Section 4.

6   Condenser - testing, removal and replacement

1   The condenser, or capacitor as it is sometimes known, is fitted to ensure that when the contact breaker points are open, there is no excessive sparking across them to cause waste voltage and additional wear. A faulty condenser will cause misfiring or complete failure. Although it is possible to test a condenser, special equipment is required. It is therefore advisable to replace a suspected faulty unit with a new one as they are relatively inexpensive.

2   If the contact points become pitted after a relatively small mileage and if starting is difficult, then it is a good idea to replace the condenser when replacing the points. Another way to check is to remove the distributor cap and rotor arm and turn the engine so that the points are closed. Then switch on the ignition and open the points, using an insulated screwdriver. There should be a small blue spark visible but if the condenser is faulty there will be a fat blue spark.

3   The condenser is external to the workings of the distributor, and can be removed by undoing the lead from the condenser to the fixing point on the side of the distributor, and the retaining screws on the distributor body.

4   Fit a new replacement in the reverse order (photo).

7   Distributor - removal and replacement

1   To assist during reassembly, the timing of the distributor can be marked before it is removed, This is achieved by turning the crankshaft to tdc (top-dead-centre), which can be seen by aligning the 'V' nick in the fan/alternator pulley with the 'O' marked on the timing chest. With a fine toothed hacksaw blade or small file, mark the position of the two flanges and, on top of the distributor body, mark the point to which the rotor arm is facing.

2   The distributor is best removed by undoing the two retaining bolts on the extension tube flange to timing chest. If disconnected at the top of the extension tube, the preset timing will be disturbed: this should be avoided if possible.

3   Remove the vacuum tube from the carburettor (photo).
4   Disconnect the low tension lead.
5   The distributor may now be withdrawn.
6   Replacement is a reversal of the above procedure, but if the engine has been turned over at all, since distributor removal, the ignition

4.5b Checking contact breaker points gap with feeler gauge

4.5c Levering the contacts, to adjust the gap

5.4 The contact breaker points, washer and retaining screw removed for inspection

6.4 Position of condenser on distributor body also showing connecting lead

7.3 Vacuum tube connection

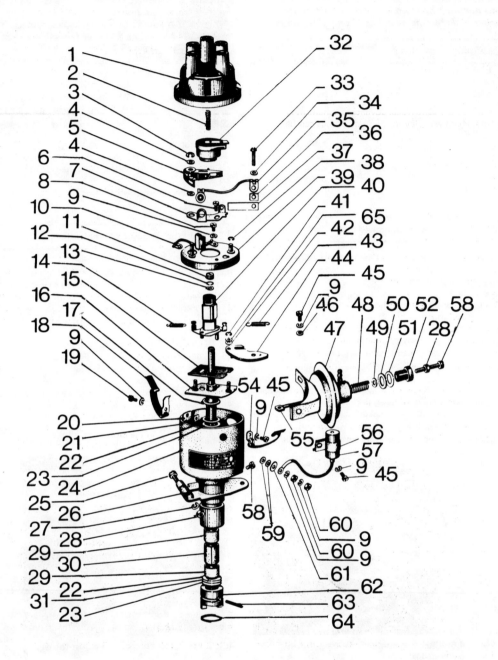

Fig. 4.4. The component parts of the distributor (Sec. 8)

1	Distributor cap assembly	17	Washer	33	Screw
2	Carbon brush	18	Holding spring	34	Washer
3	Safety washer	19	Screw	35	Arm connection
4	Distance washer	20	Packing piece	36	Insulating washer
5	Contact breaker arm	21	Nut	37	Insulating band
6	Screw	22	Washer	38	Safety ring
7	Fixed contact	23	Washer	39	Base plate
8	Screw	24	Casing of distributor	40	Cam compl.
9	Spring washer	25	Screw	41	Safety ring
10	Earthing connection	26	Bracket	42	Washer
11	Lubricating packing	27	Spring washer	43	Governor spring
12	Securing spring	28	Nut	44	Governor weight
13	Washer	29	Self lubricating bearing	45	Screw
14	Governor spring	30	Lubricating felt	46	Washer
15	Washer	31	Washer	47	Vacuum chamber
16	Shaft compl.	32	Distributor rotor	48	Spring

49	Distance washer
50	Seal
51	Distance washer
52	Reduction screw
54	Holding spring
55	Pull rod
56	Retainer
57	Capacitor
58	Screw
59	Insulating washer
60	Nut
61	Insulating washer
62	Driving coupling
63	Coupling pin
64	Securing pin
65	Distance washer

should be retimed. This is also necessary if the clamp plate at the top of the extension tube has been disturbed. See Section 9 to check and adjust ignition timing.

8 Distributor - dismantling, inspection and reassembly

Refer to Fig. 4.4.

1 If the distributor is causing trouble, it is often a good idea to fit a completely new unit. Without the proper test equipment it is difficult to diagnose whether or not the centrifugal advance mechanism is performing as it should. However, play in the shaft bushes can be detected by removing the rotor arm and gripping the end of the distributor shaft and trying to move it sideways. If there is any movement then it means that the cam cannot accurately control the contact points gap. This must receive attention.

2 With the distributor removed, take off the rotor, condenser and contact points.

3 Remove the vacuum unit complete, by undoing the two screws (one retains the condenser connector), and holding spring.

4 Undo the distributor cap retaining clip screws and remove the clips, then lift out the baseplate.

5 By now you should not have taken too much time dismantling the distributor, and after cleaning the components in petrol or carbon tetrachloride they may be examined for wear. It should be noted that individual components are not particularly easy to obtain. Serious consideration should be given to a new or exchange assembly. If, however, you feel you must proceed to dismantle and renovate your distributor further, continue as follows.

6 Remove the felt pad from its recess in the cam head and then the 'C' clip and washer.

7 From the bottom of the shaft, remove the serrated location pin from the drive coupling by drifting it out.

8 Remove the coupling from the shaft and withdraw the camshaft, complete with the governor springs and weight assembly.

9 The bushes and felt lubricator can now be removed from the distributor body.

10 Check the condition of the contact breaker points. Check the distributor cap for signs of tracking, indicated by a thin black line between the segments. Renew the cap if any signs of tracking are found.

11 If the metal portion of the rotor arm is badly burned or loose, renew the arm. If slightly burnt clean the arm with a fine file.

12 Check that the carbon brush moves freely in the centre of the distributor cover.

13 Examine the fit of the breaker plate on the bearing plate and also check the breaker arm pivot for looseness or wear and renew as necessary.

14 Examine the balance weights and pivot pins for wear, and renew the weights or cam assembly if a degree of wear is found.

15 Examine the shaft and the fit of the cam assembly on the shaft. If the clearance is excessive compare the items with new units, and renew either, or both, if they show excessive wear.

16 If the shaft is loose in the distributor bushes, it will be necessary to fit a new shaft, and bushes and felt bush (located between the bushes). The old bushes are simply pressed out and the new bushes pressed in. The felt bush should be thoroughly soaked in oil prior to assembly. It will be noted that there is a grub screw located at an angle in the exterior of the distributor body approximately in line with the bushes. This grub screw should be periodically removed and oil squirted through the aperture to re-lubricate the felt bush. This will prolong both the shaft and bush life.

17 Examine the length of the balance weight springs and compare them with new springs. If they have stretched they must be renewed.

18 Reassembly is a straight reversal of the dismantling process, but there are several points which should be noted in addition to those already given in the section on dismantling.

19 Lubricate with engine oil, the balance weights and other parts of the mechanical advance mechanism; the distributor shaft; and the portion of the shaft on which the cam bears, during assembly. Do not oil excessively but ensure these parts are adequately lubricated.

20 Check the action of the weights in the fully advanced and fully retarded positions and ensure they are not binding.

21 Tighten the micrometer adjusting nut to the middle position on the timing scale.

22 Finally, set the contact breaker gap to the correct clearance.

9.6 Fine adjustment of the ignition timing

9 Ignition timing - checking and adjustment

If it is necessary to reset the ignition timing or to check it, a 12v bulb (35 to 45w) in a holder with two leads attached, will be required in place of a voltmeter. Proceed as follows:

1 First turn the crankshaft over to get tdc (top-dead-centre). This is achieved when the 'V' mark on the fan/alternator pulley is in line with the 'O' mark on the timing chest. Number 1 piston should be at the top of its firing stroke. If the rocker cover is removed, this can be confirmed by seeing if both the inlet and exhaust valves of number 1 cylinder are both in the closed position and the rockers 'slack'.

2 Ensure that the points have been set to the recommended setting, are in good condition, and the battery is connected. Turn on the ignition and connect one test light lead to the terminal where the coil low tension lead is connected to the distributor, and then connect the other lead from the bulb to earth. The bulb should light up when the contact breaker points are open.

3 With the distributor clamp bolt loosened, turn the body of the distributor anticlockwise until the test light goes out.

4 Apply finger-pressure to the rotor arm in a clockwise direction, and then turn the distributor body in a clockwise direction until the bulb *just* lights. Hold the distributor in this position and retighten the clamp bolt.

5 Disconnect the bulb and replace the distributor cap. Static ignition timing is now complete.

6 It must be noted that to get the very best setting the final adjustment should be made on the road. The distributor vernier can be moved about ¼ of a division at a time until the best setting is obtained. The Pal Magneton distributors fitted, have a screw and locking nut for fine adjustments in place of the more usual knurled nut vernier adjustment (photo).

7 The amount of wear in the engine, grade of petrol used, and amount of carbon in the combustion chambers, all contribute to make the recommended ignition timing settings no more than nominal ones. To obtain the best setting under running conditions, first start the engine and allow it to warm up to normal temperature, and then accelerate in top gear from 30 to 50 mph, listening for heavy pinking. If this occurs, the ignition needs to be retarded slightly until just the faintest trace of pinking can be heard under these operating conditions.

8 Since the ignition timing adjustment enables the firing point to be related correctly in relation to the grade of fuel used, the fullest advantage of any change of fuel will only be attained by re-adjustment of the ignition settings.

10 Spark plugs and HT leads - general

1 The correct functioning of the spark plugs is vital for the correct running and efficiency of the engine.

White deposits and damaged
porcelain insulation indicating
overheating

Broken porcelain insulation
due to bent central electrode

Electrodes burnt away due to
wrong heat value or chronic
pre-ignition (pinking)

Excessive black deposits
caused by over-rich mixture
or wrong heat value

Mild white deposits and electrode burnt indicating too
weak a fuel mixture

Plug in sound condition with
light greyish brown deposits

Fig. 4.5. Spark plug electrode conditions (Sec. 10)

2   At intervals of 3,000 miles (5,000 km), the plugs should be removed, examined, cleaned, and if worn excessively, replaced. The condition of the spark plug will also tell much about the overall condition of the engine (see Fig. 4.5).

3   If the insulator nose of the spark plug is clean and white, with no deposits, this is indicative of a weak mixture, or too hot a plug. (A hot plug transfers heat away from the electrode slowly - a cold plug transfers it away quickly).

4   If the top and insulator nose is covered with hard black looking deposits, then this is indicative that the mixture is too rich. Should the plug be black and oily, then it is likely that the engine is fairly worn, as well as the mixture being too rich.

5   If the insulator nose is covered with light tan to greyish brown deposits, then the mixture is correct and it is likely that the engine is in good condition.

6   If there are any traces of long brown tapering stains on the outside of the white portion of the plug, then the plug will have to be renewed, as this shows that there is a faulty joint between the plug body and the insulator, and compression is being allowed to leak away.

7   Plugs should be cleaned by a sand blasting machine, which will free them from carbon more thoroughly than cleaning by hand. The machine will also test the condition of the plugs under compression. Any plug that fails to spark at the recommended pressure should be renewed.

8   The spark plug gap is of considerable importance, as, if it is too large or too small, the size of the spark and its efficiency will be seriously impaired.

9   To set it, measure the gap with a feeler gauge, and then bend open, or close, the outer plug electrode until the correct gap is achieved. The centre electrode should never be bent as this may crack the insulation and cause plug failure, if nothing worse.

10 When replacing the plugs, remember to use new plug washers, and replace the leads from the distributor in the correct firing order, which is 1, 3, 4, 2, number 1 cylinder being the one nearest the crankshaft pulley.

11 The only routine attention required by the HT leads is to be kept clean and dry. At 3,000 miles (5,000 km) intervals, remove the leads, one at a time, from the respective plug and distributor position. Then remove any corrosion or dirt from the brass end clips. Clean out the distributor cap collars and replace the leads.

12 Renew the spark plugs regularly at 12,500 miles (20,000 km) intervals.

11 Coil - general

The coil, mounted on the inside panel of the right-hand rear wing, normally requires very little attention, apart from checking that the HT and low tension lead connections are clean and secure.

The coil should always be tested at its working temperature; so, if possible, allow the engine to warm up first. To test the coil refer to the Ignition fault diagnosis Section.

If required, the coil can easily be removed by disconnecting the leads and undoing the clamp location stud nuts. Reassembly is the reverse procedure.

12 Ignition system - fault diagnosis

By far the majority of breakdown and running troubles are caused by faults in the ignition system, either in the low tension or high tension circuit. There are two main symptoms indicating ignition faults. Either the engine will not start or fire, or the engine is difficult to start and misfires. If it is a regular misfire, i.e. the engine is only running on two or three cylinders, the fault is almost sure to be in the secondary, or high tension, circuit. If the misfiring is intermittent, the fault could be in either the high or low tension circuits. If the car stops suddenly, or will not start at all, it is likely that the fault is in the low tension circuit. Loss of power and overheating, apart from faulty carburation settings, are normally due to faults in the distributor or incorrect ignition timing.

Engine fails to start

1   If the engine fails to start and the car was running normally when it was last used, first check there is fuel in the petrol tank. If the engine turns over normally on the starter motor and the battery is evidently well charged, then the fault may be in either the high or low tension circuits. First check the HT circuit. **Note:** If the battery is known to be fully charged, the ignition light comes on, and the starter motor fails to turn the engine, **check the tightness of the leads on the battery terminals and the security of the earth lead to its connection to the body.** It is quite common for the leads to have worked loose, even if they look and feel secure. If one of the battery terminal posts gets very hot when trying to work the starter motor, this is a sure indication of a faulty connection to that terminal.

2 One of the commonest reasons for bad starting is wet or damp spark plug leads and distributor. Remove the distributor cap. If condensation is visible internally, dry the cap with a rag and wipe over the leads. Replace the cap.

3 If the engine still fails to start, check that current is reaching the plugs, by disconnecting each plug lead in turn at the spark plug end, and holding the end of the cable with a pair of pliers with insulated handles about 3/16 in (5 mm) away from the cylinder block. Spin the engine on the starter motor.

4 Sparking between the end of the cable and the block should be fairly strong with a regular blue spark. (Hold the lead with rubber to avoid electric shocks). If current is reaching the plugs, then remove them and clean and regap them. The engine should now start.

5 If there is no spark at the plug leads, take off the HT lead from the centre of the distributor cap and hold it to the block as before. Spin the engine on the starter once more. A rapid succession of blue sparks between the end of the lead and the block indicates that the coil is in order and that the distributor cap is cracked, the rotor arm faulty or the carbon brush in the top of the distributor cap is not making good contact with the spring on the rotor arm. Possibly the points are in bad condition. Clean and reset them.

6 If there are no sparks from the end of the lead from the coil, check the connections at the coil end of the lead. If it is in order start checking the low tension circuit.

7 Use a 12 volt voltmeter or a 12 volt bulb and two lengths of wire. With the ignition switch on and the points open, test between the low tension wire to the coil (SW or +) and earth. No reading indicates a break in the supply from the ignition switch. Check the connections at the switch to see if any are loose. Refit them and the engine should run. A reading shows a faulty coil or condenser or broken lead between the coil and the distributor.

8 Take the condenser wire off the points assembly and with the points open, test between the moving point and earth. If there now is a reading, then the fault is in the condenser. Fit a new one and the fault is cleared.

9 With no reading from the moving point to earth, take a reading between earth and the CB or (−) terminal of the coil. A reading here indicates a broken wire which must be renewed between the coil and distributor. No reading confirms that the coil has failed and must be renewed. Remember to connect the condenser lead to the points assembly. For these tests it is sufficient to separate the contact breaker points with a piece of paper.

Engine misfires

1 If the engine misfires regularly, run it at a fast idling speed. Pull off each of the plug caps in turn and listen to the note of the engine. Hold the plug cap in a dry cloth or with a rubber glove as additional protection against a shock from the HT supply.

2 No difference in engine running will be noticed when the lead from the defective circuit is removed. Removing the lead from one of the good cylinders will accentuate the misfire.

3 Remove the plug lead from the end of the defective plug and hold it about 3/16 in (5 mm) away from the block. Restart the engine. If the sparking is fairly strong and regular, the fault must lie in the spark plug.

4 The plug may be loose, the insulation may be cracked, or the points may have burnt away, giving too wide a gap for the spark to jump. Worse still, one of the points may have broken off. Either renew the plug, or clean it, reset the gap, and then test it.

5 If there is no spark at the end of the plug lead, or if it is weak and intermittent, check the ignition lead from the distributor to the plug. If the insulation is cracked or perished, renew the lead. Check the connections at the distributor cap.

6 If there is still no spark, examine the distributor cap carefully for tracking. This can be recognised by a very thin black line running between two or more electrodes, or between an electrode and some other part of the distributor. These lines are paths which now conduct electricity across the cap, thus letting it run to earth. The only answer is a new distributor cap.

7 Apart from the ignition timing being incorrect, other causes of misfiring have already been dealt with under the section dealing with the failure of the engine to start. To recap, these are that:

    a) The coil may be faulty giving an intermittent misfire.
    b) There may be a damaged wire or loose connection in the low tension circuit.
    c) The condenser may be short circuiting.
    d) There may be a mechanical fault in the distributor (broken driving spindle or contact breaker spring).

8 If the ignition timing is too far retarded, it should be noted that the engine will tend to overheat, and there will be a quite noticeable drop in power. If the engine is overheating and the power is down, and the ignition timing is correct, then the carburettor should be checked, as it is likely that this is where the fault lies.

Chapter 5 Clutch

Contents

Specifications

Type	Dry, single plate
System of control	Hydraulically operated
Clutch diameter	7 in (177.8 mm)
Clutch pedal free-travel clearance	2 in (50.8 mm)
Clutch operating rod clearance	0.25 in (6.35 mm)

Torque wrench setting	lb f ft	kg f m
Pressure (cover) plate retaining bolts	16.6 - 20.2	2.3 - 2.8

1 General description

The dry, single plate, type clutch has been used on all models since the introduction of the 1000 MB Series in 1964.

Basically, it comprises a cover plate, incorporating the coil springs, and a pressure plate, which bolts onto the flywheel. The friction disc is positioned between the pressure plate and the flywheel and is free-floating on the gearbox input shaft splines.

The mode of operation is that when the clutch pedal is depressed, the thrust bearing moves toward the clutch. The thrust bearing acts on three levers thereby lifting the pressure plate away from the friction disc.

The friction disc is now free and the gear shift can be used. When the clutch pedal is released the thrust bearing withdraws from the clutch and the pressure plate is allowed to bear on the friction disc and flywheel. With the disc firmly retained against the flywheel by the force in the coil springs, the clutch will transmit the driving torque from the engine to the gearbox.

2 Clutch actuating mechanism - description

1   The actuating system is hydraulic, drawing on fluid from the same reservoir as the brake system.
2   The master cylinder is located in the front boot, mounted on the bulkhead panel.
3   Hydraulic lines connect the master cylinder to the slave cylinder and this is mounted on top of the gearbox. It is accessible from within the car via an inspection panel in the floor of the rear luggage compartment. A plastic cover is located in position over the slave cylinder by a spring retainer. This cover prevents the ingress of dirt into the bell-housing aperture. To remove this cover simply prise the spring back as in the photo.

3 Master cylinder - removal and dismantling

For MB Models refer to Chapter 9, Section 13.
1   To remove the master cylinder, it is first necessary to disconnect the hydraulic fluid feed pipe from the reservoir, which locates on the top of the cylinder. Place a piece of newspaper under the cylinder to prevent any spillage which might damage the paintwork. Undo the

2.3 Slave cylinder cover and retaining spring

union bolt and double the hose back on itself, with a piece of rag over the end, to prevent spillage. Tie the hose back out of the way.

2 Undo the two flange retaining nuts, and remove together with the spring washers.

3 Disconnect the feed pipe from the side of the cylinder which goes to the slave cylinder.

4 Now withdraw the master cylinder from the bulkhead leaving the piston operating rod attached to the pedal linkage.

5 The master cylinder assembly can now be removed to the workbench where the various components can be dismantled, cleaned and laid out in sequence on a sheet of clean newspaper.

6 Dismantle as follows, referring to Fig. 5.1.
Remove the rubber protection boot from the cylinder.

7 Remove the circlip, cover, piston assembly, and valve assembly.

8 If required, the valve assembly in the outlet pipe to the slave cylinder can be removed by unscrewing the end plug.

4 Master cylinder - renovation and refitting

1 Once the unit has been dismantled, thoroughly clean all parts in hydraulic fluid - never contaminate any part associated with clutch or brake hydraulic systems with any other solvent.

2 Wipe the components dry with a non-fluffy rag and carefully examine the cylinder bore for wear, scratches or score marks. Renew cylinder if necessary.

3 Always use a complete set of new rubbers and, prior to assembly on the piston, thoroughly wet the primary and secondary cups in **clean** hydraulic fluid.

4 With all components laid out on a spotlessly clean surface, make sure your hands are free from grease and foreign matter and that your tools are spotlessly clean.

5 Assembly of the master cylinder is the reverse of dismantling

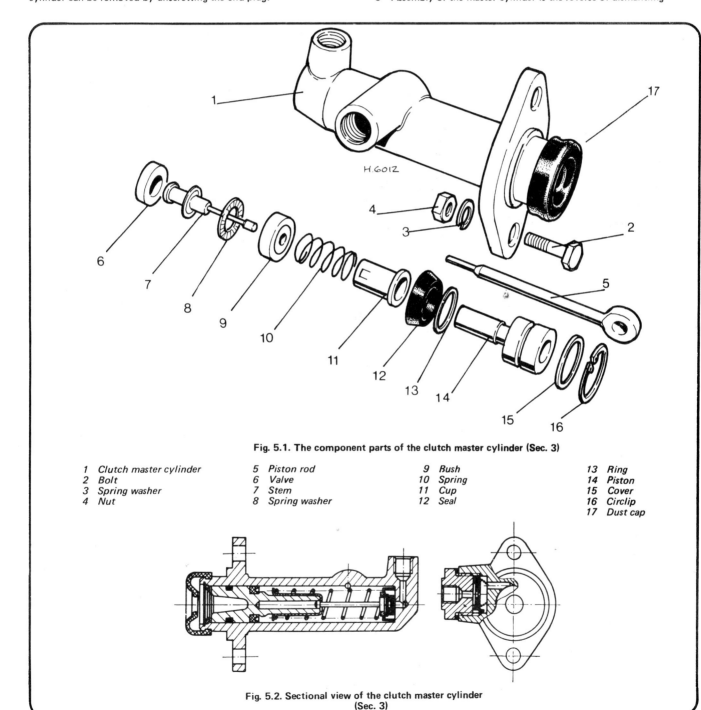

Fig. 5.1. The component parts of the clutch master cylinder (Sec. 3)

1 Clutch master cylinder
2 Bolt
3 Spring washer
4 Nut
5 Piston rod
6 Valve
7 Stem
8 Spring washer
9 Bush
10 Spring
11 Cup
12 Seal
13 Ring
14 Piston
15 Cover
16 Circlip
17 Dust cap

Fig. 5.2. Sectional view of the clutch master cylinder
(Sec. 3)

sequence - be careful not to damage the fine lips on the piston cups
when introducing the piston assembly back into the cylinder.
6   Refitting is the reverse sequence to removal, except that the
hydraulic system must be bled from the slave cylinder - see Section 7.

5   Clutch slave cylinder - removal and dismantling

1   Refer to Fig. 5.3. It is possible to remove the slave cylinder without lowering the engine or transaxle assemblies. The first step is to
disconnect the inlet pipe (plug it to prevent leakage) and then remove
the cylinder cover.
2   Unscrew the nuts which retain the cylinder to the gearbox and
remove the release fork springs (photo). With the nuts removed the
cylinder and pushrod may be lifted clear.
3   Dismantling of the cylinder assembly should be done on a clean
bench, and begins with the withdrawal of the operating rod (photo)
followed by the removal of the rubber boot over the end of the
cylinder and then removal of the circlip.
4   The piston may now be extracted and the bleed screw removed (also
the seal and spring on some early models).
5   Thoroughly clean all parts in clean brake fluid or methylated spirit,
ready for inspection.
6   Temporarily cover the aperture in the bellhousing with a piece of
rag, or similar, to prevent the entry of bolts, washers or dirt into the
housing.

6   Clutch slave cylinder - renovation, assembly and refitting

1   Having thoroughly cleaned all parts of the cylinder assembly,
examine as follows.
2   Inspect the piston and cylinder for scratching and the rubber seal
and boot for wear or perishing.
3   If the cylinder bore or periphery of the piston are badly scratched,
it is advisable to renew the whole unit, as it is not practical to repair
these items.
4   Should the rubbers only, be at fault, then these can be renewed from
a seal kit.
5   Smear all parts of the piston assembly with hydraulic fluid and
carefully reassemble and refit the slave cylinder in the reverse order of
removal and dismantling.
6   After refitting the slave cylinder, bleed the system, as described in
Section 7, and adjust, as described in Section 8.

7   Clutch system - bleeding

1   Gather together a clean glass jar, length of rubber tubing which fits
tightly over the bleed nipple in the slave cylinder and a tin of hydraulic
brake fluid. The services of an assistant will also be required.
2   Check that the master cylinder is full and if not, fill it, and cover
the bottom two inches of the jar with hydraulic fluid.

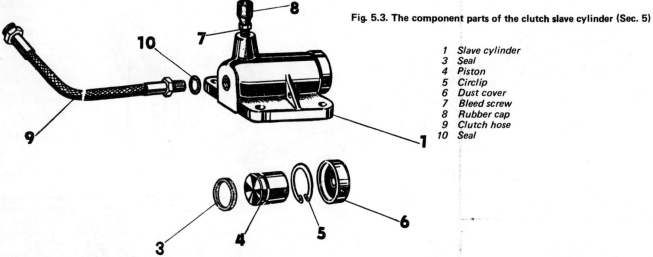

Fig. 5.3. The component parts of the clutch slave cylinder (Sec. 5)

1   Slave cylinder
3   Seal
4   Piston
5   Circlip
6   Dust cover
7   Bleed screw
8   Rubber cap
9   Clutch hose
10   Seal

5.2 Slave cylinder with release fork springs in position

5.3. Slave cylinder with the operating rod removed

3 Remove the rubber dust cap from the bleed nipple on the slave cylinder and with a suitable spanner open the bleed nipple ½ to ¾ of a turn.

4 Place one end of the tube securely over the nipple and insert the other end in the jar so that the tube orifice is below the level of the fluid.

5 The assistant should now pump the clutch pedal using a sequence of 3 long and 3 short strokes, until air bubbles cease to emerge from the end of the tubing. It is essential that the end of this tube should stay immersed at all times. Your assistant should also ensure that the fluid reservoir is kept topped-up, as if this empties, air will enter the system and it will be necessary to start again.

6 When no more air bubbles appear, tighten the bleed nipple during a slow downstroke. This done, remove the bleed tube from the nipple and replace the rubber dust cap.

7 Do not re-use hydraulic fluid bled from the system.

8 Clutch - adjustment

1 After a major overhaul of the clutch, or hydraulic circuits, the clutch operating rod and release lever should be checked for correct adjustment. The correct clearance between the two is 0.25 in (6.35 mm). The adjustment is made by undoing the locknut on the rod and turning the ball-headed nut in the direction required to obtain the correct clearance. When the correct clearance has been obtained lock the ball-headed nut in position with the locknut (photo).

2 The correct clutch pedal free-play is 2 in (50.8 mm); this is adjustable by turning the pedal stop screws. These should be locked in position when the correct clearance is obtained.

3 The clutch pedal free-play should only be re-adjusted when it is known that (a) the clutch unit is in good condition; (b) the hydraulic circuit is functioning correctly, and does not need bleeding.

9 Clutch - removal and dismantling

To renew the friction disc or examine the clutch assembly, it is necessary to remove the engine from the gearbox. To remove the engine only, follow the instructions given in Chapter 1.

With the engine removed from the car proceed as follows:

1 Mark the pressure (cover) plate in relation to the flywheel so that it can be replaced in the same relative position.

2 Slacken off the cover plate retaining bolts half a turn at a time in a diagonal sequence, to relieve the tension of the coil springs evenly thus preventing distortion.

3 On removing the bolts, the friction disc will be released, together with the cover plate (photo).

10 Clutch - inspection

To check the condition of the clutch assembly proceed as follows.

Friction disc

1 Visually inspect the facing material. There should be no evidence of oil contamination, deep scoring, pitting or signs of uneven wear. Also ensure that there is at least 1/32 in (0.8 mm) of lining material above the heads of the rivets. Glazing of the lining material is acceptable as long as the lining material pattern can clearly be seen through the glaze.

2 Next check the friction disc for distortion. Note that it can easily be damaged by the transaxle input shaft when the engine and transaxle are mated. To test the plate for distortion, slide it onto the input shaft splines. Rotate the disc against a fixed object. Any distortion will become immediately apparent. Whilst the disc is on the input shaft, ensure that it runs up and down the splines freely. Renew the friction disc if the splines are worn or if any of the previously described faults are in evidence. **Note:** If fitting a replacement friction disc, ensure that it is a good sliding fit on the input shaft splines with no tight spots.

Pressure plate assembly

3 Clean this assembly before inspection. Do not dismantle as the adjustment on the clutch fingers is preset and should not be disturbed.

4 Inspect the pressure plate friction face for any signs of scoring or pitting - if present, renew the assembly as a unit. Look for broken springs through the retaining cups, and also the finger return springs.

5 Inspect the clutch release sleeve assembly, checking for wear on the front face and the bearing.

6 Ensure that the release fork and the return and retaining springs are in good condition - any distortion, or signs of wear, will necessitate renewal (see Section 12). **Note:** Any signs of oil on the clutch assembly when dismantling, indicates that the gearbox input shaft and/or crankshaft oil seals are faulty and should therefore be renewed at this time. Also examine the camshaft core plug and oilway plug for signs of leakage.

11 Clutch - refitting

1 It is important that no oil or grease gets on the clutch disc friction linings, or the pressure plate and flywheel faces. It is advisable to refit the clutch with clean hands and to wipe down the pressure plate and flywheel faces with a clean dry rag before assembly begins.

2 Place the clutch disc against the flywheel with the longer end of

8.1 Adjusting the operating rod

9.3 Removing the clutch unit

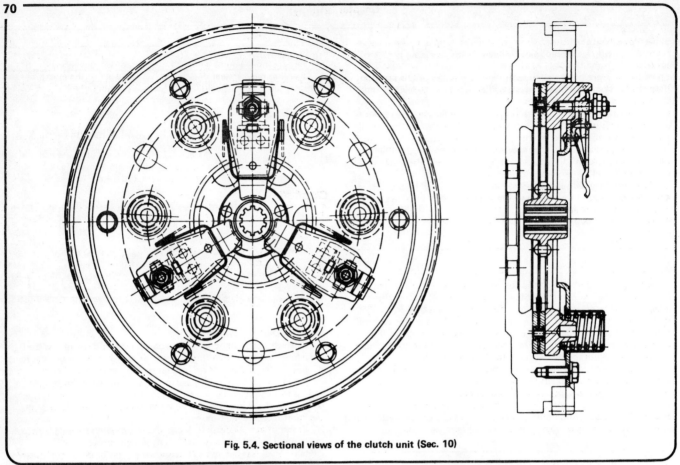

Fig. 5.4. Sectional views of the clutch unit (Sec. 10)

11.7 Reassembled clutch unit and flywheel

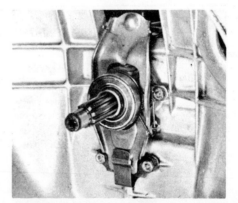

12.2 Clutch release bearing and lever assembly in position

12.3 Release bearing and lever complete, with lever retaining clip removed

12.4 Release bearing and lever on the gearbox side showing spring location

12.5 Removing the release sleeve/oil seal from gearbox

the hub facing outwards, away from the flywheel. On no account should the clutch disc be replaced with the longer end of the centre hub facing in to the flywheel as on reassembly it will be found quite impossible to operate the clutch with the friction disc in this position. Often the friction disc will be marked 'Flywheel Side' to aid refitting.
3 Refit the clutch cover assembly, with markings in line with those made on the flywheel. Replace the six retaining bolts and spring washers. Tighten them finger-tight so that the clutch disc is gripped, but can still be moved.
4 The clutch disc must now be centralised so that when the engine and gearbox are mated, the gearbox input shaft splines will pass through the splines in the centre of the friction plate hub.
5 Centralise the clutch disc by inserting a round bar or long screwdriver into the hole in the centre of the clutch, so that the end of the bar rests in the crankshaft bearing for the input shaft. Ideally an old input shaft should be used for this purpose.
6 Using the input shaft bearing in the crankshaft as a fulcrum point, move the bar sideways, or up and down, as required, to centralise the clutch disc.
7 Centralisation can be judged by removing the bar and viewing the clutch disc splined hub in relation to the input shaft bearing in the crankshaft. When the two appear in line, the clutch bolts may be tightened to the correct torque in a diagonal sequence to ensure that the pressure (cover) plate is pulled down evenly and without distortion (photo). To prevent the flywheel turning when tightening the cover plate bolts, a screwdriver may be placed to locate between the teeth at the flywheel and a bellhousing stud.

12 Clutch release bearing unit and gearbox oilseal - removal and reassembly

1 To inspect the clutch release bearing it is necessary to remove the engine from the gearbox, as described in Chapter 1.
2 The release bearing and fork form an integral unit, which is retained in position by the release fork holder at the bottom, whilst the bearing, which locates over the protruding oil seal sleeve from the gearbox, is fixed with the release fork by means of a special spring (photo).
3 To remove the release bearing and fork, simply undo and remove the two fork retaining clip nuts and remove complete (photo).
4 To disconnect the release fork and bearing, unclip the spring from the rear face (photo).
5 If oil is leaking from the gearbox, the sleeve and seal should also be removed and the seal renewed at this stage. This can be achieved by first partly draining the gearbox, undoing the two sleeve plate retaining nuts (photo), and then removing the sleeve complete with seal from its aperture.
6 After renewing the seal the sleeve can be reassembled over the spigot shaft and with a small amount of sealing solution smeared around its location housing in the gearbox, pressed into position.
7 Smear some grease over the sleeve prior to fitting the release bearing assembly into position.

13 Clutch - lubrication

1 To lubricate the clutch release lever it is necessary to remove the central floor cover under the floor covering in the compartment behind the rear seats. This done, release the spring and remove the plastic cover over the slave cylinder.
2 With a suitable oilcan, preferably having an adjustable nozzle, apply 10 to 12 drops of oil to the central slot of the clutch release lever.
3 Also lubricate the clutch release bearing sleeve recess with the pad in it. **Note:** Be careful not to squirt any oil in the direction of the clutch plate assembly!

14 Fault diagnosis - clutch

There are four main faults to which the clutch and release mechanism are prone. They may occur by themselves or in conjunction with any of the other faults. They are clutch squeal, slip, spin, and judder.

Clutch squeal
1 If on taking up the drive or when changing gear, the clutch squeals, this is a sure indication of a badly worn clutch release bearing.
2 As well as regular wear due to normal use, wear of the clutch release bearing is much accentuated if the clutch is ridden, or held down for long periods in gear, with the engine running. To minimise wear of this component the car should always be taken out of gear at traffic lights and for similar hold-ups.
3 The clutch release bearing is not an expensive item, but difficult to get at. **Note:** Ensure engine squeal does not originate from the fan belt or water pump.

Clutch slip
4 Clutch slip is a self-evident condition which occurs when the clutch friction plate is badly worn, the release arm free travel is insufficient, oil or grease have got onto the flywheel or pressure plate faces, or the pressure plate itself is faulty.
5 The reason for clutch slip is that, due to one of the faults listed above, there is either insufficient pressure from the pressure plate, or insufficient friction from the friction plate to ensure solid drive.
6 If small amounts of oil get onto the clutch, they will be burnt off under the heat of clutch engagement, and in the process, gradually darken the linings. Excessive oil on the clutch will burn off leaving a carbon deposit which can cause quite bad slip, or fierceness, spin and judder.
7 If clutch slip is suspected, and confirmation of this condition is required, there are several tests which can be made.
8 With the engine in second or third gear and pulling lightly up a moderate incline, sudden depression of the accelerator pedal may cause the engine to increase its speed without any increase in road speed. Easing off on the accelerator will then give a definite drop in engine speed without the car slowing.
9 In extreme cases of clutch slip the engine will race under normal acceleration conditions.
10 If slip is due to oil or grease on the linings a temporary cure can sometimes be effected by squirting carbon tetrachloride into the clutch. The permanent cure is, of course, to renew the clutch driven plate and trace and rectify the oil leak.

Clutch spin
11 Clutch spin is a condition which occurs when there is a leak in the clutch hydraulic actuating mechanism, the release arm free travel is excessive, there is an obstruction in the clutch either on the primary gear splines, or in the operation lever itself, or oil may have partially burnt off the clutch linings and have left a resinous deposit which is causing the clutch disc to stick to the pressure plate or flywheel.
12 The reason for clutch spin is that due to any, or a combination of, the faults just listed, the clutch pressure plate is not completely freeing from the centre plate even with the clutch pedal fully depressed.
13 If clutch spin is suspected, the condition can be confirmed by extreme difficulty in engaging first gear from rest, difficulty in changing gear, and very sudden take-up of the clutch drive at the fully depressed end of the clutch pedal travel as the clutch is released.
14 Check the clutch master and slave cylinders and the connecting hydraulic pipe for leaks. Fluid in one of the rubber boots fitted over the end of either the master or slave cylinders is a sure sign of a leaking piston seal.
15 If these points are checked and found to be in order then the fault lies internally in the clutch, and it will be necessary to remove the clutch for examination.

Clutch judder
16 Clutch judder is a self-evident condition which occurs when the gearbox or engine mountings are loose or too flexible, when there is oil on the faces of the clutch friction plate, or when the clutch pressure plate has been incorrectly adjusted.
17 The reason for clutch judder is that due to one of the faults just listed, the clutch pressure plate is not freeing smoothly from the friction disc, and is snatching.
18 Clutch judder normally occurs when the clutch pedal is released in first or reverse gears, and the whole car shudders as it moves backwards or forwards.

Chapter 6 Transaxle

Contents

Specifications

Number of gears	4 forward, 1 reverse
Synchromesh	On all forward gears

Oil capacity (gearbox and differential)
Initial filling	4.4 Imp. pints (2.5 litres)
Refill	3.5 Imp. pints (2 litres)

Filler location	Top of gearbox through filler neck

Gear ratios and mph per 1000 rpm
4th	0.96 : 1/16.1 mph
3rd	1.41 : 1/10.92 mph
2nd	2.12 : 1/7.28 mph
1st	3.80 : 1/4.1 mph
Reverse	3.27 : 1/4.7 mph

Final drive
Type	Swinging half-axles with independent suspension
Differential	Spiral bevel gears
Final drive ratio:	
Standard	4.44 : 1
Alternative	4.66 : 1
Crownwheel pinion backlash	0.003 - 0.007 in (0.15 - 0.20 mm)

Torque wrench settings
	lb f ft	kg fm
Prime motion shaft nut	25 to 31	3.5 to 4.5
Pinion nut	58 to 65	8 to 9
Pinion bearing cap nut	10 to 12	1.4 to 1.7
Release sleeve bolt nut	4 to 6	0.6 to 0.8
Speedometer shaft clamp bolt/nut	4 to 6	0.7 to 0.9
Speedometer bearing bolt/nut	4 to 6	0.7 to 0.9
Reverse pin bolt nut	11 to 14	1.7 to 2
Reverse pin bolt	4 to 6	0.7 to 0.9
Shifter fork bolt	14	2
Interlock ball cap bolt	7	0.8
Resilient mounting bolt	21 to 28	3 to 4
Differential housing bolt	14 to 21	2 to 3
Crownwheel bolt	50 to 57	7 to 8
Tapered draw plugs	21	2.5 to 3
Half-axle balljoint bolt	14 to 17	2 to 2.5

1 General description, gearbox modifications and routine maintenance

General description

The transmission unit fitted to all models contains four forward speeds and one reverse. The gearchange lever is of floor mounted, remote control type.

The gearbox and final drive unit form an integral assembly within a single aluminium casing. For inspection or repairs, this has to be removed from the car, the two halves of the casing 'split', and the front cover removed. It is not possible to remove the differential or gearbox separately from the car.

For maintenance there is a drain plug, level plug and a special filler tube projects from the top of the gearbox casing between the starter motor and clutch slave cylinder. Check the oil level regularly, as described in the Maintenance Section at the front of the book. See Fig. 6.1, for sectional views of gearbox and transmission (early type).

Gearbox modifications

Mainshaft: Since April 1975, the preload thrust on the driveshaft bearing is no longer fitted. This is due to improved machining methods during gearbox manufacture.

Synchro-hubs: From May 1975, improved synchro-hub springs were fitted to both the 1st/2nd and 3rd/4th synchro-hubs. These springs are stronger than those previously fitted. Do not interchange the two types on a hub. They are fully interchangeable as a complete set.

Pinion shaft bushes: In August 1974, the 4th and 2nd/3rd gears were no longer fitted to the bushes which located them on the shaft. They now fit directly to the splines and where there used to be two friction ring location keys (a long or short type), there is now a single long one, which locates all of the friction rings.

Crownwheel and pinion - special note

If on stripping the gearbox and differential units, the pinion or crownwheel unit are damaged and need replacement, they will have to

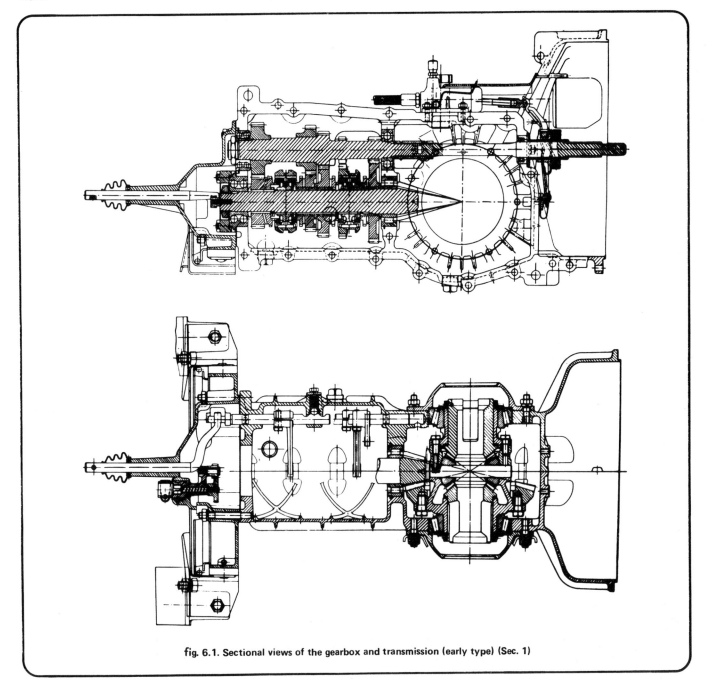

fig. 6.1. Sectional views of the gearbox and transmission (early type) (Sec. 1)

be renewed as a pair. Each crownwheel and pinion are run in together at the Skoda factory and are marked as such (see Fig. 6.2). The crownwheel is located in the differential housing between the tapered roller bearings, which are preloaded by the shims fitted between the half-axle flanges and the bearing cups.

The pinion adjustment is by half-shims fitted between the front pinion shaft bearing flange and bearing cover.

To predetermine the thickness of the shims required for accurate meshing of the two gears, special tools are required. It is not possible to accurately check the mesh of the two gears when the gearbox/differential units are fully assembled.

In view of these problems, if you have to replace the differential unit it is best left to your local Skoda agent, unless he is benevolent enough to pre-check your gearbox/differential tolerances to determine the respective shim requirements.

Similarly, if the crownwheel unit is damaged or suspect, do not strip it down but take it to your Skoda dealer for checking. The crownwheel and sunwheels have preset adjustments and require specialised tools for resetting.

Gearbox and transaxle - routine maintenance

Every 6,250 miles (10,000 km) remove the level plug and check the oil level. If the oil appears a little low top the unit up, through the filler neck on top of the gearbox (photos), with the recommended grade of oil until it runs out of the level hole. Wash the plug in petrol and check the washer. Replace the plug and tighten it firmly. Also visually inspect the transaxle for leaks and rectify as necessary.

Every 12,500 miles (20,000 km) run the car until the engine is hot and then obtain a bowl or other container of at least 5 Imp. pints (2.84 litres) capacity. Remove the transmission unit drain plug (photo) and also the filler/level plug and allow the oil to drain for at least 10 minutes. The differential unit has a separate drain plug and this should also be removed. The differential shares the same oil as the gearbox and it is therefore refilled, via the gearbox filler neck. While the oil is draining wash the plugs in petrol and check their washers (photo).

Replace the drain plugs tightening them firmly. Refill the transaxle with the recommended oil until it flows back out of the filler plug (it should take approximately 3.5 Imp. pints (1.98 litres)). Replace the filler plug and tighten it firmly.

Visually inspect the rubber transmission unit mountings for deterioration or damage.

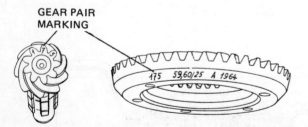

Fig. 6.2. Crownwheel and pinion showing the pair marking number (Sec. 1)

2 Transaxle assembly - removal and refitting

1   To remove the transaxle it is necessary to withdraw it from the car together with the engine and half-axle units, as described in Chapter 1. Also read Section 2 of Chapter 1, before proceeding.
2   When the transmission/engine unit has been removed the two units can be separated by undoing the nuts and bolts around the periphery of the bellhousing.
3   This done the units can be gently pulled apart and the transmission unit is ready for dismantling to begin. It is a good idea to thoroughly wash the exterior of the transmission unit with paraffin or 'Gunk'. This will simplify dismantling considerably and also help to prevent the ingress of dirt into the internal working parts.
4   Refitting of the transaxle assembly is accomplished in the reverse sequence.

3 Transaxle - removal of half-axle assemblies

With the transaxle removed from the car and disconnected from the engine unit, proceed as follows.
1   Remove the starter motor from the two location studs.
2   Place a drip tray under the axle housing to catch any oil which may remain. Now remove one of the half-axle assemblies by undoing the six nuts retaining the universal coupling cover and withdraw complete with shims, knuckle and guide blocks. The guide blocks should be kept in their respective positions; this is best achieved by retaining them on their pegs with a rubber band around them.
3   Repeat for the second half-axle assembly.

4 Gearbox front cover - removal

Undo the retaining nuts and washers, and disconnect from the gearbox, complete with gasket.

5 Gearbox bellhousing - dismantling

Dismantle the clutch release unit from the gearbox by undoing the two nuts from the studs, on which the release lever retaining plate is located. Then withdraw the release bearing and lever unit, complete, from the spigot shaft.

6 Gearbox and differential - dismantling

1   Remove the reversing light switch (photo), if fitted.
2   Remove the front cover and gasket, complete with the gear selection control rod, by undoing the six retaining nuts.
3   Remove the pinion shaft bearing cover by undoing the four nuts.
4   Carefully remove from the pinion shaft the 'half' shims (photo), keeping in order, and tie together through the holes with a piece of wire, or place in a safe spot keeping in respective positions.
5   Remove the 'C' clip and slide off the speedometer drive gear from

1a The transaxle oil level plug

1b Topping-up the transaxle

1c The gearbox drain plug

6.1 Removing the reversing light switch

6.4 Removing the pinion shaft locating half shims

6.5 The speedometer drivegear location showing the retaining 'C' clip

6.7 The gearbox flange clamp nut in the bellhousing

6.11 The gear selector detent retaining plate in position just forward of the drain plug

6.12 View showing selectors, rods and clamp bolts

7.1 Reverse gear shaft location screw and locking nut

8.3 Removing the late type locking slide bar, or locking key

its splined shaft (photo).

6   Undo the retaining nut and remove with tag washer.

7   Drain any remaining oil in the gearbox by tilting over a drip tray. The gearbox is now ready to be 'split' by undoing the six upper and eight lower housing flange nuts, the clamp nut inside the bellhousing (photo) and the nut to the right of the clutch slave cylinder. The gearbox can now be laid on its side (either), and 'split' by levering with a screwdriver in the opposing recesses in the flange bosses, wriggling the two halves free over the studs.

8   Lift out the differential unit complete.

9   Lift out the primary shaft assembly complete.

10   Lift out the pinion shaft assembly complete.

11   From the right-hand gearbox housing, remove the detent plate (photo), and the three springs and balls.

12   Slacken the selector clamp bolts and remove the 1st and 2nd, 3rd and 4th and the reverse selector fork rods (photo).

13   The interlock pins can now be extracted from their position in the end of the casing, via the selector rod holes.

7   Reverse gear - removal

1   To remove reverse gear undo the locknut and unscrew the locating stud from the casing on the outside (photo), then punch out the carrier shaft towards the front of the casing away from the differential housing.

8   Bevel pinion unit - dismantling

1   Refer to Fig. 6.3. Remove the bearing, a two row special type with a protruding flange around the outside periphery, by supporting the main assembly and applying a puller over the bearing. In order not to damage the speedometer gear shaft, place a suitable tube or socket and 'T' bar head over the shaft and locate the puller screw on it.

2   Remove fourth gear and, on earlier models, the bush.

3   Withdraw the 'locking slide bar' or friction ring key (photo), (earlier models had individual friction ring keys (37 and 27)), and the

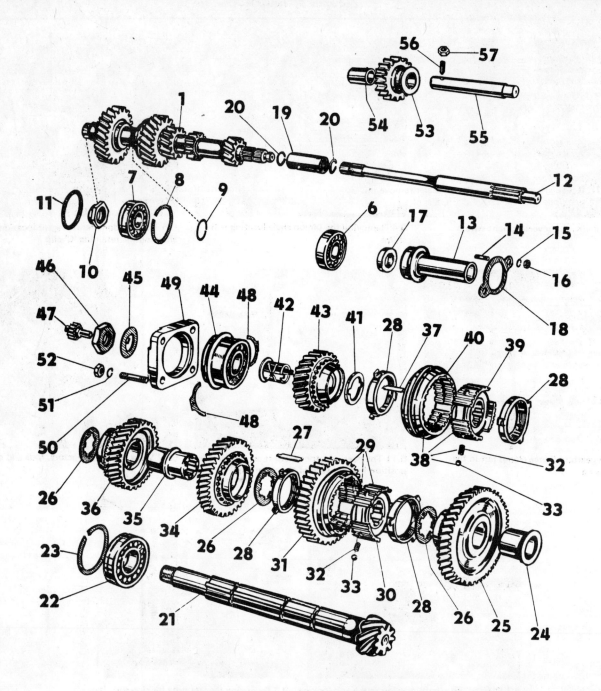

Fig. 6.3. The components of the pinion shaft, primary shaft and reverse gear shaft (Sec. 8)
Note: (a) Bush (35) for the 2nd and 3rd gears is not fitted to the later type gearbox
(b) Fourth gear bush (42) is not fitted to the later models
See 'Gearbox Modifications,' Section 1, for further details

1	Primary shaft	20	Securing clip	32	Spring	43	4th speed gear
6	Ball bearing	21	Pinion/shaft	33	Ball bearing	44	2 row ball bearing
7	Ball bearing	22	Roller bearing	34	2nd speed gear	45	Tab washer
8	Bearing distance ring	23	Bearing distance ring	35	Bush 2nd/3rd gears	46	Nut
9	Ring	24	Bush - 1st gear	36	3rd speed gear	47	Speedometer drive wheel
10	Nut	25	1st speed gear	37	Locking key - short	48	Compensating washer
11	Compensating washer	26	Friction ring	38	3rd and 4th Selector hub	50	Stud
12	Spigot shaft	27	Locking key		assembly	51	Spring washer
13	Sleeve clutch release bearing	28	Synchromesh ring	39	3rd and 4th Selector hub	52	Nut
14	Stud	29	1st and 2nd Selector hub		centre	53	Reverse gear with bush
15	Spring washer		assembly	40	3rd and 4th Selector hub	54	Bush
16	Nut	30	1st and 2nd Selector hub		sleeve	55	Reverse gear shaft
17	Oil seal		centre	41	Friction ring	56	Set screw
18	Sleeve retaining ring	31	1st and 2nd Selector hub	42	Bush 4th gear	57	Nut
19	Muff coupling		sleeve				

3rd and 4th gear friction ring.

4   After noting which way round it is fitted, remove the 3rd/4th gear synchro-hub assembly, and the 3rd gear synchro clutch centre, which can be replaced in the hub.

5   Remove 3rd gear and friction ring.

6   Remove friction ring and 2nd gear.

7   Remove synchro-ring and 1st and 2nd synchro-hub assembly.

8   Remove friction ring and 1st gear complete with synchro-ring and bush.

9   Slide off the roller bearing outer cage and, if necessary, the inner roller bearing race, taking great care not to damage the pinion teeth. The pinion is matched to the crownwheel and if damaged should be renewed complete with a matching new crownwheel assembly (see Section 1). It is suggested that your Skoda dealer remove this bearing race, as he is equipped with a special removal tool.

9 Synchro-hub - dismantling

Carefully press the synchro clutch centre through the synchro sleeve, and collect and retain the springs and balls, as they are retracted: keep in order of dismantling.

10 Input shaft - dismantling

1   This is in two sections, comprising the primary and spigot shafts, and can be split by removing the spring clips from the splined connector sleeve and parting the two shafts.

2   Remove ball bearing, if required, with a puller and at the opposing end of the shaft, undo the nut and locating ring from the outer bearing cage and then remove bearing.

11 Speedometer drive gear cluster - removal

This assembly is located in the front cover and is removed by undoing the cotter pin nut and driving out the pin.

12 Gearbox mountings - general

1   The gearbox mounting rubbers should be removed and cleaned at this stage, and if showing signs of wear, renewed.

2   They are bonded to small flat plates, which are bolted to the underside of the front cover casting. When in position the mountings are sandwiched between the casing and the mounting bracket which support the gearbox.

13 Gearbox components - examination and renovation

1   All parts should be thoroughly washed in paraffin or petrol and then laid out on a sheet of clean newspaper.

2   Generally examine the gearwheels and bearings for excessive wear, distortion, slackness of fit and damage to machined faces and threads.

3   The most likely components to be worn are the selector forks. Wear will be immediately apparent as the ends of each fork will be badly grooved. If the selector forks are badly worn, the selector should be renewed. A badly worn selector will eventually lead to jumping out of gear and difficult engagement.

4   The synchro-rings are bound to be worn and it is false economy not to renew them. New rings will improve the smoothness and speed of the gearchange considerably.

5   The reverse pinion gearwheel will possibly be badly worn and is the main cause of the familiar buzz and vibration during reversing. If your vehicle is suffering from this malady the gearwheel should be renewed.

6   If the input shaft bearings are worn they will cause the gearbox to be very noisy and to suffer from vibration. Bearings can be checked by feeling for slackness of the bearings in races and also by listening for excessive noise when the bearings are spun.

7   Always fit a new front cover gasket and input shaft seal. Also, if renewing pinion gears, renew the corresponding gear on the input shaft and vice versa.

8   Lastly check the condition of the transmission casings joint faces.

If any traces of old jointing compound are still present they should be removed with methylated spirit and **not** scraped under any circumstances.

Exchange transaxle units

9   If your gearbox has many defects it will probably be easier and more convenient to exchange the complete transaxle unit. If this is the case, make sure of getting the correct replacement unit. Certain earlier type units did not have reversing light switch attachments fitted. Otherwise they are basically the same, but check with your Skoda dealer to make sure, especially with regard to the differential bearing preload shim requirements for reassembly of the half-axles. It is vitally important that the shim requirements are accurate, or the crownwheel will be incorrectly meshed with the pinion.

14 Gearbox - reassembly (general)

Before proceeding with reassembly all parts should be laid out on a sheet of clean newspaper. Absolute cleanliness is extremely important. Each component should be lightly lubricated as it is assembled.

To reassemble the gearbox proceed as detailed in the following Sections.

15 Pinion shaft - reassembly

1   Press the needle roller bearing into position against the back of the pinion gear with the flange ring groove offset, away from the pinion gear.

2   Fit the bearing distance ring to its groove on the bearing outer race.

3   Next slide the 1st gear coupling bush down the shaft so that the flanged end butts against the bearing.

4   With the coupling bush pressed against the bearing, slide the friction ring down the shaft with the oil groove face towards the pinion, and locate in the groove in the shaft. Rotate the ring to determine its suitability. Different thicknesses of friction ring are available and a fairly tight fit in the groove, against the bush, is required (see Fig. 6.4).

5   When a ring of the correct thickness has been selected, remove it from the shaft, lubricate the bush and fit the 1st gear over it (photo), followed by the friction ring (oilways to pinion) (photo), and turn the ring, using a drift, to align with the grooves on the shaft (photo). Now check that the gear is free to rotate.

6   On earlier models, slide the locking key into its shaft groove. Later models have a single long locking key which was fitted in place of the two shorter types. Do not fit the long key at this stage, but try it in the groove to ensure the friction ring is correctly located.
Note: Each time a friction ring is fitted, slide the long key down its groove to check location.

7   Place the 1st and 2nd hub centre on the workbench so that the teeth face downwards (photo). Insert the springs into their location holes. Smear some grease round them to locate them in position, and place

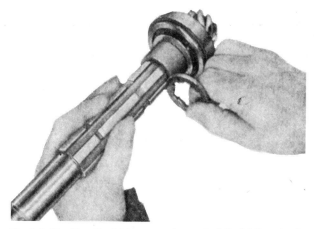

Fig. 6.4. Checking the thickness requirement of the friction ring in location groove on shaft (Sec. 15)

15.6a Fitting the 1st gear over the bush

15.6b Fitting selected friction ring

15.6c Aligning the friction ring with shaft grooves

15.7a The 1st and 2nd synchro-hub unit ready for assembly

15.7b Inserting the springs and balls into the hub centre

15.8 The assembled synchro-hub

15.9 Assembling the 1st/2nd selector hub

15.10 View showing friction ring located in shaft groove. Note oil grooves

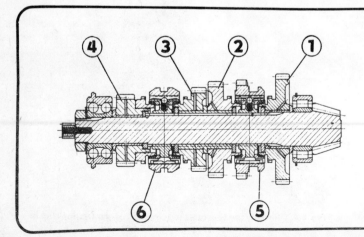

Fig. 6.5. The bevel pinion shaft unit (early type) (Sec. 15)

1 1st speed gear
2 2nd speed gear
3 3rd speed gear
4 4th speed gear
5 Synchromesh unit for 1st/2nd gears
6 Synchromesh unit for 3rd/4th gears

the balls on the springs (photo).

8   With the short end of the hub facing upwards (away from the gear-teeth), depress the balls and springs and slide the hub centre into the 1st/2nd selector hub (photo).

9   Now insert the synchro-ring into the hub centre from the reverse side of the gear, and slide the completed assembly onto the pinion shaft, with the gear facing away from the pinion (photo).

10   Fit the synchro-ring to the other side of the hub assembly and then fit a 3.5 mm thick friction ring to its groove on the shaft. The lubrication grooves face away from the pinion (photo).

11A   *Pre-1974 models (2nd/3rd gear bush):* Pre-1974 models differ at this point in that the 2nd and 3rd gear were located on a bush and not directly on the shaft splines. Therefore, having fitted the 1st/2nd synchro locking assembly complete with friction ring and synchro ring, proceed as follows:

   a)   *Slide a friction ring down the shaft to locate in its groove. Turn the ring so that it is locked in position in its groove and then fit the 2nd/3rd gear location bush onto the shaft.*
   b)   *Now select a friction ring to fit firmly into its groove and lock the bush in position.*
   c)   *This achieved, remove the friction rings and bush from the shaft.*
   d)   *Locate the 2nd gear over the bush with the teeth offset away from the pinion (to the centre of the bush) and slide the bush and sleeve onto the shaft. Then locate 3rd gear, with the teeth facing towards the pinion, onto the bush.*
   e)   *Refit the previously selected friction ring with its lubrication groove facing towards the pinion.*
   f)   *Turn it in the groove and check that the gears rotate freely.*
   g)   *Insert the short location key into the spline groove to lock the friction ring in position.*

11B   *Post-1974 models (2nd/3rd gear location):* Fit 2nd speed gear, with teeth offset away from the pinion, followed by the friction ring 'c' (Fig. 6.6). Again select a friction ring that is a tight fit in the shaft

groove. With a feeler gauge check the clearance between the friction ring and 2nd gear; this should be between 0.001 in (0.05 mm) to 0.005 in (0.15 mm) (photo). If required, adjust by fitting an alternative friction ring in groove 'b'. **Note:** Friction ring 'c' differs from the others in that it has oil grooves on both faces.

Fit the 3rd gear to the shaft, with the teeth offset, towards the pinion, and a friction ring to its groove.

Again, the clearance between the gear and friction ring must be checked to ensure it is between 0.001 in (0.05 mm) to 0.005 in (0.15 mm).

12   Assemble the 3rd/4th selector hub unit in a similar fashion to the 1st and 2nd, and insert the synchro with its locking tabs offset to the pinion. Slide the unit onto the shaft with the larger flange on the inner hub facing away from the pinion (photo). Then insert the synchro-ring into the opposite side of the hub with its lock tabs facing away from the pinion.

13A   *Pre-1974 models (4th gear bush):* Pre-1974 models were fitted with a bush on which 4th gear was located. Under extreme conditions this bush can seize. It is, therefore, of utmost importance to lubricate it with a molybdenum-disulphide type grease, prior to assembly. Then, proceed as follows:

   a)   *With the 3rd and 4th gear selector unit in position on the shaft, complete with the synchro-ring, place the friction ring of the 4th gear onto the shaft, with the lip of the inserted location key engaging into the ring slot. Note that this friction ring differs from those previously fitted.*
   b)   *Smear the 4th gear bush with molybdenum-disulphide type grease and locate the 4th gear over it with the teeth offset to the bush flange.*
   c)   *Slide the bush and gear over the shaft with the gearteeth and bush flange offset away from the pinion, and turn the bush so that its locating lug fits into the vacant slot in the friction rim. Now press the double ball bearing onto the shaft so that the flange on the outer bearing race is offset away from the pinion.*

13B   *Post-1974 models:* Fit the friction ring 'e' (Fig. 6.6) and slide the long locating key down its shaft groove until it is fully in position. This is apparent when the end of the key is level with the shaft splines (photo).

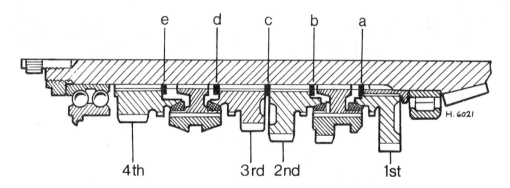

Fig. 6.6. Sectional view of later type bevel pinion shaft unit, showing respective gear positions and frictions discs (Sec. 15)

15.11 Checking the clearance between friction rings and 2nd gear

15.12 The 3rd/4th synchro-hub unit in position

15.13 Friction ring (e) in position on shaft with the locking key fully inserted in its groove

15.14 Locknut, bearing and 4th gear positioned on shaft

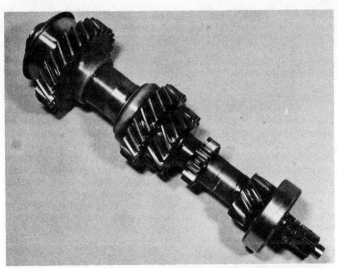

16.2 The input shaft, with gears and bearings fitted. Note the location ring on the periphery of the bearing adjacent to 4th speed gear

16.4a The primary and spigot shaft with interconnecting collar

16.4b The primary and spigot shaft assembled and retained by two spring clips

Fit the 4th speed gear onto the shaft with the teeth offset away from the pinion. Now press the double row ball bearing onto the pinion shaft. The clearance between the 4th gear and the bearing should be between 0.001 to 0.005 in (0.05 to 0.015 mm), with the bearing fully positioned. Any adjustment necessary is made by changing the friction ring in groove 'e'.

14 Fit the locking nut (photo) and tighten to the specified torque wrench setting. Bend over the locking tab in the nut with a punch to lock in position in the wedged slot in shaft.

15 If the speedometer driving gear has been removed, this can now be relocated with its splined shaft in the end of the pinion shaft, and locked in position with the 'C' clip.

16 Input shaft - reassembly

1 Assuming the 3rd and 4th gear are in place on the shaft and the bearings in position, proceed as follows.

2 Fit the location ring (Fig. 6.3) to its bearing location groove. (photo).

3 Fit the retaining nut and tighten to the specified torque; lock by bending the locking tab in the nut boss into the wedged slot in shaft.

4 Join the primary and spigot shafts by fitting the intermediate collar (photo) and retain with the spring clips (photo).

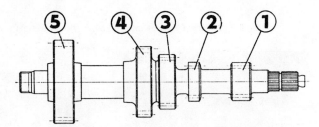

Fig. 6.7. Sectional view of the primary shaft (Sec. 16)

1 1st gear	4 3rd gear
2 Reverse gear	5 4th gear
3 2nd gear	

17 Reverse gear - reassembly

1 The reassembly sequence of the reverse gear and shaft, is a reversal of the dismantling instructions, but ensure that all parts are thoroughly cleaned and well lubricated.

2 Check that the gear runs freely on completing the assembly (photo).

17.2 The reverse gear in position on shaft in gearbox

18.2 Locating the reverse gear selector onto shaft and gear guide groove

18.5 The pinion shaft assembly placed in position in the gearbox half-casing

18.6 Placing the input shaft into position

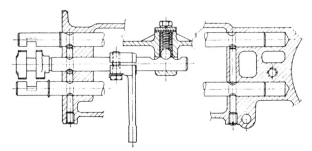

Fig. 6.8. Diagram showing selection rod location, interlocking pins and detent springs and balls (Sec. 18)

18 Selector shaft - reassembly

1   Stand right-hand half of the gearbox casing on the clutch housing.
2   Insert the circlip into its groove on the reverse selector shaft, and pass the shaft through the aperture, in the forward end of the gearbox. As it passes through, place the reverse selector onto the shaft (photo).

The shaft continues through the gearbox and locates in the gearbox to differential wall. Locate the selector clamp locking bolt in position - there is a slight recess in the shaft to locate it.
3   Insert the interlock pins into the aperture within the selector rod location holes (Fig. 6.8).
4   Insert the 1st/2nd selector rod circlip to its groove, pass the rod through the box and fit the selector and then do the same with 3rd/4th selector rod.
5   Place the pinion shaft assembly into position in the selectors and gearbox bearing locations. Rotate the assembly to ensure it spins freely (photo).
6   Insert the input shaft assembly, checking that the selectors engage correctly and that the gears do not bind (photo).

19 Differential - reassembly

1   The crownwheel unit is now fitted into position (crownwheel teeth facing down to mesh with pinion) (photo).
2   Ensure that the gearbox mating flanges are perfectly clean and smear with jointing compound.
3   Ensure that all the gears are well lubricated.
4   Slide the spigot shaft seal into position on the shaft to locate in the half-aperture in the differential housing wall (photo).

19.1 Position of crownwheel in the differential housing

19.4 The spigot shaft seal in position in gearbox half-casing

19.5 Reassembling the gearbox half casings

20.1 Placing shim over the driveshaft bearing

20.2a View inside end cover showing selector rod and speedometer gears

20.2b The rubber dirt seal with wire twisted by pliers to retain it

5   Refit the left-hand gearbox half casing into position over the studs, and use a soft-headed hammer or block of wood to tap lightly home. Ensure flanges are a neat fit all round (photo).
6   Refit the flange nuts and bolts, do not tighten at this stage (do not forget the clamp bolt in the bellhousing).
7   Re-insert the pinion half shims, exactly as they were removed, or has been specified by your Skoda specialist (see special note regarding crownwheel and pinion).
8   Replace the end housing bearing cover over the four location studs and retain with nuts and spring washers. Torque tighten the nuts to the specified pressure. Note that the housing does not fit flush to the gearbox endhousing, but against the bearing. Do not overtighten.
9   Ensure the crownwheel and pinion movement is free by rotating the halfshaft location housings.
10 Now tighten the gearbox casing nuts to the specified torque pressure.

20 End-cover - reassembly

1   Place shim over the driveshaft bearing (photo).
2   If removed, oil and replace the selector rod into the end cover housing so that it protrudes through the guide tube (photo). Replace the rubber protection boot and retain with a length of wire twisted to grip the rubber over the cover tube (photo). Do not overtighten the wire, it will distort and possibly cut the rubber.
3   Smear some sealing compound over the end cover and gearbox mating faces and fit the gasket over the studs.
4   Initially hold the selector rod back, and place the end-cover over the location studs, then as the cover closes onto the end face of the gearbox, guide the selector rod into the selector channels. Secure the end-cover with the nuts and washers. Check that the selector mechanism is working correctly by gripping the end of the protruding selector rod and push, pull and turn it to ensure correct engagement. Due to the lack of leverage the movement will be stiff, but if it fails to engage as required, do not force or hit with a hammer. Undo and remove the

20.5 The detent springs and balls in their respective housings prior to fitting the retaining plate

end-cover to check that the selector rod is correctly engaged.
5   Fit the three detent balls and springs into their respective apertures in the gearbox outer casing just forward of the level plug (photo). Retain with plate, gasket and two bolts, which should be tightened to the specified torque.
6   Refit the reversing switch into position.

21 Bellhousing - reassembly

1   Check that the half-casings clamping bolt is in position and tightened.

2 Reassemble the clutch release fork assembly by fitting the spring round the groove in the clutch release sleeve, and locate the sleeve and spring into the fork.
3 Clip on the release fork holder to the fork.
4 Refit the release sleeve guide retaining plate over the two studs and tighten the two nuts and spring washers.
5 Replace the clutch release fork into position and retain the support over the two lower studs with nuts and spring washers.
6 Assuming the end-cover mounting suspension rubbers are bolted in position, the transaxle is now ready for reassembly to the engine. To prevent the ingress of foreign matter into the aperture in which the slave cylinder is located, place a piece of cardboard over the studs.

22 Gearshift mechanism - general

Refer to Fig. 6.9. The gear selection lever is of floor-mounted type, situated on the central floor tunnel between the front seats. Selection movements are transmitted to the rear mounted gearbox by means of a control rod. Normally, this rod should never need to be removed, but if it has to be extracted it can only be withdrawn from the rear with the gearbox removed. The rear end of the control rod is connected to the selection rod in the gearbox end-cover via a rubberised connection piece (photo). This fits over the 'T' section end of the forward control rod and has a sleeve with locking bolt and nut,

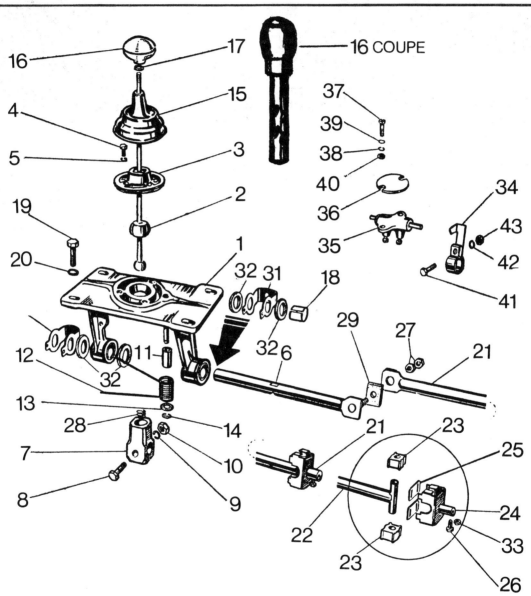

Fig. 6.9. The components of the gearshift mechanism (sec. 22)

1 Lever bracket with sleeve	12 Bias spring	23 Bush rubber	34 Contact finger
2 Gear change lever	13 Washer	24 Cover	35 Switch
3 Cover	14 Ring	25 Cover plate	36 Washer
4 Screw	15 Cuff	26 Securing screw	37 Screw cheesehead
5 Washer	16 Knob	27 Nut	38 Spring washer
6 Change rod	17 Washer	29 Rubber washer	39 Washer
7 Sleeve	18 Bush	30 Clip	40 Nut
8 Screw	19 Screw	31 Clip	41 Bolt
9 Washer	20 Washer	32 Packing ring	42 Spring washer
10 Nut	21 Tie rod assembly	33 Securing nut	43 Nut
11 Guiding pin	22 Tie rod		

22.0 Selection rod and connection incorporating a rubber shock absorber

23.1 The speedometer cable connection

which fits over the selection rod from the gearbox.

The selector mechanism is the same on all models except the Coupe which has a different selector lever.

Gear selection lever and bracket - removal, inspection and replacement

1   Remove the carpet from the central tunnel to reveal the gearbox mounting bolts, and engage neutral.

2   Unscrew the two bolts from the rear of the gearchange bracket. The tunnel cover may now be removed by pulling forward and lifting clear.

3   Remove the bracket securing bolts and the tie-rod to selector rod nuts and prise the two rods apart.

4   Now remove the lever and bracket assembly complete, by lifting clear through the aperture, tilting the gear lever forwards to clear the tie-rod at the rear.

5   Unscrew the three lever flange bolts from the bracket and lift the lever clear.

6   To remove the tie-rod, undo and remove the selector lever to control rod location piece clamp bolt and nut.

7   Withdraw the tie-rod through the bracket lugs and retain the washers, springs and 'U' section clips noting their order of dismantling.

8   Clean all parts thoroughly and inspect for signs of wear. Re-insert the tie-rod into the bracket lugs and check for excessive slackness in the bushes. Renew the bushes, if necessary.

9   To reassemble, lubricate all the parts and rebuild the unit in the reverse order to dismantling.

10 Ensure that the rubber washer is fitted between the connecting and tie-rods and that the tie-rod nuts are securely locked.

11 Ensure the lever is in the neutral position, when tightening the tie-rod location clamping piece.

12 Prior to replacing the cover, smear grease onto the sliding parts of the tie-rod.

23 Speedometer cable - general

1   This is attached to the gearbox front cover by a bolted clamp (photo).

2   The driving gear unit is driven by a small gear located on its own shaft, which is fully splined and fits into the rear end of the pinion shaft.

3   The cable is routed along the underneath of the car in the same channel as the gearshift, clutch and brake systems run. It finally passes through the floor at the front into the car below the dashboard. The cable then screws into the back of the speedometer.

4   The cable rarely needs attention, but it sometimes may need removing if in need of lubrication, when it will make a squeaking noise dependent on the speed of the car.

5   The remedy is to liberally coat the inner cable with thick oil or grease before refitting into the outer cable and reassembly onto the car.

24 Fault diagnosis - gearbox

Symptom	Reason/s	Remedy
Poor gear selection/synchromesh	Worn pinion shaft thrust washers	Renew the thrust washers to take up excessive endfloat
	Selector forks worn due to:	
	a) Continuous resting of hand on gear lever	Don't!
	b) Incorrectly adjusted gearlever bracket	Reposition bracket.
	c) Loose selector rod/gearchange linkage locating bolt	Position and tighten location bolt.
	d) Selector forks incorrectly adjusted	Remove and 'split' gearbox to check selector locations and centralise in hub grooves as required.
	Synchronising cones worn or damaged	Dismantle and overhaul transmission unit. Fit new gear wheels and synchronising cones.
	Defective clutch or spigot bearing	Check clutch adjustment.
	Gearbox level plug screwed in too far and fouling the 1st/2nd selector fork	Unscrew plug sufficiently to free the action of the selector fork. If loose in thread apply small amount of thread locking compound or fit new plug.
	Bent selector operating rod	Replace with new rod.
Jumping out of gear	Worn selector fork (see above)	As above.
	Worn or broken detent springs	Dismantle and renew.
Excessive noise	Lack of maintenance:	
	a) Oil level low	Top-up transmission unit with correct grade oil.
	b) Incorrect oil grade used	Change oil to correct type.
	c) General wear of bushes or roller bearings, or gearteeth	Dismantle and overhaul unit.

Chapter 7 Driveshafts, hubs, wheels and tyres

Contents

Specifications

Driveshafts ... ...   Each halfshaft has a slip joint at the differential end, while, at the wheel end, it has a taper and thread on which the hub and retaining nut are located. Each halfshaft is fully enclosed in a tubular casing. Suspension of the swinging half-axles is independent.

Wheels
Type ... ...   Pressed-steel disc, 4 stud fixing
Wheel rim ... ...   4½J x 14

Tyres
Tyre size (radial) ... ...   155 x 14
Tyre inflation pressures (radial) :*
    Front ... ...   20 lb/sq in (1.4 Kg/sq.cm)
    Rear ... ...   26 lb/sq in (1.8 Kg/sq.cm)

* For high speed or heavy loads add 3 lb/sq in (0.2 Kg/sq.cm)

Torque wrench settings

	lb f ft	Kg f m
Wheel nut	45 - 50	6 - 7
Half-axle ball joint nut	15 - 20	2 - 2.5
Half-axle shaft nut	122 aprox. to nearest s/pin hole	17 approx. to nearest s/pin hole.
Brake backplate bolt	15 - 20	2 - 2.5
Front hub nut	11	1.5

1 General description and routine maintenance

Refer to Fig. 7.1. Drive is transmitted from the differential unit to the rear wheels by means of driveshafts, enclosed in their respective casings which incorporate the wheel bearing hub carrier flange and differential housing swivel flange.

The axial movement of the half-axles is controlled by strut arms which are located round the half-axle tubes and the underbody just forward of the rear wheel arches in a rubber mounted swivel joint.

Telescopic shock absorbers are located to the rear of the half-axles between the strut arms and body mounting and are enclosed within the coil springs.

Routine maintenance

Very little maintenance is required, but the following points should not be neglected:

Tyres: A weekly check should be made on the tyre pressures (including the spare) and tyre treads. Any small stones lodged between the treads must be removed. Look for signs of uneven tyre wear and scuffing, and if these are apparent the suspension and steering must be checked for alignment. Ensure that the tread depths meet the legal requirements.

Front hubs: Every 31,000 miles (50,000 km) remove the hub grease caps and refill with a wheel bearing grease of suitable type. Check the endfloat and adjust if necessary.

2 Special notes

1   Never remove the strut arm connection from the half-axle as this is preset to give the correct rear drive wheel alignment. If removal is ever necessary, it should be left for your Skoda dealer to do.

2   It is not possible to extract an axle driveshaft from the differential through the casing, due to the locating pin guide blocks, located on its inner end, within the axle housing. These can be removed after the withdrawal of the driveshaft from the casing. Therefore, remove the half-axle assembly complete.

3   We found it virtually impossible to remove the rear brake drum/hub on either side, even with a substantial universal type puller. It is therefore suggested that if any work is to be carried out on the rear half-axle units, it is best left to your Skoda agent. However, it may be possible to borrow the Skoda special tool required to remove the brake drum (Jig no. MP5 - 111). If the special tool is available then the brake drum should be removed prior to removing the half-axle unit from the car. Do not try to force the brake drum off by hitting with a hammer!

3 Half-axle units - removal and refitting (transmission in car)

1   Jack-up the rear of the car and support the body on firmly based axle stands or blocks. The front wheels should be chocked to prevent any possible movement of the car.

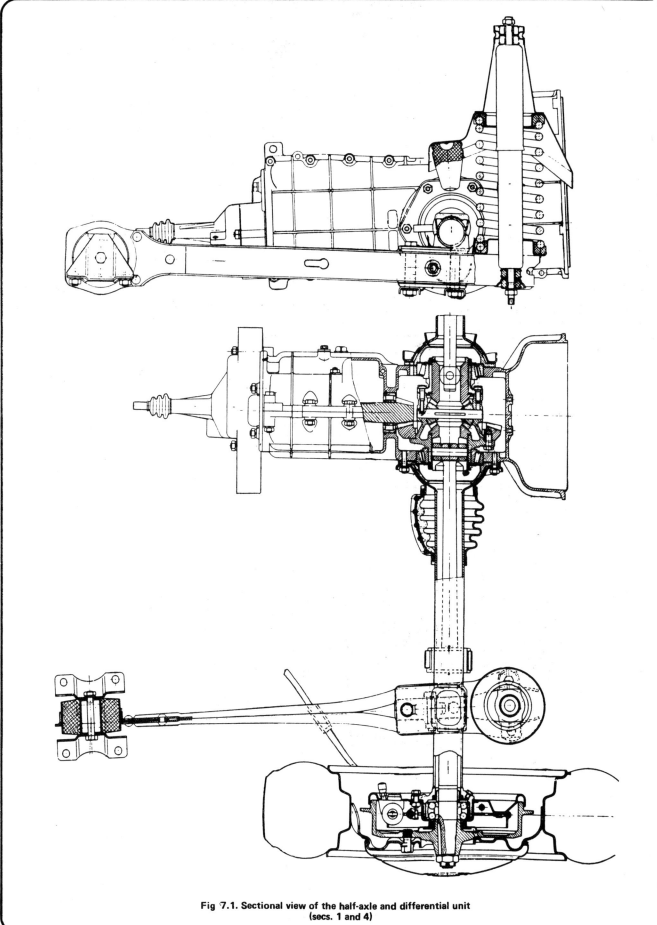

Fig 7.1. Sectional view of the half-axle and differential unit
(secs. 1 and 4)

2   From inside the car, disconnect the handbrake cable/s by undoing
the cable adjusting nuts, on the handbrake linkage, located at the rear
end of the central tunnel in front of the rear seats. Pull the cable/s
through the guide holes in the body to hang free under the car.
3   Remove the roadwheels, and place a jack under the brake drum to
support.
4   Disconnect the telescopic shock absorber from the strut arm.
Insert a 12 mm open jaw spanner through the coil spring and locate on
the nut on the base of the shock absorber body to prevent it from
turning whilst undoing the retaining nut.
5   Disconnect the rear brake hydraulic pipe/s unions.
6   Remove the yoke limiting strap/s for the driveshaft.
7   Undo the four nuts retaining the forward end of the thrust arm
(photo), and carefully lower and remove the jack. The coil spring can
now be removed.
8   Place a container under the differential housing and drain the oil.
9   Support the half-axle in line with the differential housing and
remove the axle housing flange bolts, and withdraw the half-axle unit
complete.
10 Refitting is the reverse sequence of the above, but note the
following:
   When refitting the half-axle to the differential housing, be sure to
fit the same number and thickness of taper bearing preload shims as
were originally fitted! A new gasket must be used. The gaskets differ in
thickness according to requirements. If on assembly the half-axle

3.7 Thrust arm forward mounting point

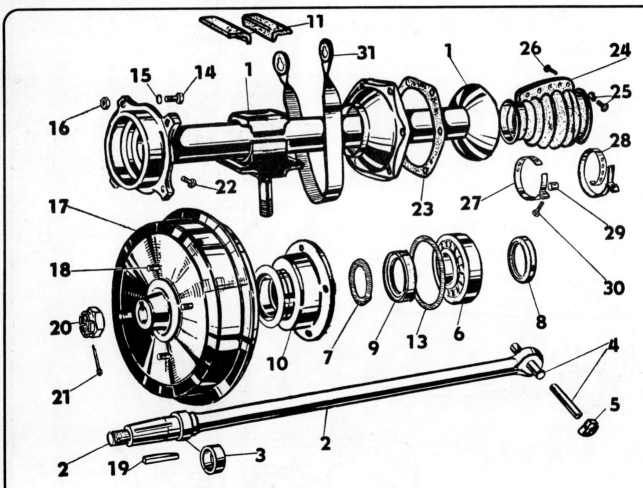

Fig. 7.2. Component parts of the half-axle unit (Sec. 4)

1 Half-axle housing	9 Oil seal	18 Wheel stud	26 Screw/washer/nut
2 Halfshaft assembly	10 Cover assembly	19 Key	27 Clip
3 Support ring	11 Rubber bush	20 Nut	28 Clip
4 Pin	13 Rubber 'O' ring	21 Split pin	29 Nut
5 Guide block	14 Bolt	22 Bolt	30 Screw
6 Ball bearing (self align)	15 Spring washer	23 Gasket	31 Axle retaining strap
7 Washer	16 Nut	24 Rubber protection boot	
8 Oil seal	17 Hub/brake drum assembly	25 Rivet/nut	

radial movement is stiff, a thicker, or additional, gasket is required. The gasket should be fitted so that the breather hole in the top of the differential housing flange face is not obstructed.

11 If a replacement protective rubber boot is being fitted ensure that the joint flange is positioned facing upwards and approximately 45° from the half-axle. The old flange faces may have been retained by rivets. However, as a special riveting tool is required, these may be replaced by bolts, flat washers and nuts, but do not overtighten.

12 Top-up the transaxle oil level, and bleed the brakes. Adjust the hand and foot brakes.

4 Half-axle units - dismantling, inspection and reassembly

1 Having removed the half-axle complete with the thrust arm (assuming that the brake drum has been removed, as described in Section 2), proceed as follows.

2 Refer to Fig. 7.2. Remove the Woodruff key from the axle-shaft.

3 Remove the brake shoes and actuating mechanism, as described in Chapter 9.

4 Unscrew the four nuts/bolts securing the hub cover to the back-plate/bearing housing, and remove the cover.

5 If it is just the outer seal or 'O' ring that has to be renewed, these can now be removed.

6 If the inner seal or bearing has to be renewed then the half-shaft will have to be pressed into the housing approximately 0.40 in (10 mm) and then reverse pressed out of the housing complete with bearing. This will enable a puller to be located with its jaws behind the bearing to pull it off the shaft..

7 The inner seal can now be removed and the various components cleaned and inspected.

8 Having dismantled to this stage, alway renew the oil seals and 'O' ring. Check the oil seal support ring on the halfshaft. If damaged or marked, so as to affect the seal, remove from the shaft and replace with a new one - ensure that the new seal is located in exactly the same position as the old one. If the bearing is suspect, this should also be renewed.

7 Reassembly is the reverse procedure of dismantling, but be sure to refit the oil seals facing the correct way round. The inner seal must have its sealing edge and spring facing towards the axle. Lubricate the seals prior to assembly and smear the shaft and housing aperture with grease prior to fitting the bearing. Also lightly smear the tapered face of the shaft before fitting the brake drum/hub. Ensure that the retaining nut is torqued to the specified pressure and a new split pin is used to retain it.

5 Wheel hub/brake drum unit - dismantling and reassembly

1 To inspect the wheel hub unit only it is not necessary to remove the complete half-axle assembly from the car. However, a special puller will probably be required to remove the brake drum/hub, as mentioned in Section 2.

2 If a puller is available then jack-up the car and remove the wheel.

3 Place an axle-stand or blocks under the half-axle to support, and chock the front wheels to prevent movement of the car.

4 Remove the split pin and undo the castle nut.

5 The brake dum/hub can now be removed from the tapered axle-shaft, using the special puller. To remove the bearing cover and seals assembly, refer to Section 4.

6 Refitting is the reverse of the above procedure, but fit a new split pin after torqueing the hub nut to the specified pressure.

6 Front wheel hubs - dismantling, inspection and reassembly

1 Jack-up the front of the car and chock the rear wheels to prevent movement of the car.

2 Remove the relevant roadwheel.

3 Prise the hub cap from the hub (photo), using a screwdriver.

4 Remove the split pin and undo the castle nut and the special washer.

5 *Drum brake models:* On the earlier models fitted with drum brakes at the front, the hub/drum may now be removed. If the drum does not

6.3 Removing the front wheel hub cap

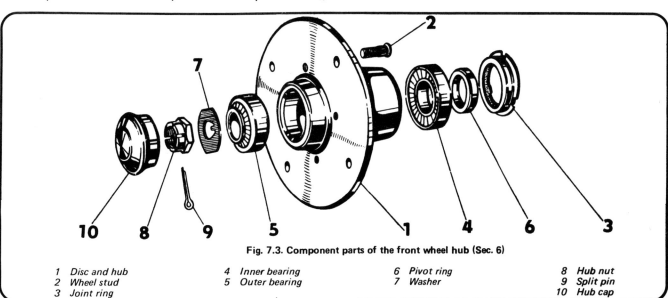

Fig. 7.3. Component parts of the front wheel hub (Sec. 6)

1 Disc and hub	4 Inner bearing	6 Pivot ring	8 Hub nut
2 Wheel stud	5 Outer bearing	7 Washer	9 Split pin
3 Joint ring			10 Hub cap

readily pull off, lightly tap the protruding flange of the outer periphery of the drum with a hide or wooden mallet.

Disc brake models: On models fitted with disc brakes at the front, the brake unit will have to be removed, as described in Chapter 9. The hub complete with disc can then be removed.

6   The outer bearing cone and cup may now be extracted from the hub for inspection.

7   The inner bearing cone and cup may be withdrawn after the oil seal is removed (note which way round it is fitted). If the inner bearing cone has remained on the stub axle it will have to be removed with a suitable puller. The bearing cups can be knocked out of their respective housings using a narrow drift or suitable puller.

8   All parts of the hub should now be washed in clean paraffin and inspected.

9   Check the bearings for excessive looseness in their cages, and the bearing cups for marks or scratches. If any part is in a doubtful condition it should be renewed. The seal must be renewed regardless of condition.

10   Reassembly commences by packing the hubs with wheel bearing grease of the correct type.

11   To replace the bearing cups place the housing onto a firm surface and place the cup squarely over its aperture. Place a block of wood over the cup and tap with a hammer until the cup is fully home in its housing.

12   The remaining reassembly is a reversal of the dismantling procedure. Once reassembly is complete, the hub/brake drum can be refitted to the stub axle and the hub endfloat adjustment made. Refit and bleed the brakes on later models.

---

7   Front hub - endfloat adjustment

1   This is achieved with the roadwheel fitted but the grease cap and split pin locking the hub nut, removed. Obviously the wheel must be off the ground and free to rotate. Slowly tighten the hub nut until the wheel cover rotates freely. Back off the nut until the wheel is *just* able to rotate freely, without perceptible play in the bearings. Tap the wheel hub and (brake disc on later models) to ensure correct bedding of the bearings.

3   When the correct adjustment is achieved, insert the split pin to lock the nut. If it is necessary, back off the nut slightly to allow insertion of the split pin. Do not further tighten the nut.

4   Fill the cap with wheel bearing grease of the correct type and refit.

---

8   Wheels - general

Because of the design of the suspension of the car the strength and

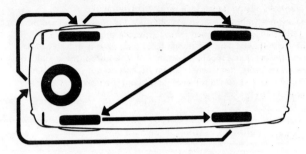

Fig. 7.4. Sequence for interchanging roadwheels (Sec. 9)

trueness of the roadwheels is critical, particularly at the front. A great deal of excessive wear on the wheel bearings and driveshaft joints can be attributed to buckled and deformed wheels. Check, whenever there is a sudden difference in the feel at the steering wheel, that the wheels are not buckled or dented. Check also that the wheels are balanced, statically and dynamically; most garages and tyre specialists have balancing equipment. If any deformity is noticed the wheel should be replaced by a new one. Do not attempt to repair wheel rims.

---

9   Tyres - general

In the same way that the condition and suitability of the wheels fitted is critical so it is with the tyres. Because of the design of the suspension it is advisable to fit radial ply tyres on this car.

It is good practice to regularly - daily - inspect the tyres on your car because some tyre faults can become dangerous very quickly. When wall blisters are found, or cuts or foreign objects deep in the tyre, remove the wheel at once and take it to a garage so that the tyre can be inspected and repaired.

Periodically check the pressure of the spare tyre. It is a good idea to occasionally interchange the wheels to ensure even tyre wear, as shown in Fig. 7.4. **Note:** This does not apply where fabric belted radial tyres are fitted. However, excessive uneven tyre wear is probably due to a suspension fault or misalignment and a check should be made as described in Chapter 8.

It is obviously necessary to periodically check the tyre treads to ensure that their condition complies with current legislation regarding maximum wear limits.

Chapter 8 Suspension and steering

Contents

Specifications

Front suspension	Independent, wishbone and coil spring
Rear suspension	Independent, swing half-axles with coil springs and strut arms
Shock absorbers	Telescopic, front and rear
Front shock absorber type	Pal model T26 X110
Rear shock absorber type	Pal model 2T26 x 175
Coil spring (front), free length	281 mm
Coil spring (rear), free length	303 mm
Steering	Direct, worm and nut - symmetrical
Toe-in	0.157 - 0.236 in (4 to 6 mm)
Toe-in (full load)	0.039 - 0.118 in (1 to 3 mm)
Camber	1° 30' $\pm$ 15'
Caster	6° 30'
King-pin inclination	7° 30'
Track (front)	4 ft 2.5 in (1 m 282.7 mm)
Track (rear)	4 ft 1 in (1 m 244.6 mm)
Wheelbase	7 ft 11 in (2 m 413 mm)
Ground clearance	7 in (177.8 mm)
Steering box lubricant capacity	0.45 Imp. pint (0.25 litre)

Torque wrench settings
Front suspension and steering

	lb f ft	kg fm
Bottom wishbone:		
Swivel pin to body nut	48 to 53	6.5 to 7
Swivel pin to inner (rubber bushed) joint nut	33 to 43	4.5 to 6
Swivel pin locknut (outer)	53 to 64	7 to 9
Upper wishbone:		
Inner swivel pin nut (rubber bush)	43 to 48	6 to 6.5
Swivel pin locknut (outer)	53 to 64	7 to 9
Swivel pin to knuckle nut	53	7
Eccentric pin nut	53 to 64	7 to 9
Lower wishbone bracket bolt nut	28 to 38	4 to 5
Lower shock absorber nut	38 to 40	5 to 5.5
Upper shock absorber nut	8 to 10	1.2 to 1.4
Axle/body nut	27 to 33	4 to 4.5
Stabilizer clamp bolt	8 to 10	1.2 to 1.4
Upper wishbone bracket bolt	14 to 18	1.9 to 2.5
Lower shock absorber bracket bolt	15 to 18	2 to 2.5
Steering wheel nut	23 to 38	3 to 5
Steering link nut	72	10
Idler lever pin nut (14 mm)	43	6
Idler lever pin nut (10 mm)	27	4

Torque wrench settings

	lb f ft	kg fm
Steering arm nut	53	7
Steering rod nut	38 to 43	5 to 6
Steering rod ball joint nut	38 to 43	5 to 6
Steering box retaining bolts	27 to 38	4 to 5
Steering box cover retaining bolt (7 mm)	11 to 13	1.5 to 1.7
Steering box bearing cover bolt (6 mm)	5	0.7
Rear suspension		
Strut rod bolt nut (14 mm)	43 to 53	6 to 7
Strut rod bolt nut (12 mm)	38 to 43	5 to 6
Strut rod to body nut	27 to 33	4 to 4.5
Shock absorber to body nut	10	1.4
Shock absorber to strut rod nut	15	2
Strut rod rubber bush bolt nut	17 to 25	2.4 to 3.2

1 General description and routine maintenance

See Fig. 8.1. The front suspension has remained conceptually unchanged since the introduction of the 1000 MB series.

The independent suspension is of the double-wishbone type, having coil springs controlled by double-acting telescopic shock absorbers.

The steering knuckle units, on later models, are fitted with Glacier DX friction rings and self-lubricating bushes.

The steering box is of worm and nut or peg type and the steering column is of the safety type.

The rear suspension is also independent, having swinging half-axles pivoting from the transaxle unit. Coil springs and double acting shock absorbers are fitted and strut rods located on the half-axle casings at the rear, are located under the body just forward of the rear wheel arches, and are flexibly mounted.

Routine maintenance

It is essential to maintain the suspension and steering in good order if the safety of your car is to be preserved. Even small amounts of wear in the suspension joints and steering mechanism will affect the handling of the car to a dangerous extent. It is for that reason that the Department of Transport (DoT) test examines the condition and serviceability of the suspension and steering particularly, as well as the more obvious components such as the lights, tyres and chassis.

Regular checks should be made therefore to discover slackness and wear in the suspension and steering at the earliest moment. The components most likely to wear are:

Steering control rod ball joints
Stub axle knuckle bushes and king-pin bushes
Upper and lower wishbone pivot pin bushes
Front and rear hydraulic dampers

All of those points should be tested with a tyre lever or screwdriver to see whether there is any movement between them and the fixed component. The tests should also be carried out with the front or back of the car jacked up so as to remove the imposed loads on the suspension assemblies. It will then be easier to detect small amounts of movement.

Together with the mechanical tests on the suspension and steering joints, the components themselves should be examined for serviceability - particularly:

a) *Steering box mounting bolts for looseness*
b) *Steering column to steering box coupling*
c) *Steering wheel to column joint*
d) *Anti-roll bar bushes (if applicable)*
e) *Front and rear wheel hub bearings (Chapter 7)*
f) *Front spring mounting*

There should be no play - or failure - in any single part of any of the aforementioned components. It is dangerous to use a vehicle in a doubtful condition.

Every 6,250 miles (10,000 km) lubricate the king-pins and steering joints, together with the front hubs.

Every 12,500 miles (20,000 km) lubricate as per 6,250 miles (10,000 km) and check the steering box oil level, topping-up if necessary.

2 Front axle and suspension unit - removal and refitting

1 If a comprehensive inspection and rebuild of the front axle and suspension unit is to be carried out it is advisable, in the interest of working comfort, to remove the complete unit from the car. This can be achieved fairly easily and without any specialised tools. Proceed as follows, referring to Fig. 8.2 as necessary.

2 Jack-up the front of the car and support, on the underside of the body, with blocks or axle stands so that no part of the suspension will be obstructed during dismantling or assembly. Remove the roadwheels.

3 From inside the forward luggage compartment, unscrew completely the two retaining nuts for the right and left-hand shock absorbers.

4 Unscrew the castle nuts from the steering coupling and then remove the toe board lid from within the car. Remove the steering column facia cover by slackening the dipswitch and flasher switch retaining nuts (on the Coupe models, unscrew the under panel crosshead screws and lower the panel), and then the two bearing holder bracket screws. Undo the steering lock retaining bolts, and withdraw the steering column into the car to disconnect from the steering box input shaft coupling.

5 From underneath the car, undo the wishbone arm pin retaining nuts just sufficiently to release the washers on the brackets of the stiffener panel (front) and underbody (rear) (photo).

6 Disconnect the anti-roll bar connections to the brackets of the fuel tank stiffener unit.

7 Disconnect the hydraulic brake hoses (place a polythene bag over the ends and retain with a rubber band to prevent the ingress of dirt into the pipes).

8 Support the axle centrally with a trolley jack, and remove the four retaining bolts (two on each side of the telescopic shock absorbers) (photo).

9 Compress the respective telescopic shock absorber piston rods through their apertures in the body and then carefully lower the axle unit complete, and remove from under the car.

10 Refitting of the axle unit is the reversal of removal procedure, however, the following points should be noted:

a) *Renew, if necessary, the rubber boot and, when fitting, smear with grease round its location on the shaft.*

b) *Before connecting the steering box to column coupling, ensure that the wheels are pointing straight-ahead and the steering wheel is in the corresponding position. Prior to tightening the coupling bolts, turn the steering wheel to full lock to the right and left to ensure that the steering lock is limited by the king-pin socket stops.*

c) *Ensure that the wheels are correctly aligned (see Section 8).*

3 Front axle and suspension unit - dismantling and reassembly (general)

1 If the front axle and suspension unit is removed from the car for dismantling, it can be cleaned with Gunk or a similar solvent and hosed

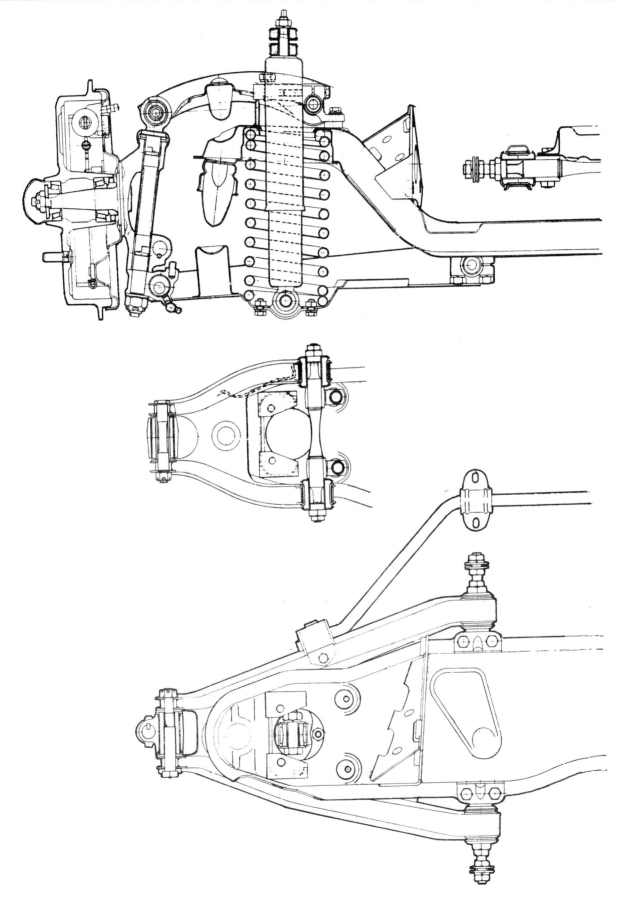

Fig. 8.1. Sectional layout of front suspension and stub axle (Sec. 1)

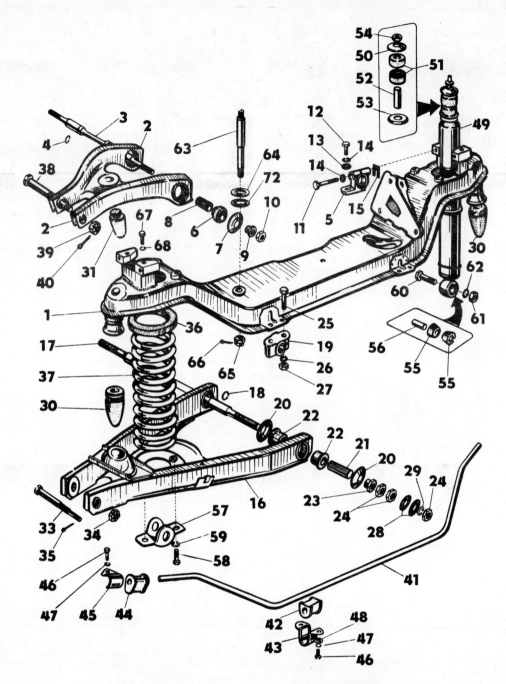

Fig. 8.2. Component parts of the front axle and suspension unit (Sec. 2)

1 Front axle assembly	19 Lower pivot pin holder	38 Upper wishbone pin	56 Distance tube
2 Top wishbone	20 Cap	39 Castellated nut	57 Damper holder
3 Pin	21 Distance tube	40 Split pin	58 Bolt
4 Wire circlip	22 Rubber bush	41 Stabiliser	59 Spring washer
5 Top wishbone support	23 Nut	42 Rubber bush	60 Bolt damper bracket
6 Rubber bush	24 Nut	43 Stabiliser bracket	61 Nut
7 Cup washer	25 Bolt	44 Rubber bush	62 Spring washer
8 Distance tube	26 Spring washer	45 Stabiliser bracket	63 Idler pin
9 Nut	27 Nut	46 Bolt	64 Idler thrust washer
10 Nut	28 Washer	47 Spring washer	65 Castellated nut
11 Bolt	29 Spring washer	48 Washer	66 Split pin
12 Bolt	30 Rubber bump stop	49 Hydraulic damper	67 Bolt
13 Washer	31 Rubber stop	50 Cup washer	68 Spring washer
14 Spring washer	33 Eccentric bolt	51 Rubber bush	72 Rubber washer
15 Camber adjustment washer	34 Castellated nut	52 Distance tube	
16 Lower wishbone	35 Split pin	53 Cup washer	
17 Lower pivot pin	36 Rubber washer	54 Nut/spring washer	
18 Wire clip	37 Front axle spring	55 Rubber bush	

2.5 View of the lower wishbone arm swivel pin mounting points

2.8 The front axle mounting bolts, in the wing channel

4.1 The anti-roll bar inner location bracket bush

5.1 The front shock absorber location retaining nut

off, but be sure to cover the brake connections first to prevent dirt and water entering the hydraulic system.

2   No special tools are absolutely necessary, but a ball pin extractor and selection of drifts will be of assistance.

3   If required, the brakes can be removed as described in Chapter 9, and the hubs as described in Chapter 7.

4   If only minor work is to be carried out then, obviously, it will not be necessary to remove the complete axle unit from the car but generally the instructions, in the following Sections, for dismantling the various sub-assemblies will be the same.

5   If the same shims and spacing washers are used on reassembly as were originally found in the steering and suspension joints, then the camber and caster angles should be good enough to drive the car to your Skoda dealer for checking.

4   Anti-roll bar - removal and refitting

1   The anti-roll bar is located in rubber bushes which are retained in clamps bolted to the lower wishbones on the outside, and within brackets attached to the underside of the fuel tank stiffener unit (photo).

2   The first action in the task of removing the anti-roll bar is to jack-up the front of the car and to place axle stands under the two coil spring locations in the wishbone.

3   With the underside of the front of the car now accessible, the

necessary clamp retaining bolts can be removed, and the anti-roll bar disconnected.

4   Clean and inspect the rubber bushes: if perished, split or generally worn, they should be replaced with a new set.

5   Refit the anti-roll bar to the suspension in the reverse sequence of removal.

5   Front shock absorbers - removal and refitting

1   To remove a front shock absorber, first unscrew the retaining nut of the piston rod which is located in the front luggage compartment (photo), by one complete turn to relieve the pressure.

2   From underneath unscrew and remove the shock absorber lower retaining bracket bolts from the wishbone.

3   Unscrew the top retaining nut completely and remove the shock absorber through the wishbone aperture.

4   If there are signs of oil leakage and/or the compression resistance is low, then it should either be repaired or exchanged by your local Skoda agent.

5   Refitting is the reversal of removal.

6   Front coil springs - removal and refitting

1   Before commencing work on dismantling the coil springs, a

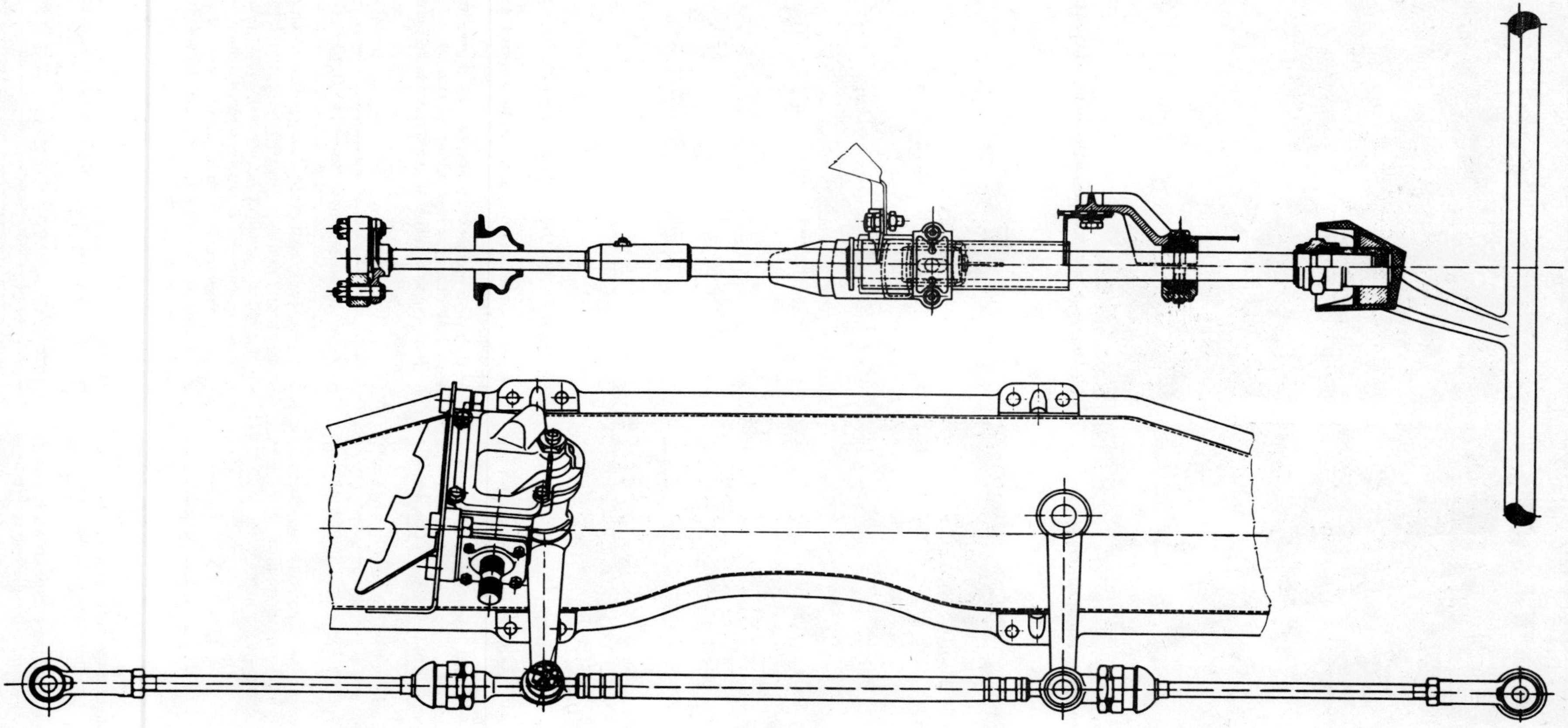

Fig. 8.3. Sectional views of the steering column and trackrods (Sec. 7)

suitable coil spring compressor should be at hand. Various proprietary types are available from most good accessory shops and tool factors.

2 Remove the shock absorber as described in Section 5.

3 Have an assistant sit on the front wing and whilst the spring is compressed, fit the spring compressor clips over two or three adjacent coils, ensuring that it is firmly located.

4 With the spring compressed, jack-up the front of the vehicle and support the bodyframe and crossmember adequately on axle stands. Remove the roadwheel.

5 Withdraw the spring complete with compressor. With certain types of spring compressor it may be necessary to lower the wishbone in order to withdraw the spring complete with compressor.

6 It is advisable to renew the rubber washer located at the top of the spring within the axle housing.

7 Refitting of the front springs is a reversal of the removal procedure.

7 Trackrods - removal, inspection and refitting

1 Fig. 8.3. If the trackrod or joints are being disconnected for cleaning and inspection only, be extra careful not to damage the rubber protector sleeves during dismantling.

2 Remove the steering and idler rod castle nuts split pins and then unscrew the nuts. If a ball pin extractor is available, remove the nuts and split the tapered joints with the aid of the extractor. If an extractor is not available, slightly loosen the nuts and then firmly support the connecting steering rod and idler rod by placing a block hammer, or similar, against it. Using a hide headed mallet, strike the castle nut to split the joint. Do not continue to hit the nut if it does not split the joint as this will damage the threads.

3 On removing the track rod unit, the respective joints can be cleaned and inspected. The ball joints should not show any signs of ovality; if they do, they should be replaced with new ones. The rubber seals and their retaining rings should also be inspected for signs of deterioration, and renewed if necessary.

4 If the bushes in the connecting rod have to be renewed, drive the old bushes out with a suitable drift, and press the new ones in carefully — ensuring that they enter their location bore squarely and without binding.

5 On earlier models, the trackrod ends and idler rod joints have grease nipples fitted. These should be checked to ensure they are not damaged or blocked, and the oilways in the rod ends cleaned out with a pipe cleaner or blown clear with compressed air.

6 If the trackrod-ends have to be removed, note their relative positions prior to dismantling from the control rod. This will assist during reassembly and ensure that the track settings will be approximately correct, although the track will still have to be checked and adjusted for accuracy prior to using the car on the road.

7 Reassembly of the trackrods is a reversal of the dismantling procedure. Tighten the castle nuts to the specified torque and always use new split pins to lock them.

8 Wheel alignment - general

1 Provided that reassembly of the steering and suspension system involved only renewal of joints and/or bushes and not disturbance of the lengths of any of the steering rods or trackrods, then you should be able to drive carefully to your nearest Skoda dealer, where the wheels may be aligned with the specialized equipment that is absolutely necessary for this task.

2 If on reassembly steering rods or suspension arms have been renewed, then it will be necessary to check the alignment with simple equipment, before the car is driven to the local Skoda dealer for the final accurate alignment.

3 The settings are given in the Specifications Section of this Chapter.

4 Of all the settings to be considered, only the toe-in is likely to be seriously affected during repair work on the car.

5 The toe-in setting of the wheels is checked, as follows. The car should be positioned on a flat level area and be unladen. The tyres should be at their correct pressures and the car should be level on the suspension.

6 The front wheels are correctly aligned when they are turning in 0.15 to 0.23 in (4 to 6 mm). This toe-in figure is the difference in distance between the middle of the two front wheel rims when measured at hub level on the most forward tip and the most rearward tip of the

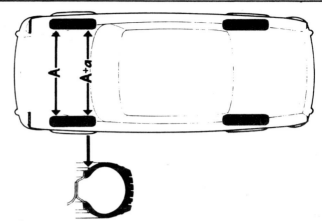

Fig. 8.4. Diagram showing wheel alignment check points (Sec. 8)

a = toe-in

wheel rims (Fig. 8.4).

7 Adjustment is made by slackening the nuts locking the trackrod relative to the ball joint sockets and screwing the trackrod into, or out of, the ball joint socket, as necessary. Retighten the locknuts when the correct adjustment is made. On some models the adjustment is made on the central trackrod. After releasing the locking nut the rod is adjusted by turning with a pipe wrench. If the adjustment required is considerable, distribute the adjustment equally between both trackrods.

Mark the position checked with a piece of chalk and then move the car forwards so that the wheels are turned through 180° and recheck the alignment.

If incorrect, it may be that a wheel, or both wheels, are buckled, in which case get the adjustment to as near as possible to the correct setting and have the alignment rechecked by your Skoda agent.

9 Steering box - removal, dismantling and inspection

1 Refer to Fig. 8.5. If for any reason the steering box has to be removed it will be necessary to disconnect it from the steering column, as described in Section 2.

2 To disconnect the ball joint between the steering box drop arm and the trackrod, remove the split pin and undo the castle nut. Proprietary split wedges or a ball joint separator can then be used to 'split' the ball joint.

3 Undo the three bolts securing the steering box, and remove the box complete with drop arm.

4 Remove the tapered plug from its location in the steering box top cover and drain out the oil.

5 Remove the flexible column joint hub from the splines of the steering worm.

6 Remove the split pin and unscrew the drop arm retaining nut to remove the drop arm and its locating Woodruff key from the rocker arm shaft. It may be necessary to use a universal puller.

7 Loosen the nut and setscrews in the steering box cover and then remove the retaining bolts and lift the cover clear.

8 Now lift the rocker arm shaft out of the box, complete with the special worm actuating nut.

9 If the bearings are to be removed, unscrew the end cap retaining bolts and withdraw the bearings, complete with worm, by drifting out.

10 Remove the bearings from the shaft with a puller.

11 Clean all parts of the steering box thoroughly, and inspect for excessive wear in the worm and nut (or peg in some models). Test the rocker arm fit in its locating bush and if required, drift out the bush and replace with a new one. The bearings do not normally wear to any extent, but they should also be checked. Always renew the 'O' rings and cover gaskets.

10 Steering box - reassembly and refitting

1 Assuming the rocker arm bush to have been renewed and pressed into position, replace the 'O' ring and dust cap into their aperture.

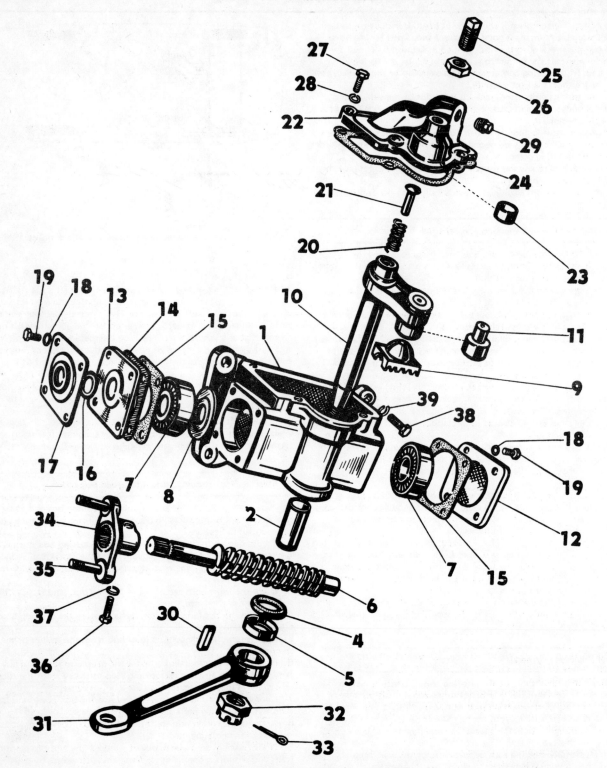

Fig. 8.5. Components of the steering box (Sec. 10)

1	Steering box	12	Bottom box cover	21	Spring pin	30	Key
2	Bush	13	Top box cover	22	Steering box top	31	Drop arm
4	'O' ring	14	Preload adjustment washer	23	Cover bush	32	Castellated nut
5	Dust cap	15	Preload adjustment gasket	24	Cover gasket	33	Split pin
6	Steering worm	16	'O' ring	25	Set screw	34	Input shaft coupling
7	Ball bearing	17	Cover plate	26	Nut	35	Stud
8	Bearing washer	18	Fan washer	27	Bolt	36	Screw
9	Steering nut	19	Bolt	28	Washer	37	Washer
10	Rocker shaft	20	Rocker shaft spring	29	Taper filler plug	38	Bolt
11	Rocker shaft pin					39	Spring washer

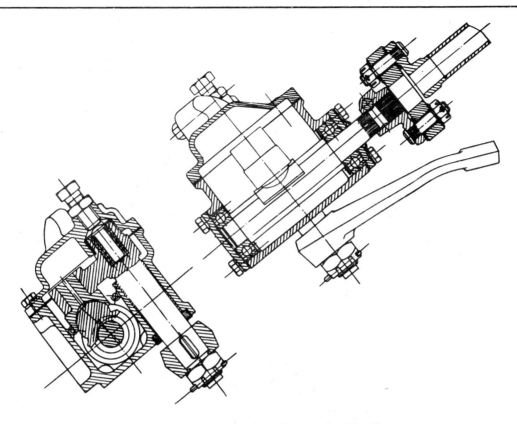

Fig. 8.6. Sectional views of steering box (Sec. 9)

2 Press fit the bottom bearing into position in the box.
3 Smear both sides of the bottom cover gasket with a sealing compound, refit with the cover and retain with bolts and spring washers.
4 Fit the bearing washer onto the top of the shaft, and then press fit the top bearing into position on the end of the worm shaft. Insert the shaft into position in the box and press into the bottom bearing, then fit the top bearing into position within its orifice in the box.
5 Measure the thickness of the bearing protrusion from the box, and fit the appropriate number of washers required to offset this thickness; smear with sealing compound. Refit the top cover, 'O' ring and the cover plate and tighten to the specified torque.
6 Check the worm shaft for smooth rotation, endfloat and axial play.
7 Now reassemble the rocker arm and nut (or peg) into the box and also the spring and pin to the arm shaft. Coat the joint faces with sealer and fit the gasket and cover, securing with retaining bolts and washers.
8 Refit the drop arm and Woodruff key, then tighten the retaining castle nut firmly to the nearest split pin hole. Insert and divide the split pin to lock the nut.
9 Now insert the adjustment screw into the top cover and turn the drop arm to its limit. With the drop arm in this position, first tighten the adjustment screw fully and then unscrew it by 120° to ensure the correct amount of free-play in the steering. Lock in position with the locknut.
10 Fit the column coupling to the worm shaft and retain with clamp bolt.
11 Try the steering action, which should be quite smooth. If tight, unscrew the adjustment screw to suit, and then lock with the nut.
12 Refit the steering box to the car and refill with oil (SAE 90) to the brim of the filler hole.
13 Reconnect the trackrod ball joint to the drop arm.

11 Steering wheel and column shaft - removal and refitting

1 Refer to Fig. 8.7. To remove the steering wheel and column complete, it will be necessary to jack-up the front of the car and place on axle stands or blocks. This will allow access to underside of the car, in order to disconnect the steering column shaft to worm shaft coupling from the steering box. Before disconnecting, ensure the road-wheels are facing straight-ahead.
2 Now follow the instructions given in Section 2, paragraph 4.
3 Alternatively, on later models, if the upper column shaft and steering wheel only are to be removed, loosen the upper to lower shaft location screw locknut and remove the screw (36 and 37). Then remove the steering column facia cover screws and cover, the bearing holder bracket screws and the steering lock clamp retaining bolts. The upper column and wheel can now be withdrawn from the splines of the lower shaft. Although the car will not have to be jacked-up in this instance, the wheels should still be set to the straight-ahead position.
4 To remove the steering wheel from the column, undo the nut at the top of the column; under the wheel. When withdrawing the wheel, ensure that the two collets do not fall out. MB models require a special puller to remove the steering wheel, therefore, this task should be entrusted to your Skoda agent.
5 Refitting is a reversal of the removal procedure.

12 Stub axle, king-pin and wishbones - removal, inspection and refitting

1 See Fig. 8.8. If the axle assembly is still on the car, jack-up at the front and support with stands. Chock the rear wheels to prevent car movement.
2 Remove the brakes (see Chapter 9), and wheel hub units (Chapter 7).
3 Remove the coil spring/s and shock absorber/s, as described in Sections 5 and 6.
4 Disconnect the trackrod.
5 Remove the brake backplate.
6 Withdraw the split pin from the steering rod castle nut and loosen the nut. To remove the steering rod, which is located in the stub axle on a taper and Woodruff key, hit the nut with a soft-headed mallet. When the tapered joint is free, remove the nut and withdraw the steering rod. Remove the Woodruff key.
7 Remove the upper wishbone from the axle and stub axle by removing the respective split pin and castle nut and locking nuts from the wishbone pins. Remove the dust cap and rubber bush from the axle pin and disconnect the circlips from the pin grooves within the

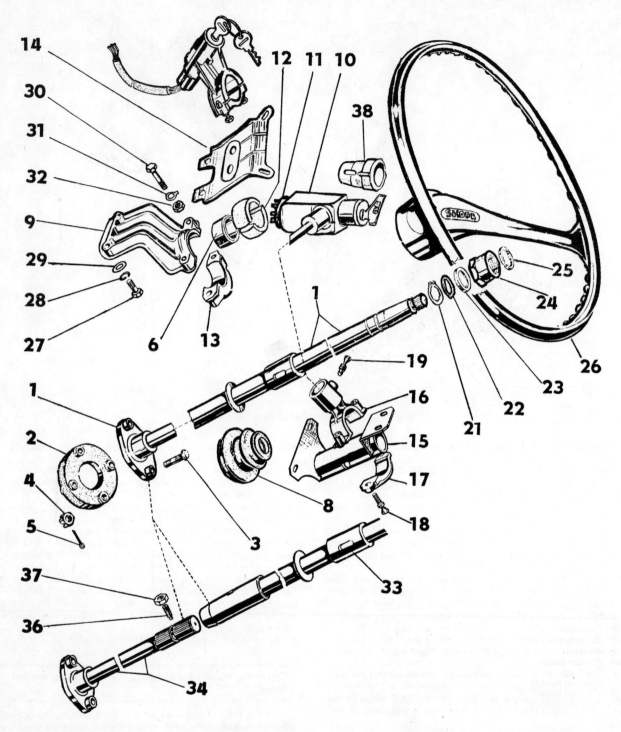

Fig. 8.7. Steering wheel and column components (Sec. 11)

1	Steering column shaft	11	Switch box	21	Lock washer	30	Bolt
2	Flexible coupling	12	Rubber insert	22	Concave washer	31	Lock washer
3	Bolt	13	Bearing cover	23	Washer	32	Nut
4	Nut	14	Holder for steering rod cover	24	Nut	33	Upper shaft
5	Cotter pin	15	Lock holder	25	Segment	34	Lower shaft
6	Bearing	16	Lock holder with screws	26	Steering wheel	36	Screw
8	Sealing cup	17	Lock holder clamp half	27	Bolt	37	Nut
9	Bracket	18	Shear head bolt	28	Washer	38	Cover
10	Lock c/w switchbox assembly	19	Shear head bolt	29	Washer		

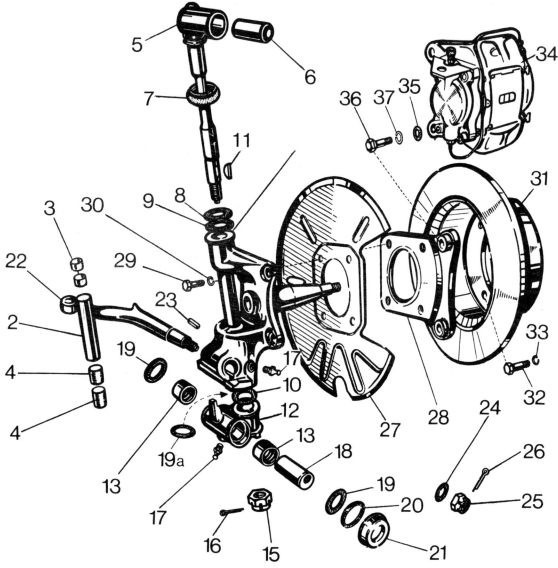

Fig. 8.8 Stub axle and king-pin components (Sec. 12)

1	Stub axle	11	Key	20	Dust seal
2	Distance piece	12	Steering knuckle	21	Dust cap
3	Top bush	13	Knuckle bush	22	Steering lever
4	Bottom bush	15	Nut	23	Key
5	King pin	16	Split pin	24	Washer
6	Rubber bush	17	Lubricating nipple	25	Nut
7	Dust cap	18	Eccentric insert	26	Split pin
8	Friction washer	19	Adjusting washer	27	Disc brake shield
9	Friction washer	19a	Washer polythene	28	Caliper bracket
10	Friction washer				

29	Bolt
30	Washer
31	Brake disc
32	Bolts
33	Washer
34	Brake caliper
35	Adjusting washer
36	Bolt
37	Washer

wishbone.

8   With a soft drift and hammer, drive the pins through the wishbone, stub axle and axle locations, and remove the upper wishbone.

9   Remove the lower wishbone by removing from the axle pivot pin the retaining nuts, washers, rubber bush and cap, and from within the wishbone, the circlips from their grooves. Clean and keep the respective adjustment washers in order, for reassembly. Remove the split pin and castle nut from the eccentric bolt, and with a soft drift and hammer, drive the pin and bolt through the wishbone and stub axle to remove.

10   To dismantle the stub axle and king-pin unit, remove the castle nut and split pin from the king-pin at the bottom. Prise the Woodruff key from its groove.

11   Remove the steering knuckle and then withdraw the king-pin from the stub axle.

12   Clean all parts thoroughly and inspect for excessive wear of the king-pin and bushes.

13   If the bushes and king-pin are to be renewed, it is a task for your Skoda dealer as the new bushes will have to be reamed to suit the new king-pin. The dealer will also have the equipment to remove and replace the bushes. The steering knuckle bush will also have to be replaced, and this should be taken for attention at the same time.

If the eccentric bush and eccentric bolt are to be renewed, this task should be entrusted to your Skoda dealer. This is because the bush setting is critical in terms of its effect on camber angle; the dealer will also advise on the shim thickness requirements.

14   Remove the knuckle and stub axle grease nipples and clean out the oilways to ensure good lubrication of the new bushes.

15   The king-pin top wishbone location bolt bush, should be renewed at this stage; also a job for your Skoda dealer.

16   Fit new seals and dustcaps as required, and always use new split pins on reassembly.

17   Reassembly of stub axle and wishbones is a reversal of dismantling,

but the following points should be noted:

a) *Always lubricate with a good quality multi-purpose grease, the swivel pins, bushes and king-pin prior to assembly.*

b) *When fitting the rubber bush to the upper wishbone, insert the bushes into hot, soapy water first, to ease entry into the wishbone arm 'eyes'. When fitted the bushes should protrude equally each side of the eye. Any wet soapy solution remaining should be wiped or blown off with compressed air.*

c) *Always renew the circlips and ensure that they are correctly fitted in their respective grooves.*

d) *Connect the wishbones to the axle first and then insert the coil spring and rubber washer. It is advisable to smear the top of the coil spring and the washer joint faces with a rubber solution to ensure correct final location within the wishbone arm and axle. Having located the coil spring, compress it so that when the lower wishbone arm is raised the gap between the stop rubber in the axle and the wishbone stop is 0.79 in (20 mm), then refit the stub axle unit.*

e) *When fitting the steering knuckles, do not interchange the right or left-hand knuckles.*

f) *Refit the wheel hub and brakes, as described in Chapters 7 and 9. Bleed the brakes prior to using the car on the road.*

g) *When the trackrods are reconnected, check the toe-in, as described in Section 9.*

h) *After the repair of any unit from the front suspension or steering assembly, it is most important that an alignment check should be made by your Skoda agent. He is fully equipped to do this, and for the comparatively small cost involved, it will save you money on tyre wear and ensure the correct handling and safety of your car.*

13 Rear suspension - general

1   Each side of the rear suspension basically consists of a coil spring and telescopic shock absorber, which are located between the car body and the half-axle strut arms. The strut arms are located on the half-axle casings at one end, and the forward end hinges in a flexible mounting bolted to the underbody, just forward of the rear wheel arches (photo).

2   As previously mentioned, **on no account must the strut arm be disconnected or relocated on its half-axle mounting, as this will affect the rear wheel alignment.** Should it ever be necessary to remove the strut arms, work beyond this point should be left to your Skoda dealer.

3   Note that the rear coil springs are a heavier gauge than those of the front and they should never be interchanged.

14 Coil spring and shock absorber (rear) - removal and refitting

1   Jack-up the rear of the car until the half-axle is lowered into the suspension yoke limiting strap. Further support the underbody with blocks or axle stands as a safety measure.

2   Remove the relevant roadwheel.

3   Unscrew the shock absorber retaining nut at the bottom (photo) and, to prevent the shock absorber turning, insert a 17 mm open-ended spanner through the spring and locate on the nut at the base of the shock absorber body, whilst undoing the bottom nut.

4   Push the shock absorber up, and compress the spring to remove.

5   The shock absorber can now be removed by unscrewing its retaining nut at the top.

6   If on removal the upper and lower coil spring rubber locating washers are perished, or worn, they should be renewed on assembly.

13.1 General view showing rear coil suspension and half-axle unit

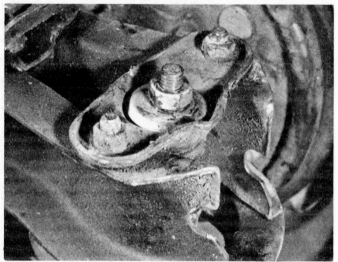

14.3 Rear shock absorber retaining nut and washer in strut arm

7   Refitting the coil springs and shock absorbers is a reversal of the removal procedure.

15 Strut arm flexible mounting bushes - general

The rubber bushes fitted to the forward end of the strut arms are inserted during manufacture and cannot be removed or refitted without specialised equipment. Therefore, any such work should be taken to your Skoda dealer. **Do not remove the strut arms from the half-axle.**

16 Fault diagnosis - suspension and steering

Before diagnosing faults from the following chart, check that any irregularities are not caused by:

1 *Binding brakes*
2 *Incorrect 'mix' of radial and crossply tyres*
3 *Incorrect tyre pressures*
4 *Misalignment of the body frame or rear axle*

Symptom	Reason/s	Remedy
Steering wheel can be moved considerably before any sign of movement of the wheels is apparent	Wear in the steering linkage, gear and column coupling	Check movement in all joints and steering gear and overhaul and renew as required.
Vehicle difficult to steer in a consistent straight line - wandering	As above Wheel alignment incorrect (indicated by excessive or uneven tyre wear) Front wheel hub bearings loose or worn Worn ball joints, trackrods or suspension arms	As above. Check wheel alignment. Adjust or renew as necessary. Renew as necessary.
Steering stiff and heavy	Incorrect wheel alignment (indicated by excessive or uneven tyre wear) Excessive wear or seizure in one or more of the joints in the steering linkage or suspension arm ball joints Excessive wear in the steering gear unit	Check wheel alignment. Renew as necessary or grease the suspension unit ball joints. Adjust if possible or renew.
Wheel wobble and vibration	Roadwheels out of balance Roadwheels buckled Wheel alignment incorrect Wear in the steering linkage, suspension arm ball joints or suspension arm pivot bushes	Balance wheels. Check for damage. Check wheel alignment. Check and renew as necessary.
Excessive pitching and rolling on corners and during braking	Defective shock absorbers and/or broken torsion bar, anti-roll bar broken away	Check and renew as necessary.

Chapter 9 Braking system

Contents

Specifications

Type
Early models	Hydraulic, single leading shoe drum brakes all round
Later models	Hydraulic, dual line, disc brakes front, drum rear

Adjustment
Drum brakes	Eccentric cam, via adjusters on backplate
Disc brakes	Automatic

Handbrake
Handbrake	Hand operated levers, actuating rear brakes via adjustable cables

Drum brakes
Diameter	8.97 in (230 mm)
Width of lining	1.56 in (40 mm)

Disc brakes
Diameter	9.84 in (252.5 mm)

Torque wrench settings
	lb f ft	Kg f m
Disc brake bolt	35 to 43	4.8 to 6
Brake clamp bolt (12 mm)	53 to 68	7 to 9.5
Brake clamp bolt (8 mm)	13 to 18	1.9 to 2.5
Brake cylinder bolt	5	0.07
Brake backplate bolt	14.5 to 18	2 to 2.5
Pipe unions	15	2.04
Bleed nipples	6	0.9
Inner cylinder bolts	20	2.75

1 General description

Earlier model Skodas have drum brakes on all wheels, these being operated hydraulically by means of the brake pedal coupled to the brake master cylinder.

Both front and rear brakes are of the single leading shoe type with one brake cylinder per wheel for both shoes. Both the front and rear brakes are individually adjustable by turning the adjusters on the backplates.

The handbrake lever is located between the front seats and this actuates the rear brakes only, by means of cables.

The hydraulic circuit operates when pressure on the foot brake pedal moves a piston in the master cylinder. The moving piston pumps the fluid in the cylinder into the pipe lines under pressure, and thus forces the wheel slave cylinder pistons to move out, pushing the shoe against the brake drum as they do so.

When the brake pedal pressure is released the brake shoes retract under spring tension and the fluid displaced from the master cylinder is returned.

Later models have disc brakes at the front (Fig. 9.1). These are also hydraulically operated, but adjustment is automatic. The braking system is otherwise basically the same.

The master cylinder is of tandem type, incorporating two pistons and seal assemblies, which operate simultaneously. The front piston operates the forward brakes and the rear piston the rear brakes. The advantage of this type of braking unit is that if the front circuit should fail for any reason, the rear circuit will still operate and vice versa.

2 Routine maintenance

1 Weekly, carefully clean the brake/clutch fluid reservoir cap and surround, remove the cap and inspect the level of the fluid which should be level with the top of the separator in the centre of the reservoir.
2 If the fluid is below this level, top-up the reservoir with the correct

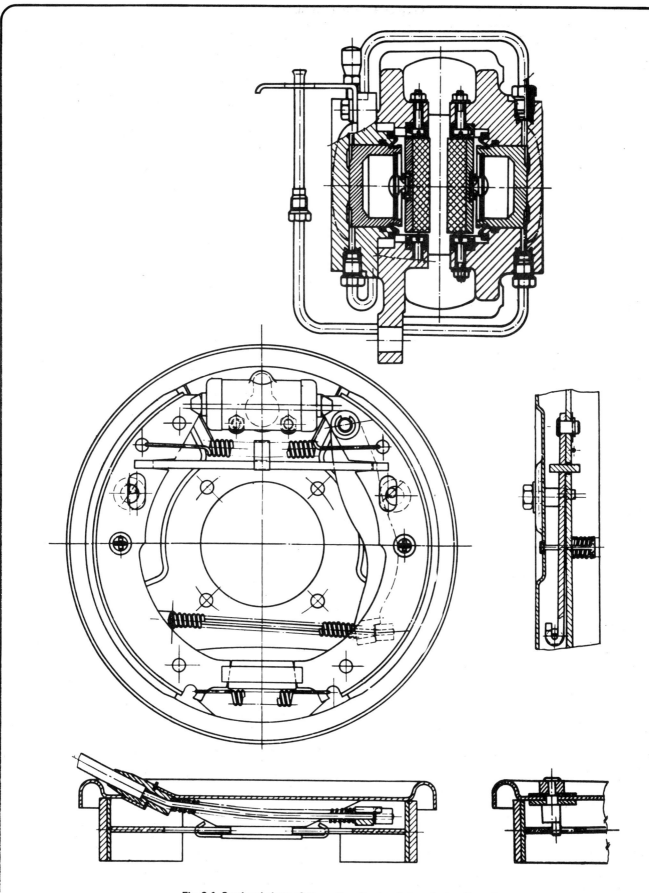

Fig. 9.1. Sectional views of disc caliper (top) and drum brakes (Sec. 1)

type of brake fluid. It is vital that no other type of brake fluid is used. Use of a non-standard fluid will result in brake failure caused by the perishing of the special seals in the master and brake cylinders. If topping-up becomes frequent then check the metal piping and flexible hose for leaks, and check for worn brake or master cylinders which will also cause loss of fluid. **Note:** Take great care not to spill hydraulic fluid on the paintwork when topping-up the reservoir, as the fluid will damage any paintwork it comes into contact with.

3   Every 12,500 miles (20,000 km) check the brake linings for wear. If the surface of the lining is almost at rivet level, then the linings must be replaced or damage to the drums will ensue. However, if the linings are in good condition, take this opportunity to brush and blow any dust off the linings, backplate and drum. For this purpose use a clean brush and, if available compressed air.

4   If it is found that excessive brake pedal travel is needed to operate the brakes then the front and rear brakes should be adjusted (rear brakes only for disc brake models).

5   If handbrake operation is not satisfactory, the rear brakes should be adjusted. This will normally effect a cure. If after rear brake adjustment the handbrake is no better, then there is a strong possibility that the handbrake cables have stretched. If this is the case it is necessary to adjust the handbrake itself.

6   The front disc brakes on later models require a minimum of maintenance. Every 12,500 miles (20,000 km) or 6 months, remove the disc pads and inspect for wear, renewing the four if necessary. With compressed air blow the caliper unit through, to remove collected dust, then clean and de-rust the pad retaining clips and lightly smear with grease prior to re-assembly. If badly rusted, renew the clips.

7   Check the hydraulic pipes and connections for leaks, or signs of corrosion and renew as required.

3   Drum brakes - adjustment

1   Jack-up the rear of the car and chock the front wheels to prevent movement of the car.

2   Release the handbrake to the off position and move the gearlever to the neutral position.

3   Spin the rear wheel and from underneath turn the two adjuster nuts on the backplate (Fig. 9.2) with a ring-spanner one at a time, until both shoes are locking the wheel. Then slacken each in turn so that the wheel is *just* free to spin freely. Apply the brakes to centralise the shoes.

4   Repeat the procedure on the other wheel to complete rear brake adjustments.

5   Adjust front drum brakes in the same manner, but chock the rear wheels and place in gear, to prevent car movement.

4   Rear brakes - removal, inspection and refitting

1   The brake drums at the rear also serve as the hubs. As mentioned in Chapter 7, Section 2, a special puller is required to remove the drums before any work may be carried out on the brakes or hubs. If the puller is available proceed as follows:-

2   Jack-up the rear of the car, support firmly on axle stands and remove the roadwheel. Release the handbrake.

3   Withdraw the split pin and unscrew the hub nut.

4   With the special puller, remove the brake drum/hub. The brake shoes and slave cylinder are now exposed.

5   The brake linings should be renewed if they are so worn that the rivet heads are flush with the surface of the linings, or will be before the next inspection. If bonded linings are fitted they must be removed when the material has worn down to 1/32 in (0.8 mm) at its thinnest point. If the shoes are being removed to give access to the wheel cylinders, then cover the linings with masking tape to prevent any possibility of their becoming contaminated with grease.

6   Remove each brake shoe locating pin by turning the dished washer with a pair of pliers, so that the slot aligns with the head of the pin and then withdraw the whole assembly.

7   Unhook the retractor spring which connects the two shoes at the top, by prising with a screwdriver and then unhook the lever spring in a similar fashion.

8   Now remove the brakes shoes complete with the distance lever.

9   Tie a piece of string or place an elastic band around the slave cylinder to prevent piston movement. Do not apply pressure to the brake pedal

Fig. 9.2. Drum brake adjusters (Sec. 3) black arrows indicate direction in which to turn adjusters to move shoes towards the drum (Sec. 6)

while the shoes are removed, as this will eject the pistons necessitating brake bleeding.

10 Thoroughly clean all traces of dust from the brake shoes, backplate and brake drums, using a dry paint brush.

11 Check that the rubber dust covers are in good order on the slave cylinders, and that there are no hydraulic fluid leaks.

12 Before reassembly, smear a trace of brake grease to the sliding surfaces. Ensure that the shoes are free to slide on the closed end of the cylinder and the piston anchorage point.

13 Refitting is a straightforward reversal of the removal procedure, but note the following points:

   a) *Do not omit to replace the shoe steady pins and springs.*
   b) *Ensure that the return springs are in their correct holes.*
   c) *Adjust the rear brakes, as described in Section 3, but if new shoes were fitted, back off the adjusters slightly more than normal to allow for shoe expansion.*

14 After two or three hundred miles, check and readjust the brakes in the normal manner.

5   Front brakes (drum) - removal, inspection and refitting

1   Remove the hub caps, loosen the wheel nuts, jack-up the front of the car, supporting on axle stands, and remove the wheel.

2   Slacken off the brake adjustment.

3   Prise off the hub grease cap with a screwdriver and withdraw the split pin from the castle nut. Undo and remove the earth nut and special washer, and then withdraw the tapered bearing cone. Lightly tap the outside rim of the brake drum from the inside with a soft-headed mallet, striking evenly in a diagonal fashion, and remove the drum/hub unit.

4   Note the fitted positions of the two brake shoe return springs and remove them by prising from each shoe with a screwdriver.

5   Remove the brake shoe locating pins by turning the dished washers so that the slot aligns with the head of the pin and then withdrawing the complete pin assembly.

6   Now follow the instructions given in Section 4, paragraphs 8 to 13.

7   Having reassembled the brake unit and hub, adjust the brakes as described in Section 3, apply the brakes to centralise the shoes and recheck adjustment.

8   After two or three hundred miles, check and readjust the brake adjustment.

6   Wheel slave cylinder - removal, inspection and refitting

1   To inspect, remove or replace the rear wheel slave cylinder, it is necessary to remove the rear wheels, brake drums/hubs and brake shoes, as described in Section 4. On early models with front drum brakes, the wheel cylinders are removed and serviced in the same manner, but follow the instructions given in Section 5 to remove the brake drum and shoes.

2   Before disconnecting the hydraulic hose connection from the back-plate, remove the hydraulic fluid reservoir filler cap and place a piece of

polythene over the seal and replace the cap. This restricts the flow of the fluid from the disconnected pipe.

3   Now remove the connecting pipe from the backplate. Note that the pipes are angled at approximately 30° down from the horizontal, and be sure to refit at this angle to prevent chafing of the hose on the strut arm. Temporarily tie the hose out of the way and plug the end to prevent the ingress of dirt.

4   Remove the brake bleed nipple and disconnect the cylinder from the backplate by undoing the two bolts (photo).

5   Thoroughly clean off the outside of the cylinder or remove to the workbench, where it may be stripped down on a sheet of clean paper.

6.4 Hydraulic hose connection to wheel cylinder. Note the bleed nipple at the top and the cylinder retaining bolts

Cleanliness during dismantling, inspection and reassembly is essential.

6   To strip for inspection, remove from each end of the cylinder, the two dust seal rubbers, then remove the pistons and slotted rods and finally the inner seals and spring.

Clean all parts thoroughly and inspect the seals for signs of wear or perishing, and the pistons and cylinder bore for scratches or pitting - renew as required. Replacement seals are usually readily available and are relatively inexpensive.

7   Reassembly of the cylinder unit is a straight reversal of dismantling, but when fitting the seals, smear with some hydraulic fluid to ease entry into the bore. The lip of the seal should face away from the piston.

8   On refitting the cylinders to the backplate, reconnect the hydraulic pipe, brake shoes, drum/hub and wheel and then bleed the hydraulic system, as described in Section 10, and if necessary re-adjust the brakes (Section 3).

7   Disc brake caliper unit - removal and refitting

1   Jack-up the front of the car and remove the relevant roadwheel.

2   Unscrew the filler cap of the hydraulic fluid reservoir and stretch a piece of thin polythene over the top of the neck and replace the cap. This prevents excessive leakage of brake fluid when the flexible hose connecting the front brake is removed.

3   Remove the disc pad cover by withdrawing the two 'R' clips (photo) and extracting the cover retaining pins (photo).

4   Now remove the disc pads by simply pulling out, (noting from which side each pad came if they are to be replaced) (photo).

5   Disconnect the flexible brake hose and cover the open end to prevent ingress of dirt.

6   Unscrew the caliper unit retaining bolts and remove the unit from the disc.

7   The caliper unit can now be cleaned and inspected. If there is any leakage of hydraulic fluid past the piston seals the unit should be taken to your Skoda dealer for attention.

8   Refitting is the reverse of the removal procedure. However, on final

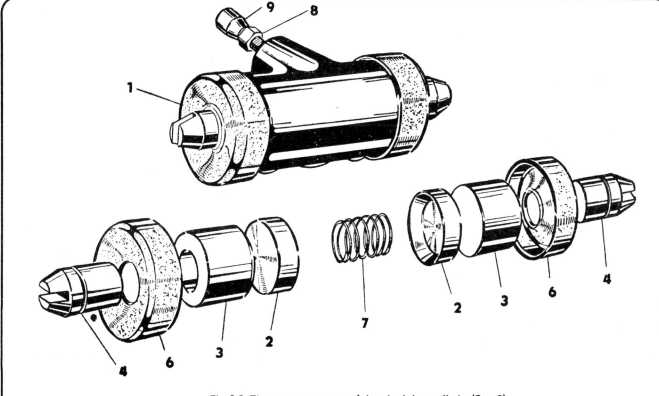

Fig. 9.3. The component parts of the wheel slave cylinder (Sec. 6)

| 1 | Wheel cylinder | 3 | Piston | 6 | Dust cover | 8 | Bleed nipple |
| 2 | Seal | 4 | Push rod | 7 | Spring | 9 | Bleed nipple cap |

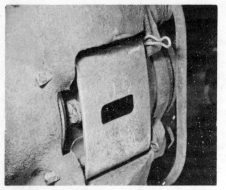

7.3a Disc brake pad retaining cover, showing position of 'R' clip

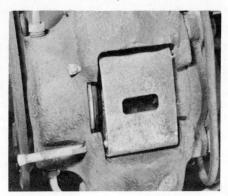

7.3b Disc brake pad cover - removing the retaining pins

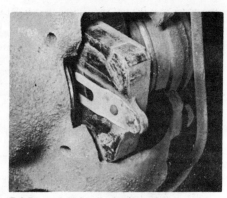

7.4 Removing the disc brake pads

assembly, remember to remove the polythene from the hydraulic reservoir and bleed the brake/s.

8 Brake disc - removal, inspection and refitting

1   To remove the brake disc, follow the instructions given in Section 7. Remove the brake caliper unit, but leave its hydraulic connections intact.
2   Then remove the wheel nut as described in Chapter 7.
3   Undo the four retaining bolts and remove the disc from the hub.
4   If the disc is badly scored it should be renewed, but it is sometimes possible to have the disc re-machined in an engineering machine shop to remove normal wear marks. The minimum permissible disc thickness is 0.28 in (7.4 mm), and if re-machined the amount of machining should be uniform on each face. Run-out should not exceed 0.005 in (0.15 mm) - this can be checked with a dial guage.
5   Refitting the disc is a reversal of the removal procedure.

9 Disc brake pads - removal, inspection and refitting

1   If the disc pads are to be removed for inspection, or renewal, follow the instructions given in Section 7, paragraphs 1, 3 and 4.
2   The pads should be renewed when they are worn to a minimum thickness of 0.275 in (7 mm), or if they will be before the next inspection.
3   There are three different types of pads available, these being as follows:

Type 1	Marking
Don 12	No marking
Osinek 10	White paint marked
Klinger 1390	Green paint marked

It is most important that disc pads of the same type are used in pairs on an axle. **Never interchange them.**
4   Refitting the pads is a reversal of removal. However, if new pads are being fitted in place of worn ones it may be necessary to push the caliper piston lock into their bores to allow sufficient clearance. This action can cause the brake fluid reservoir to overflow, so remove its cap and wrap a rag around the reservoir to catch spilt fluid.
5   Disc brakes are self-adjusting.

10 Hydraulic system - bleeding

1   The system should need bleeding only when some part of it has been dismantled which would allow air into the fluid circuit; or if the reservoir level has been allowed to drop so far that air has entered the master cylinder.
2   Ensure that a supply of clean non-aerated fluid of the correct specifications is to hand in order to replenish the reservoir during the bleeding process. It is advisable, if not essential, to have someone available to help, as one person has to pump the brake pedal while the other attends to each wheel. The reservoir level also has to be continuously watched and replenished. Fluid bled out should not be

re-used. A clean glass jar and a 9 - 12 inch (225 - 300 mm) length of rubber tube that will fit tightly over the bleed nipples is required.
3   Bleed the rear brakes first as these are furthest from the master cylinder.
4   Make sure the bleed nipple is clean and put a small quantity of fluid in the bottom of the jar. Fit the tube onto the nipple and place the other end in the jar under the surface of the liquid. Keep it under the surface throughout the bleeding operation.
5   Unscrew the bleed screw ½ turn and get the assistant to depress and release the brake pedal in short sharp bursts when you direct him. Short sharp jabs are better than long slow ones because they will force any air bubbles along the line ahead of the fluid rather than pump the fluid past them. It is not essential to remove all the air the first time. If the whole system is being bled, attend to each wheel for three or four complete pedal strokes and then repeat the process. On the second time around operate the pedal sharply in the same way until no more bubbles are apparent. The bleed screw should be tightened and closed with the brake pedal fully depressed which ensures that no aerated fluid can get back into the system. Do not forget to keep the reservoir topped-up throughout.
6   When all four wheels have been satisfactorily bled depress the foot pedal which should offer a firmer resistance with no trace of 'sponginess'. The pedal should not continue to go down under sustained pressure. If it does there is a leak or the master cylinder seals are worn out.

11 Stop light switch - removal and refitting

1   On late models the stoplight switch is screwed into the side of the brake master cylinder and can be removed with the cylinder in place. On earlier models the switch is located in the rear brake fluid distributor junction to the right of the transaxle housing.
2   Remove only when it is firmly established that the switch itself is malfunctioning, and that there is no other electrical fault. Begin removal by disconnecting the two cables; mark their position. Place a piece of polythene sheet over the reservoir and replace its cap - this will stop, to some extent, the loss of fluid. Place a rag underneath the switch and with the correct sized open-ended spanner unscrew the switch.
3   Refit always using a new washer and tighten sufficiently. Refit the cables and bleed the brakes, having removed the polythene sheet.

12 Hydraulic fluid pipes - inspection, removal and refitting

1   Refer to Fig. 9.4. Periodically and certainly well in advance of the DoT Test, if due, all brake pipes, connections and unions, should be completely and carefully examined..
2   Examine first all the unions for signs of leaks. Then look at the flexible hoses for signs of fraying and chafing (as well as for leaks). This is only a preliminary inspection of the flexible hoses, as exterior condition does not necessarily indicate interior condition which will be considered later.
3   The metal pipes must be examined equally carefully. They must be thoroughly cleaned and examined for signs of dents or other percussive damage, rust and corrosion. Rust and corrosion should be scraped off, and, if the depth of pitting in the pipes is significant, they will need

renewal. This is most likely in those areas underneath the body and near the rear suspension arms where the pipes are exposed to the full force of road and weather conditions. Also check the pipe connections at the three-way joint junctions at the front and rear (photo).

4   In particular inspect the front feed pipe to the disc brake caliper flexible hose joint. The metal pipe must be close fitting to the inner wing panel to avoid the tyre rubbing against it when on full lock (photo). Also check this pipe to ensure it is not being fouled by the wishbone arm and, if necessary, reposition the pipe by bending out of the way. The loop pipe over the disc brake caliper unit has also been known to rub against the disc and there should therefore be a clearance of at least 0.25 in (5 mm).

5   At the rear, check that the flexible pipes are not rubbing against the strut arms when the suspension is compressed.

6   If any section of pipe is to be removed, first take off the fluid reservoir cap, line it with a piece of polythene film to make it airtight and screw it back on. This will minimise the amount of fluid dripping out of the system when the pipes are removed.

7   Rigid pipe removal is usually quite straightforward. The unions at each end are undone and the pipe drawn out of the connection. The clips which hold it to the car body are bent back and it is then removed. Underneath the car the exposed union can be particularly stubborn, defying the efforts of an open-ended spanner. As few people will have the special split ring spanner required, a self-grip wrench (mole) is the only answer. If the pipe is being renewed, new unions will

be provided. If not, then one will have to put up with the possibility of burring over the flats on the union and of using a self-grip wrench for refitting also.

8   Flexible hoses are always fitted to a rigid support bracket where they join a rigid pipe. The rigid pipe unions must first be removed from the flexible union, releasing the end of the pipe from the bracket. As these connections are usually exposed they are, more often that not, rusted up and a penetrating fluid is virtually essential to aid removal. When undoing them, both halves must be supported as the bracket is not strong enough to support the torque required to undo the nut and can be snapped off easily.

9   Once the flexible hose is removed, examine the internal bore. If clear of fluid it should be possible to see through it. Any specks of rubber which come out, or signs of restriction in the bore, mean that the inner lining is breaking up and the pipe must be renewed.

10 Rigid pipes which need renewal can usually be purchased at your local garage where they have the pipe, unions and special tools to make them up. All that they need to know is the pipe length required and the type of flare used at the ends of the pipe. These may be different at each end of the same pipe.

11 Refitment of pipes is a straightforward reversal of the removal procedure. It is best to get all the sets (bends) in the pipe made preparatory to installation. Also any acute bends should be put in by the garage on a bending machine, otherwise there is the possibility of kinking them and restricting the bore area and fluid flow.

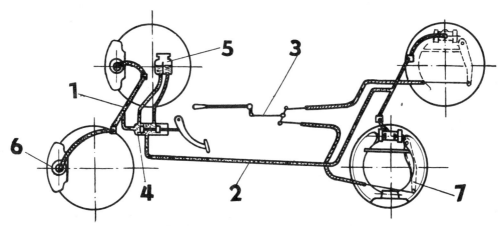

Fig. 9.4. Layout of the hydraulic circuit (Sec. 12)

1 Front brake circuit	3 Handbrake - linkage to cables	5 Hydraulic fluid reservoir	7 Rear drum brakes
2 Rear brake circuit	4 Brake master cylinder	6 Front disc brakes	

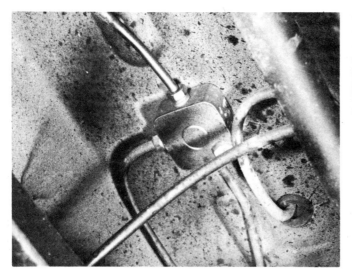

12.3 Hydraulic circuit three way connector - front

12.4 General view of disc brake showing the flexible to metal hydraulic pipe connection

12 With the pipes refitted, remove the polythene from the reservoir cap and bleed the system as described in Section 10.

13 Master cylinder (MB models) - removal and refitting

1   The brake and clutch master cylinders have a common reservoir, and are mounted to the bulkhead directly in front of the operating pedals.
2   To remove the complete clutch/brake master cylinder unit, it is necessary to drain or siphon out the fluid into a clean container. Do not spill any fluid onto the car bodywork.
3   Undo the relevant hydraulic pipe connections.
4   From inside the car undo the retaining clips and remove the piston actuating rods from the pins on each of the operating pedals.
5   Undo the cylinder unit flange nuts and remove the cylinder taking care not to spill the fluid remaining in the reservoir. Place the unit on the workbench which should be cleaned down with newspaper sheets laid on the work surface to ensure cleanliness during the dismantling process.
6   Refitting is the reversal of the removal procedure. Top-up the reservoir and bleed the system on completion. Ensure on reassembly of the actuating rods that correct pedal adjustments are made. The piston rod to master cylinder piston clearance is 0.025 in (1 mm) and this is set by turning the pedal adjustment bolt to suit, and locking in position with the locknut.

14 Master cylinder (tandem) - removal and refitting

Refer to Fig. 9.5. The braking system of later models incorporates a dual hydraulic circuit in which there are effectively two control cylinder in line with each other. Each piston within its respective part of the cylinder moves simultaneously. The front piston operates the front wheel disc brakes and the rear piston the rear drum brakes. If one circuit fails the other still operates.

It will be noted on dismantling the hydraulic pipe unions that two types of valve are used. The rear circuit valve does not have a hole in it, unlike the front circuit valve which has. **The two valves must not be interchanged.**

Cleanliness is essential during all operations when working on the hydraulic circuits.

Remove and refit the unit as follows:
1   To remove the master cylinder it is first necessary to drain the reservoir fluid into a clean container. This can be done by siphoning out through the filler neck or by undoing the feed pipe to the master cylinder. Be careful not to spill any brake fluid onto the car bodywork.

2   Undo the relevant hydraulic pipe connections from the body of the cylinder, and disconnect leads from the brake light switches (photo).
3   From inside the car, undo the retaining clips and remove the piston actuating rod from the locating pin on the brake pedals.
4   Undo the two cylinder flange nuts and remove the cylinder, taking care not to spill fluid.
5   Refitting is a reversal of the removal procedure but ensure on reassembly of the actuating rod that the correct adjustment is made. This adjustment is set by means of the pedal stop screw to allow for 0.012 - 0.020 in (0.3 - 0.5 mm) clearance, or free-travel, of the rod. If this clearance is absent the piston cannot return fully, and the operation of the system will be seriously effected.

15A   Master cylinder (MB models) - dismantling, overhaul and reassembly

1   Thoroughly clean the outside of the master cylinder unit prior to dismantling.
2   Remove the rubber boot from the end of the cylinder, and extract the circlip from the bore of the cylinder.

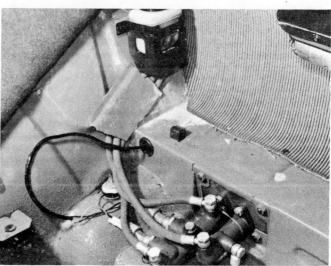

14.2 General view of brake (tandem) and clutch master cylinders, and the hydraulic fluid reservoir

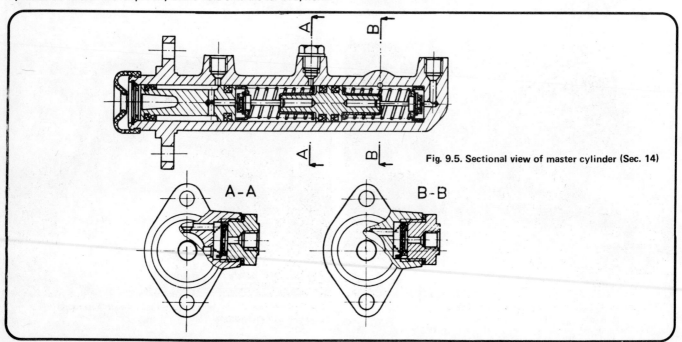

Fig. 9.5. Sectional view of master cylinder (Sec. 14)

A-A   B-B

3   The piston and its respective components may now be withdrawn carefully; take note of the order of dismantling and the position of all components relative to each other as they are withdrawn. Then lay out the respective parts in order, and throughly clean each component.
4   Inspect carefully the cylinder bore for pitting or scratches. If present, the cylinder will have to be renewed. The seals will need to be renewed as a matter of course.
5   Reassembly is the reverse order, but note first the following points:

a) Lubricate all parts prior to assembly with clean hydraulic fluid.
b) Do not force or distort the seals during assembly.
c) On refitting the unit to the car, top-up the reservoir with clean fluid and bleed the system. Check the pedal clearances and inspect the connecting pipes to the reservoir for any signs of leakage.

15B   Master cylinder (tandem) - dismantling, overhaul and reassembly

1   Refer to Fig. 9.6. Thoroughly clean the outside of the cylinder unit before dismantling.
2   Remove the rubber boot from the rear of the cylinder and take out the circlip from the bore of the cylinder.
3   The two pistons and their respective components may then be extracted from the cylinder. Do this carefully, taking note of the order

of dismantling and the relative positions of all components as they are withdrawn.
4   Having dismantled, lay the parts out in order of dismantling on a clean surface after cleaning them thoroughly with hydraulic fluid. Inspect the cylinder bore and pistons for pitting or general wear, renew as necessary. Piston seals should be renewed as a matter of course.
5   Reassembly is the reverse order to dismantling, but note the following points:

a) Special care should be taken not to overstretch the new seals when fitting to the pistons.
b) Ensure that the valves and stems are correctly located and do not distort the piston cups when fitting.
c) Lubricate all parts in clean hydraulic fluid prior to assembly.
d) On refitting, top-up the reservoir and bleed the system. Adjust the brake pedal to allow for a 0.012 - 0.020 in (0.3 - 0.5 mm) actuating rod clearance, and check the master cylinder and connections for any signs of leakage.

16 Brake and clutch pedals - removal and refitting

1   Remove the circlip from the clevis pin retaining the master cylinder actuating rod to the pedal and withdraw from the clevis pin. Repeat this operation on the clutch pedal. It is necessary to remove both pedals

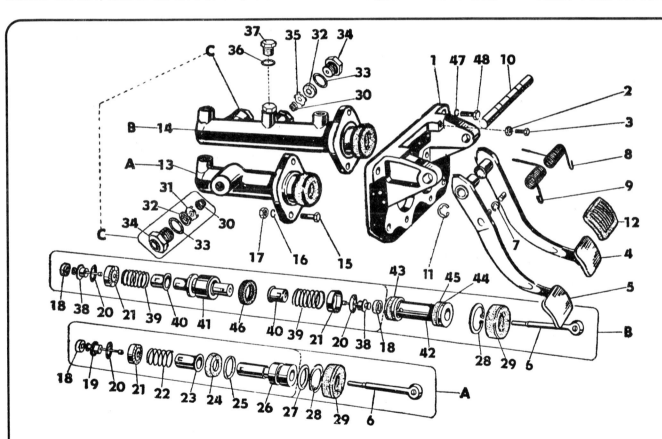

Fig. 9.6. The brake master cylinder (tandem) and clutch master cylinder component parts (Sec. 15B)

1 Pedal bracket	13 Clutch master cylinder	25 Ring	37 Plug
2 Lock nut	14 Brake master cylinder	26 Piston	38 Stem
3 Adjusting bolt	15 Bolt	27 Cover	39 Spring
4 Brake pedal	16 Washer	28 Locking ring	40 Cup
5 Clutch pedal	17 Nut	29 Dust cap	41 Floating piston
6 Piston actuating rod	18 Valve	30 Spring	42 Piston
7 Circlip	19 Stem	31 Valve body and opening	43 Sealing cup
8 Return spring	20 Washer	32 Seal	44 Slip on ring
9 Return spring	21 Bushing	33 Sealing ring	45 Piston ring
10 Pedal shaft	22 Spring	34 Plug	46 Pin/sealing ring
11 Circlip	23 Cup	35 Valve body	47 Washer
12 Pedal rubber	24 Sealing cap	36 Sealing ring	48 Screw

17.4 Handbrake cables - adjustment nuts

18.2 Pulling the handbrake cable through body channel

as they are retained by the same shaft.
2   Ease the tension springs off the pedals with a pair of pliers, noting
how they are located.
3   Remove the circlips from the end of the pedal pivot shaft and
withdraw the shaft through the pedals and mounting bracket to remove.
4   Reassembly is the reversal of dismantling but be sure to re-locate
the pedal tension springs correctly, and smear the shaft lightly with a
universal grease.

17 Handbrake - adjustment

1   The handbrake does not normally require adjustment as it is
automatically adjusted when the rear brakes are adjusted. However, if
there is play in the handbrake mechanism after rear brake adjustment
proceed as follows.
2   Jack-up the rear of the car so that the rear wheels clear the ground,
and place chocks in front of, and behind the front wheels.
3   Adjust the rear brakes, as described in Section 3.
4   From inside the car, fold forward the carpet over the central tunnel
just in front of the rear seat, and remove the cover plate to reveal the
handbrake tie-rod and cable mechanism (photo).
5   Position the handbrake in the fully off position, and then apply it so
that it is located on its second notch.
6   The cables to each rear brake can now be adjusted in turn by
tightening the regulating nuts as required to take up any slack in either
cable.
7   When the adjustment has been made, release the handbrake to the
fully off position and spin the wheels to ensure that the handbrake is
fully released.

18 Handbrake cable - removal and refitting

Handbrake cable removal entails the withdrawal of the rear brake
drum/hub. As mentioned in earlier Sections, this requires the use of a

special puller to release the hub/drum from the tapered shaft. If the
puller is available from your Skoda agent proceed as follows.
1   To remove the handbrake cables, follow the instructions given in
paragraphs 2 and 4, of Section 17, and then unscrew the regulating nuts
fully to remove.
2   From underneath the car, pull the cables clear, through the body
channels (photo). Should the right-hand cable stick, lift the right-hand
rear seat out of the way, and guide the cable round the heater radiator
unit and out of the rear body orifice.
3   Jack-up the rear of the car and remove the brake drum/hub unit
with the special puller (see Section 5, Chapter 7).
4   Remove the circlip in the end of the Bowden casing and disconnect
the cable nipple from the operating lever. The cable can now be withdrawn for inspection or replacement. Repeat this procedure on the
opposite rear wheel.
5   Refitment is the reverse procedure. but be sure to re-adjust the
handbrake, as detailed in Section 17, on final reassembly.

19 Handbrake lever - removal and refitting

1   Little attention is ever needed by the handbrake lever unit apart
from occasionally lubricating the lever hinge pin and ratchet. If it is to
be removed, proceed as follows.
2   Remove the floor covering from the central tunnel to reveal the
handbrake mounting point and handbrake cable adjustment access just
forward of the rear seats.
3   Unscrew the regulating nuts from the cables.
4   Undo the handbrake ratchet plate bolts.
5   Remove the split pin and disconnect the hinge pin of the handbrake
to relay cover, and lift the lever clear.
6   Disconnect the handbrake lever from the ratchet plate by removing
the split pin and withdrawing the locating pin. The tie-rod, spring and
press button may also be removed, if required.
7   Refitting is a reversal of removal, but the handbrake must be
re-adjusted, as described in Section 17, on completion.

20 Fault diagnosis - Braking system

Symptoms	Reason/s	Remedy
Pedal travels almost to the floor before brakes operate		
Leaks and air bubbles in hydraulic system	Brake fluid level too low	Top up master cylinder reservoir. Check for leaks.
	Wheel cylinder leaking	Dismantle wheel cylinder, clean, fit new rubbers and bleed brakes.
	Master cylinder leaking (bubbles in master cylinder fluid)	Dismantle master cylinder, clean, and fit new rubbers. Bleed brakes.
	Brake flexible hose leaking	Examine and fit new hose if old hose leaking. Bleed brakes.
	Brake line fractured	Replace with new brake pipe. Bleed brakes.
	Brake system unions loose	Check all unions in brake system and tighten as necessary. Bleed brakes.
Normal wear	Linings, pads over 75% worn	Fit replacement shoes and brake linings/ disc pads.
Incorrect adjustment	Brakes badly out of adjustment	Jack-up car and adjust brakes.
Brake pedal feels 'springy'		
Brake lining renewal	New linings not yet bedded-in	Use brakes gently until springy pedal feeling leaves.
Excessive wear or damage	Brake drums badly worn or cracked	Fit new brake drums.
Lack of maintenance	Master cylinder securing nuts loose	Tighten master cylinder securing nuts. Ensure spring washers are fitted.
Leaks or bubbles in hydraulic system	Wheel cylinder leaking	Dismantle wheel cylinder, clean, fit new rubbers, and bleed brakes.
	Master cylinder leaking (bubbles in master cylinder reservoir	Dismantle master cylinder, clean, and fit new rubbers and bleed brakes. Replace cylinder if internal walls scored.
	Brake pipe line or flexible hose leaking	Fit new pipeline or hose.
	Unions in brake system loose	Examine for leaks, tighten as necessary.
Excessive effort required to stop car		
Lining type or condition	Linings/disc pads badly worn	Fit replacement brake shoes and linings/pads.
	New linings/disc pads recently fitted - not yet bedded-in.	Use brakes gently until braking effort normal.
	Harder linings fitted than standard causing increase in pedal pressure	Remove linings/disc pads and replace with normal units.
Oil or grease leaks	Disc pads/linings and brake drums contaminated with oil, grease or hydraulic fluid	Rectify source of leak, clean brake drums/discs fit new linings/pads.
Brakes action uneven and pulling to one side		
Oil or grease leaks	Pads/linings and discs/brake drums contaminated with oil, grease, or hydraulic fluid	Ascertain and rectify source of leak, clean brake drums, fit new linings.
Lack of maintenance	Tyre pressures unequal	Check and inflate as necessary.
	Radial ply tyres fitted at one end of car only	Fit radial ply tyres of the same make to all four wheels.
	Brake backplate loose	Tighten backplate securing nuts and bolts.
	Brake shoes fitted incorrectly	Remove and fit shoes correct way round.
	Different type of linings/pads fitted at each wheel	Fit the pads/linings specified by the manufacturers all round.
	Anchorages for front suspension or rear axle loose	Tighten front and rear suspension pick-up points including spring anchorage.
	Brake drums/discs badly worn, cracked or distorted.	Fit new brake drums.
Lack of maintenance	Wheel cylinder and piston seized	Remove cylinder and overhaul or replace as necessary.

Chapter 10 Electrical system

Contents

Specifications

Battery

Type	Lead acid
Model	Akuma 6N35 or 6SST 35
Capacity	35 amp hr
Polarity	Negative earth - all MB and S series
Voltage	12

Dynamo

Make and type	Pal Magneton 443.111 - 044.14
Output	300 watts
Working revolution range	2,200 - 7,500 rpm
Maximum current	22 amps
Brush spring pressure	450 ± 5 gr

Alternator

Make	Pal Magneton
Type	443.113 - 516.00
Charge commences at	1000 rpm
Speed at 26amp	2,600 rpm
Maximum speed	12,000 rpm
Maximum current	35 amp

Starter motor

Make	Pal Magneton
Type	443.115 - 142.07
Control type	Solenoid
Rated output	0.58 kw (0.8 hp)

Regulator relay

Make	Pal Magneton
Type	443.116 - 407.610 - models 100, 100L & 110L
	443.116 - 417.00 - models 110LS, R
Cut in voltage	12.5 volts
Current limit	22 amps
Reverse current	5 amps max.
Service voltage	14 volts
Rated output	300 watts

Horns

Make	Pal Magneton
Type	Electro-magnetic
Maximum current consumption	4 amps

Bulbs

Headlights	12V, 45/40 W twin filament
Sidelights	12V, 4W T8/4
Direction indicators	12V, 21W P25-1
Direction indicators (side)	12V, 4W T8/4
Tail lights	12V, 5W R 19/5
Stoplights	12V, 21W P25-1
Number plate light	12V, 5W R 19/5
Instrument lights	12V, 1.5 or 2W
Warning lights	12V, 1.5 or 2W
Reversing lights	12V, 21W P25-1
Interior light	12V, 5W
Door warning light	12V, 4W T8/4
Luggage compartment light	12V, 5W

Windscreen wiper

Rated current	3.3A
Starting torque	95 kpcm
Cycles per minute	70 ± 15%

Heater unit motor

Motor type	09 - 9540.59
Service voltage	14V
Output	28 watts
Speed (rpm)	4000

1 General description

The electrical system is of 12 volt type and the major components comprise a 12 volt battery with a negative earth (for dynamo and alternator models), a regulator relay unit, a dynamo or alternator driven by a 'V' belt from the crankshaft pulley and a starter motor which is located on the engine/transaxle bellhousing.

The potential power output of the dynamo/alternator or battery is sufficient to severely damage the electrical wiring if a short circuit occurs, therefore, most are protected by fuses.

Systems not protected by fuses are associated with the engine and include the ignition and starter motor circuits.

2 Battery - removal and refitting

The storage battery is situated in a recess under the rear luggage compartment. On models fitted with an alternator, do not disconnect the battery with the engine running.

1 To inspect or remove, tilt the rear seat backrest forwards and remove the compartment floor covering, to reveal the battery recess lid on the left-hand side (from the rear). Unclip the lid and remove the battery by undoing and disconnecting the positive and negative terminals.

2 Note which way round the battery is situated and lift it clear of the recess. Keep it the correct way up to prevent spillage of the highly corrosive electrolyte.

3 Refitting is a reversal of removal, but it is advisable, prior to connection of the two terminals, to smear them with petroleum jelly (not grease) to prevent future corrosion (photo).

3 Battery - maintenance and inspection

1 Normal weekly battery maintenance consists of checking the electrolyte level of each cell to ensure that the separators are covered by ¼ in (6.3mm) of electrolyte. If the level has fallen top-up the battery using distilled water only. Do not overfill. If a battery is overfilled, or any electrolyte spilled, immediately wipe away the excess as electrolyte attacks and corrodes any metal it comes into contact with very rapidly.

2 As well as keeping the terminals clean and covered with petroleum jelly, the top of the battery, and especially the top of the cells, should be kept clean and dry. This helps prevent corrosion and ensures that the battery does not become partially discharged by leakage through dampness and dirt.

3 Once every three months remove the battery and inspect the battery tray, and battery leads for corrosion (white fluffy deposits on the metal which are brittle to touch). If any corrosion is found clean off the deposits with ammonia and paint over the clean metal with an anti-rust/anti-acid paint.

4 At the same time inspect the battery case for cracks. If a crack is found, clean and plug it with one of the proprietary compounds marketed by firms such as Holts for this purpose. If leakage through the crack has been excessive then it will be necessary to refill the

2.3 A badly corroded battery terminal

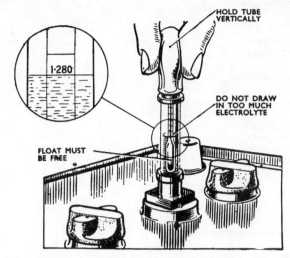

Fig. 10.1. Method of taking hydrometer readings. Take readings at eye level (Sec. 3)

appropriate cell with fresh electrolyte as detailed later. Cracks are frequently caused to the top of the battery case by pouring in distilled water in the middle of winter *after* instead of *before* a run. This gives the water no chance to mix with the electrolyte and so the former freezes and splits the battery case.

5   If topping-up the battery becomes excessive and the case has been inspected for cracks that could cause leakage, but none are found, the battery is being overcharged and the voltage regulator will have to be checked and reset.

6   With the battery on the bench at the three monthly interval check, measure its specific gravity with a hydrometer to determine the state of charge and condition of the electrolyte. There should be very little variation between the different cells and if a variation in excess of 0.025 is present it will be due to:

a) *Loss of electrolyte from the battery at some time caused by spillage or a leak resulting in a drop in the specific gravity of the electrolyte when the deficiency was replaced with distilled water instead of fresh electrolyte.*

b) *An internal short circuit caused by buckling of the plates or a similar malady pointing to the likelihood of total battery failure in the near future.*

7   The specific gravity of the electrolyte for fully charged conditions at the electrolyte temperature indicated, is listed in Table A below. The specific gravity of a fully discharged battery at different temperatures of the electrolyte is given in Table B.

8   Specific gravity is measured by drawing up into the body of a hydrometer sufficient electrolyte to allow the indicator to float freely (see Fig. 10.1). The level at which the indicator floats indicates the specific gravity.

Table A

Climate ordinarily below 26.7ºC (80ºF)

Cell fully charged	1.28
Cell half charged	1.23
Cell fully discharged	1.14

Table B

Climate ordinarily above 26.7ºC (80ºF)

Cell fully charged	1.210
Cell half charged	1.130
Cell fully discharged	1.050

Note: Electrolyte specific gravity alters with its temperature. The figures quoted above are for an electrolyte temperature of 15.6ºC (60ºF). Therefore, if the electrolyte temperature is above 15.6ºC add 0.002 to the hydrometer reading for every additional 2.8ºC (5ºF) rise to obtain a true reading. Similarly, deduct 0.002 for every 2.8ºC below 15.6ºC.

4 Battery - charging

1   During the winter months a heavier demand is placed upon the battery, such as when starting from cold, and additional electrical equipment is used more continually. It is therefore a good idea, especially with an older battery, to occasionally charge the battery from an external source. Several types of proprietary battery chargers are available from good accessory shops. Alternatively, your local garage will charge a battery for you at a nominal cost. The charging rate required is 3.5 amp.

2   Continue to charge the battery at this rate until no further rise in specific gravity is noted over a four hour period.

3   Alternatively a trickle charger of 1.5 to 2 amps output can be safely used overnight.

4   Special rapid 'boost' charges which claim to restore the battery power in 1 to 2 hours are not advised as they can seriously damage the battery plates through overheating.

5   On models fitted with an alternator, the battery should be completely disconnected before charging. This is to protect the diodes of the alternator during high voltage peaks.

5 Dynamo - routine maintenance

1   The dynamo fitted to all models (except those having an alternator) is of four-pole, shunt-wound type. It provides electrical current for all the electrical components and charges the battery.

2   Periodical maintenance consists of checking the drivebelt and tension, the mounting nuts/bolts are secure, and checking the connecting leads.

3   These items should be checked every 3,000 miles (5,000 km). The fan belt should be taut enough to ensure no slip between the belt and the dynamo pulley. If a shrieking noise comes from the engine when the unit is accelerated rapidly, it is likely that it is the fan belt slipping. On the other hand, the belt must not be too tight or the bearings will wear rapidly and cause dynamo failure or bearing seizure. Ideally ½ inch (13 mm) of free-movement should be available in the centre of the longest run between the crankshaft and dynamo pulley.

4   To adjust the drivebelt tension, slacken the mounting flange bolts, front and rear, and tilt the dynamo away from the engine to tighten, or towards the engine to slacken the tension.

5   Retighten the mounting flange bolts and recheck the drivebelt tension.

6   The front and rear bearings are pre-packed with grease on assembly and therefore require no lubrication, unless the dynamo is being dismantled.

6 Dynamo - removal, overhaul and reassembly

Removal and refitting

To remove the dynamo proceed as follows:
1 Disconnect the dynamo leads from their terminals.
2 Undo the mounting bolts and hinge the dynamo towards the engine to slacken and remove the drivebelt from the dynamo pulley.
3 Support the dynamo and remove the mounting bolts and dynamo.
4 Replacement is a reversed sequence of removal and the drivebelt is retensioned, as described in Section 5.

Dismantling, repair and reassembly

Having removed the dynamo from the car dismantle it on the workbench as follows:
1 Unscrew the drivebelt pulley nut and remove the pulley which is a split type incorporating a cooling fan on its inner half.
2 Unscrew its clamp screw and remove the brush compartment inspection cover.
3 If the brushes only are to be inspected at this stage, they can be removed from their location housings by pulling the springs clear of the slotted housing aperture, and then pulling the brushes out of the housings.
4 To disconnect the dynamo endplate, unscrew and remove the two tie-rod screws.
5 Unsolder the field winding wire from terminal 'M' and unscrew the bolt securing the connector to the positive brush.
6 Mark the position of the commutator endplate in relation to the main body and then tap the endplate clear of the body and off the armature.
7 To remove the armature, mark the endplate in relation to the main body, and carefully extract the armature complete with endplate.
8 At this stage, the various components can be cleaned to remove any oil or carbon deposits prior to inspection.
9 Never attempt to release the field coils inside the dynamo casing, a special screwdriver is necessary. If the field coils are faulty, the whole dynamo should be exchanged for a reconditioned unit.
10 Do not dismantle the dynamo any further, the only exceptions being the two end-bearings. If they show any signs of wear, they can be removed and replaced with new ones.
11 Inspect the brushes. If they are badly worn renew them. If they are scratched or marked on the contact faces they can be cleaned by placing a piece of fine emery cloth over the commutator, with its coarse side out, and lightly rubbing the brush along the curved emery cloth to retain the correct profile in the brush. If in doubt about brush condition fit a new brush set. Brushes worn down to a length below 0.47 in (12 mm) must automatically be replaced.

12 Clean the commutator with a petrol dampened rag. The mica (mikanite) must undercut the level of the commutator segment faces. If the commutator segments show signs of being burnt, it is an indication of an open circuited armature. The armature windings will also be badly discoloured if this is the case, and it should, therefore, be checked by your local auto-electrician or Skoda agent.
13 If the commutator is in good condition the surface will be smooth and free from pits or burnt areas, and the insulated areas will be clearly defined. If any pitting or burn spots are present, but are not too severe the commutator can be cleaned as follows. Mount the commutator in a lathe and when turning at a fairly high speed, skim the surface as finely as possible to remove the pittings and marks. The minimum diameter the commutator can be turned down to is 1.45 in (37mm). Also the mikanite in the segment gaps should be 0.016-0.032 in (0.4 to 0.8mm) below the surface line, at least. If the commutator has worn so that the insulating mikanite between the segments is level with the top of the segments, undercut the insulators to 0.032 in (0.8mm). A handy tool to use for this purpose is half a hacksaw blade ground to the segment gap width. The handle end can be wound with insulating tape, or similar, to make it comfortable to hold. Carefully cut the mica down to the depth required taking care not to scratch the commutator.
14 Check all internal wiring insulation, as far as possible, prior to reassembly.
15 The bearings should be packed with grease of the correct type. Do not over grease! If the bearings have been removed refit the sealing washers and shims that were removed, when dismantling, prior to the assembly of the bearings.
16 Insert the armature into the casing and refit the endplate over the shaft and onto its bearing, complete with the shim, packing ring and sealing washer.
17 Ensure that the brushes are free in their holders then lift the springs and brushes while refitting the commutator endplate to the casing.
18 Refit and tighten the two long through bolts.
19 Replace the pulley assembly.
20 Resolder the field wire to terminal 'M' and screw the field wire connector to the brushholder.
21 Turn the commutator by hand to ensure the brushes are seating correctly and then replace the cover.
22 Reconnect the dynamo to the car and adjust the drivebelt tension.

7 Dynamo/alternator drivebelt - removal and refitting

1 When renewing the dynamo/alternator drivebelt it is necessary to remove the fanbelt first, as they are both driven from the twin pulley on the water pump, and the fan belt is located on the outer pulley. Follow the removal notes in Section 10 of Chapter 2.

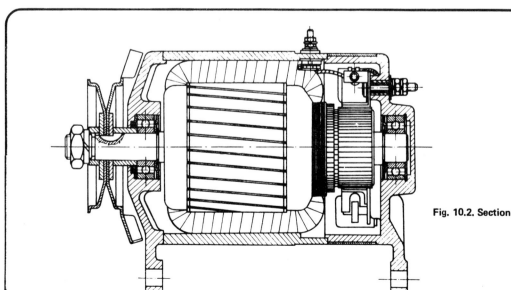

Fig. 10.2. Sectional view of dynamo (Sec. 6)

2   Loosen the dynamo/alternator on its pivot and the slotted link
lockbolt and hingebolt, then swing the dynamo towards the engine.
3   Remove the old drivebelt and carefully fit the new replacement
over the pulleys.

8   Dynamo/alternator drivebelt - adjustment

1   It is important to keep the dynamo/alternator belt correctly adjusted
and the tension should be checked regularly at 3,000 miles (5,000 km)
or 6 month intervals.
2   A slack drivebelt will slip, wear rapidly and cause the dynamo/
alternator to malfunction.
3   If the belt is too tight, the bearings of the water pump, alternator
or dynamo will wear rapidly and premature failure will result.
4   The belt should therefore be tensioned to allow for the correct
lateral movement at the mid-point position between the two pulleys
(photo).
5   To adjust the belt tension slacken the dynamo/alternator bolts just
sufficiently for the unit to be gently levered with a long screwdriver
away from the engine. Once a new position of the dynamo/alternator
has been obtained for the correct belt tension, the unit's bolts can be
tightened.
6   The respective tensions for the belt are as follows:

Dynamo lateral belt movement   0.5-0.75 in (12.7-19mm)
Alternator lateral belt movement   0.5 in (12.7mm)

8.4 Method of checking the alternator/dynamo drivebelt tension

9   Alternator - general

1   The later model cars have an alternator fitted in place of the
dynamo. The main advantage of the alternator lies in its ability to
supply a relatively high charge at low revolutions. Driving slowly in
heavy traffic with a dynamo fitted, invariably means that little or no
charge is reaching the battery. In the same conditions, an alternator
will ensure an adequate charge rate, even with lights, windscreen
wiper, heater, fan unit, etc in operation.
2   The alternator is a three phase type having semi-conductor
rectifiers.
3   Although the alternator has many advantages over the dynamo
it must be treated with the utmost respect as it is comparatively
delicate. The following points must be observed if an alternator is
fitted to the car:

a) Never arc-weld any part of the car structure without
    first disconnecting the alternator and battery.
b) If using an additional battery with jump leads to start
    the car, ensure the two batteries are connected positive-
    to-positive and negative-to-negative and that the body-
    work of the two cars is not in contact.
c) If charging the battery from an external source, discon-
    nect the battery terminals completely first.
d) Never run the engine with the battery or alternator
    leads disconnected.
e) Do not disconnect the battery with the engine running.
f) Always renew a defective ignition warning light as
    soon as is possible. The voltage control of the alter-
    nator depends on this circuit.

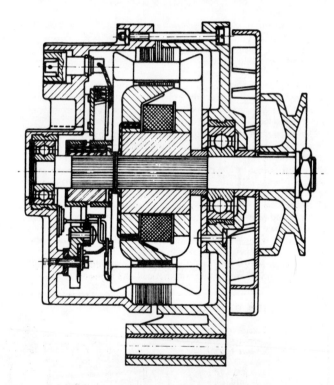

Fig. 10.3. Sectional view of alternator (Sec. 9)

10   Alternator - maintenance

No maintenance is required on the alternator apart from checking
the electrical connections for security and cleanliness and checking the
drivebelt condition and tension periodically. Also the alternator
mounting bolts should be checked for security at fairly regular
intervals.

11   Alternator - removal, refitting and fault diagnosis

Removal and refitting
1   Disconnect the battery terminals.
2   Note the terminal connections at the rear of the alternator and

disconnect the electrical leads (photo).
3   Undo and remove the adjustment arm bolts and slacken the
alternator mounting bolts and then hinge the alternator towards the
engine. Disconnect the drivebelt from the pulley.
4   Remove the mounting bolts and lift the alternator clear.
5   Refitting the alternator is the reverse sequence to removal as
described in Section 8.

Alternator - fault diagnosis
Due to the specialist knowledge and equipment required to test
or service an alternator, it is recommended that if the performance
is suspect, the car be taken to an auto-electrician who will have the
facilities for such work. However, prior to taking this course of

11.1 The alternator lead connections

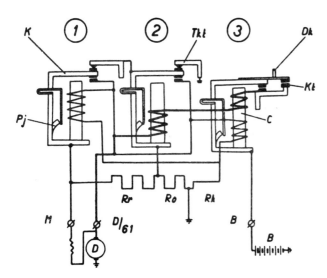

Fig. 10.4. Diagram of regulator relay (Sec. 12)

1   Voltage regulator
2   Current regulator (limiter)
3   Cut-out for voltage and reverse current - terminals
    M and D/61 - lead for dynamo D; terminal B - lead
    for battery B
C   Electromagnetic (solenoid) coils
Tkt Contact clamps
Kt Contact points
K   Armatures
Dk Cut-out armature holder
Pj Yoke regulation finger
Rr Regulator resistor
Ro Limiter resistor
Rk Compensation resistor

action, check the following points:

  a) Check the drivebelt tension.
  b) Check the battery condition.
  c) Check all electrical lead connections for cleanliness
      and security.
  d) Check that the warning lamp is not defective.

12 Regulator relay unit - description, removal and replacement

1   A regulator relay unit, to control the alternator voltage, is fitted to the inner rear wing panel. Together with the alternator or dynamo it supplies the necessary current to the battery and electric circuits in the car. No maintenance is required apart from occasionally checking its electrical terminals for cleanliness and secure fitting.
2   To remove the regulator unit, disconnect the battery terminals and then the respective wires to the regulator unit, noting where they are fitted.
3   Unscrew the regulator unit retaining screws and remove the unit, but handle with care - it should not be dropped.
4   Replacement is the reversal of removal procedure.

13 Regulator relay unit - fault diagnosis

As with the alternator, specialist knowledge and equipment is required to test or service the regulator unit. Therefore if it is suspected of being defective, it should be left to an auto-electrician, who will have the necessary facilities. Prior to taking this course of action, however, check the following:

  a) Check the regulator unit wiring connections, they
      should be clean and secure.
  b) Check that the warning lamp is not defective.

14 Starter motor - general description

The starter motor is mounted to the transaxle bellhousing on two studs and is situated directly over the right-hand half-axle. It is an electrically operated, pre-engaged type starter motor.
The method of engagement is that when the ignition is switched on, current flows from the battery to the solenoid which is fitted to the starter motor body. The plunger in the solenoid moves inward, in turn moving the pivoted lever in such a manner that the forked end engages a clutch thus transmitting movement to the flywheel.
When the flywheel solenoid plunger reaches the end of its travel, it closes an internal contact and full current flows to the starter field coils. The armature is then able to rotate the crankshaft to start the engine.
A one way clutch device is fitted to the starter drive pinion so that the engine on starting does not continue to drive the starter motor.

15 Starter motor - maintenance

1   Very little maintenance is required as the bearings are self lubricating, and apart from occasionally checking the cable connections, the starter motor should not need attention.
However, it is not a bad idea to remove the starter motor every other year to check the following:

  a) Carbon brushes
  b) Carbon brush springs
  c) The pinion and idler condition.

16 Starter motor - removal and refitting

1   The starter motor with the solenoid is removed from the transaxle as follows.
2   Remove the rear seat backrest and fold the rear luggage compartment floor covering out of the way. Remove the central inspection cover from the floor, and also the battery panel.
3   Disconnect the battery.
4   Disconnect the cables from their terminals on the solenoid (photo) after noting how they are fitted.
5   Undo the flange mounting nuts and withdraw the starter motor unit from the location studs (photo).
6   Refitting is a reversal of removal.

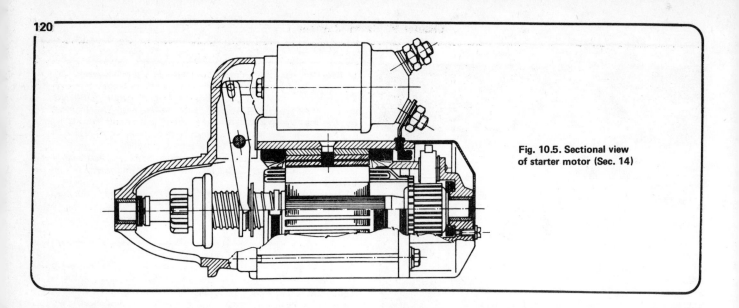

Fig. 10.5. Sectional view
of starter motor (Sec. 14)

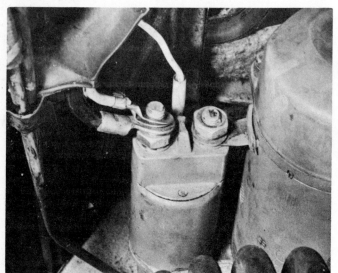

16.4 Starter motor solenoid - removing the connecting cables

16.5 Removing the starter motor and solenoid

18.4a Starter motor brush location showing retaining spring in position

18.4b Holding back the spring to remove the brush

17 Starter motor - fault diagnosis

1   If the starter motor fails to turn the engine when the switch is operated there are four possible reasons why:

a) *The battery is flat.*
b) *The electrical connections between switch, solenoid, battery and starter motor are somewhere failing to pass the necessary current from the battery to the starter.*
c) *The solenoid switch is defective.*
d) *The starter motor is either jammed or electrically defective.*

2   To check the battery, switch on the headlights. If they go dim after a few seconds the battery is in a low state of charge. If the lamps glow brightly, next operate the starter switch and see what happens to the lights. If they go dim then you know that power is reaching the starter motor but failing to turn it. Therefore, check that it is not jammed by placing the car in gear and rocking it to-and-fro. If it is not jammed the starter will have to come out for examination. If the starter should turn very slowly go on to the next check.
3   If, when the starter switch is operated, the lights stay bright, then the power is not reaching the starter. Check all connections from battery to solenoid switch and starter for perfect cleanliness and tightness. With a good battery installed this is the most usual cause of starter motor problems. Check that the earth link cable between the engine and frame is also intact and cleanly connected. This can sometimes be overlooked when the engine has been taken out.
4   If no results have yet been achieved turn off the headlights, otherwise the battery will go flat. You will possibly have heard a clicking noise each time the switch was operated. This is the solenoid switch operating but it does not necessarily follow that the main contact is closing properly. (**Note:** If no clicking has been heard from the solenoid it is certainly defective). The solenoid contact can be checked by putting a voltmeter or bulb across the main cable connection on the starter side of the solenoid and earth. When the switch is operated, there should be a reading or lighted bulb.
    If not, the solenoid switch is no good. (Do not put a bulb across the two solenoid terminals. If the motor is not faulty the bulb will blow). If, finally, it is established that the solenoid is not faulty and 12 volts are getting to the starter then the starter motor must be the culprit.

18 Starter motor brushes - removal and refitting

1   Dismantling the starter motor completely is not a job for the home mechanic. Although not too difficult to dismantle, the reassembly and adjustments required before refitting are beyond his scope, due to the specialised equipment necessary. It is, therefore, preferable to have the starter motor or solenoid checked or overhauled by a specialist auto-electrician.
2   The exception to the above note is the removal and refitting of the commutator brushes. Remove as follows.
3   Unscrew the small central retaining bolt in the end cover and prise the cover off with a screwdriver.
4   To remove the brush for inspection, prise the retaining spring (photo) back with a small screwdriver and withdraw the brush from its guide (photo).
5   If the brushes are badly worn, remove them after unscrewing the connecting lead screw and replace with new brushes. Whilst the brushes are removed, inspect their contact faces and if badly worn the starter motor should preferably be checked by an auto-electrician - there is little point in fitting new brushes to a worn out starter motor.
6   Reassembly of the starter motor brushes and endcover is the reversal of dismantling, but check that the brushes are free to move in their guides before retaining with the springs.

19 Fuses - general

1   The respective electrical circuits are protected against overloading by fuses which are located in a common block under the dashboard.
2   To inspect the fuses, unscrew the cover retaining bolt and remove the cover.
3   To remove a fuse simply prise it from its holder.
4   All fuses are 15 amp rating, and their positions are numbered accordingly, as follows:

1) *Interior light, horn, inspection lamp socket, stoplights, stoplight pilot light, and warning flash signal.*
2) *Direction indicators and pilot light, windscreen wiper, heater fan, reversing lamps, battery charge and oil pressure warning lights, temperature gauge and fuel reserve warning light.*
3) *Left-hand tail light and left-hand parking light.*
4) *Right-hand tail light and right-hand parking light, instrument panel light, fog lamps, and number plate light.*
5) *Headlamp left-hand dip.*
6) *Headlamp right-hand dip.*
7) *Headlamp left-hand main beam and main beam warning light.*
8) *Headlamp right-hand main beam.*

5   Never substitute tin foil, or similar, for blown fuses. A fuse blows for a reason and if the fault is not located and rectified immediately, serious damage to the wiring circuit will result.
6   A fuse failure is easily identified as all the systems it protects will be inoperative.

20 Windscreen wiper mechanism - fault diagnosis

1   If the wipers fail to operate, check first that the current is reaching the motor. This can be done by switching on and using a voltmeter or 12 volt bulb and two wires between the (+) terminal on the motor and earth (car body adjacent to motor).
2   If no current is reaching the motor check whether there is any at the switch. If there is, then a break has occurred in the wiring between switch and motor.
3   If there is no current at the switch go back to the ignition switch and so isolate the area of the fault.
4   If current is reaching the motor but the wipers do not operate, switch on and give the wiper arms a push - they or the motor could be jammed. Switch off immediately if nothing happens otherwise further damage to the motor may occur. If the wipers now run, the reason for them jamming must be found. It will almost certainly be due to wear in either the linkage of the wiper mechanism or the mechanism in the motor gearbox.
5   If the wipers run too slowly it will be due to something restricting the free operation of the linkage or a fault in the motor. In such cases it is well to check the current being used by connecting an ammeter in the circuit. If it exceeds three amps something is restricting free movement. If less, then the commutator and brush gear in the motor are suspect. The shafts to which the wipers are attached run in bushes and often suffer from lack of lubrication. Regular application to each shaft of a few drops of light penetrating oil, preferably graphited, helps to prevent partial or total seizure. First pull outwards the rubber grommets, afterwards, wipe off any excess.
6   If wear is obviously causing malfunction or there is a fault in the motor it is best to remove the motor or wiper mechanism for further examination and repairs.

21 Windscreen wiper blades and arms - removal and refitting

1   The wiper blades should be renewed every year or whenever they fail to wipe the windscreen cleanly.
2   To remove the blades, lift the arm and blade away from the screen and pull the rubber blade from the bridged retaining clamps.
3   If the arm is to be removed also, unscrew the pivot shaft nut on each wiper arm and pull clear (photo).
4   When refitting the arms, operate the wiper motor and stop it so that it is in the extreme rest position. Fit the wiper arms so that the blades are 0.4in (10mm) from the windscreen channel and tighten.
5   Operate the motor and check the action of the blades and re-adjust to suit if necessary.

22 Windscreen wiper linkage - removal and refitting

1 Remove the windscreen wiper arms, as described in Section 21.
2 From the wiper arm shafts, remove the washers, seals and nuts on the outer body.
3 Then push the shafts into the body for removal of the linkage unit.

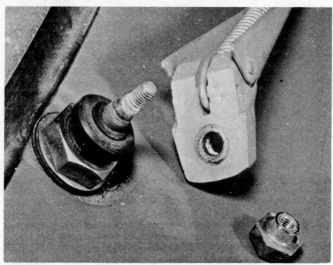

21.3 The windscreen wiper arm and retaining nut removed

23.2 The windscreen wiper motor in position

4 Check all the pivots, bearings and levers of the mechanism in your hands, to locate wear or troublesome mechanical interference.
5 It will soon be obvious if anything has broken, and if the whole mechanism is worn then it will be wise to replace it as a whole rather than mend the worst individual faults.
6 It is worth noting too that wiper spindles should be replaced as pairs and lubricated with graphite oil.
7 Assembling the mechanism and motor is an exact reversal of dismantling.

23 Windscreen wiper motor - removal and refitting

1 Disconnect the battery connection by removing the earth lead.
2 The wiper motor is located in the front luggage compartment and is attached to a tray protruding from the bulkhead (photo). Remove the tray cover for access to tie-rods.
3 Undo the segment locking bolt and lift, complete with short tie-rod, off the wiper motor driveshaft (photo). Unscrew the stand plate bolt nuts and lower the wiper motor unit from the tray.
4 Take a note of the respective connector positions and disconnect the connecting leads from their terminals on the wiper motor, and remove from car.
5 Replacement is the reversal of removal but before reconnecting the tie-rod, operate the motor, and switch off so that the driveshaft is in the parked position, and then, assuming the blades are similarly positioned, reconnect the segment and lock in position on the shaft by tightening the bolt.

24 Windscreen wiper motor - dismantling and reassembly

1 Having removed the wiper motor unit from the car a check can be

23.3 The linkage connecting arm to segment

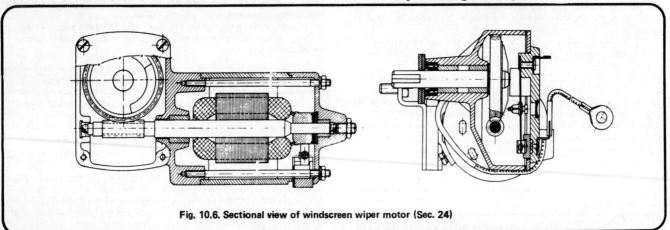

Fig. 10.6. Sectional view of windscreen wiper motor (Sec. 24)

25.1 The electric windscreen washer unit

27.1 The horn in position on mounting bracket behind the front bumper

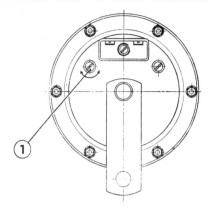

Fig. 10.7. Horn tone adjusting screw (1) (Sec. 29)

made to see if the commutator brushes are faulty.

2   To do this undo the two end cover retaining nuts complete with spring washers and cable clip. Mark the position of the cover in relation to the wiper motor body and remove the cover.

3   The brushes may be stuck or just simply worn down. If so, replace with a new pair and clean out the cover prior to fitting.

4   With the motor disconnected, also check the gear housing by unscrewing the four cover retaining screws and spring washers. Remove the cover and inspect the gearwheel and shaft. If the gear or shaft are badly worn they should obviously be renewed, together with the appropriate rubber sealing washers and cover gasket.

5   If the unit as a whole is badly worn it should be checked by your local auto-electrician or simply exchanged for a reconditioned or new unit.

6   Reassembly of the unit is the reversal of dismantling.

25 Windscreen washer unit - general

1   Two types of washer unit are fitted, one being a standard hand-pump type, and the other an electric pump unit in the water container (photo).

2   Dependent on usage the container, located in the front luggage compartment, should be checked and topped-up regularly.

3   If the washers should fail to function check the following points:

   a)   The bonnet nozzles are not blocked.
   b)   The supply tubes are not blocked, the connections are good and there are no splits or air leaks anywhere.
   c)   The water level in the container is correct.

4   If all the above points are in order, it probably means that the hand pump or distribution valve is defective and need renewal on the manual type of system. On the electric type check the wiring and current to the pump; if this is in order, the pump unit must be defective and should be renewed. To remove the pump simply unscrew from the container and lift clear. Disconnect the wires and water tube.

26 Windscreen washer jets - removal and refitting

1   From underneath the bonnet, remove the heater supply tubes and unscrew the retaining nut.

2   Now remove the jet unit from the top.

3   Refitting the jet is a reversal of removal. Adjust the position of the jet before finally tightening the retaining nut.

27 Horn - fault diagnosis

1   If the horn operates weakly or fails to sound at all, check the wiring leading to the horn, which is located within the front bumper channel, mounted on a bracket attached to the lower front grille panel (photo).

2   Check that the horn is secure on its mounting, and that there is nothing lying on the horn body.

3   If the fault is not an external one, remove the horn cover and check the leads inside the horn. If these are sound, check the contact breaker

Fig. 10.8. Replacing bulbs in the lamp group - MB models (Sec. 30)

points. If burnt or dirty, clean them with a fine file and wipe all traces of dirt away.

28 Horn - removal and refitting

1   To remove the horn, simply undo the retaining nuts to the bracket and lift the horn clear.

2   Disconnect the leads if necessary.

3   Refitting is the reverse procedure.

29 Horn - adjustment

1   Before adjusting the horn ensure that its securing nuts are tight and that nothing is lying against the horn body to impair its tone.

2   Adjustment is made by turning the screw (1) in the back of the horn in the required direction. Refer to Fig. 10.7.

30 Rear lights/indicators (MB models) - removal and refitting

1   The tail, stop and indicator lights together with the reflector on the MB models are located in the corner of each rear wing, on a common cluster panel.

2   To remove the cluster panel, unscrew the retaining screws from inside the wing and remove from the engine compartment side. Disconnect the relevant leads (note respective positions) from the panel to remove from the car.

3   To remove the outer panel cover or to replace/inspect the bulbs, unscrew the two retaining screws and disconnect from the wing.

4   Remove the bulbs by pushing down into their holders and twisting anti-clockwise, then lift clear.

5   Refitting is the reverse of removal.

31 Headlights and sidelights (MB models) bulb renewal

1   Unscrew and remove the headlight rim securing screw and rim.
2   Raise the springed lip at the top of the light unit and tilt the headlight, then pull upwards to remove from the adjusting screws.
3   Remove the wire socket from the bulb holder.
4   To remove the side or headlight bulbs push and twist.
5   Refitting is the reverse of removal.

32 Parking light (MB models) - removal and refitting

1   Turn the light cover anticlockwise so that the central division piece is horizontal, and pull clear.
2   Remove the bulb by pushing and twisting to release from its holder.
3   Remove the holder unit by unscrewing the retaining screws, pull clear and disconnect the wires.
4   Replace in the reverse sequence.

33 Direction indicator lights, front (MB models) - removal and refitting

1   These are located in the front wing panel and are removed by loosening the retaining screw, turning the unit from the horizontal to vertical position and withdrawing from the aperture. The bulb can then be removed. Refitting is the reverse procedure.
2   To remove the bulb only, unscrew the cover retaining screws, remove the cover and then the bulb from its socket.

34 Number plate light (MB models) - bulb renewal

1   Remove the lamp unit fixing screw, move the unit to the right and

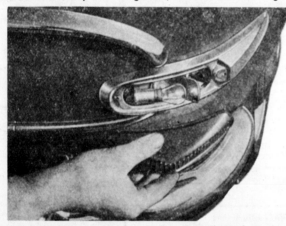

Fig. 10.9. Bulb in front flashers - MB models (Sec. 33)

unscrew its lower retaining screws.
2   The bulb is withdrawn by pushing and twisting.
3   Refitting is the reversal of removal.

35 Headlights and sidelights (S models) - bulb renewal

1   The headlight and sidelight bulbs are located in the rear of the semi-sealed beam light unit. Remove as follows.
2   Unscrew the retaining screw of the headlight rim and remove (photo).
3   Loosen the retaining screws of the unit at its base (photo).
4   With a screwdriver prise the unit to the left (photo), so that the small screwhead clears the slotted hole. The headlight lens unit can now be pushed at its lower edge to rotate on its pivots so that it can in effect be turned inside out, without being disconnected completely.
5   To remove the respective bulbs simple twist the bulb holders and pull clear of the lens (photo). The bulbs are disconnected from their holders in the same way.
6   Refitting is the reversal of removal.

36 Headlights (S models) - removal and refitting

1   Disconnect the battery by removing the negative earth lead.
2   Unscrew the chrome surround retaining screw.
3   Remove the surrounding light retaining and adjusting screws to remove the unit. Disconnect the headlight and integral sidelight bulbs and sockets and the respective connecting wires and remove the unit.
4   Refitting is the reverse procedure but adjust the headlight alignment (Section 37) prior to refitting the surround rim.

37 Headlights (all models) - adjustment

1   It is always advisable to have the headlamps aligned on proper optical beam setting equipment but if this is not available, the following procedure may be used.
2   Position the car on level ground 16.4ft (5 metres) in front of a dark wall or board. The wall or board must be at right angles to the centre line of the car.
3   Draw a vertical line on the board in line with the centre line of the car.
4   Bounce the car on its suspension to ensure correct settlement and then measure the height between the ground and the centre of the headlamps ('H' - Fig. 10.10).
5   Draw a horizontal line across the board at this measured height, less 2.3 in (60 mm).
6   On this horizontal line mark a cross on either side of, and equidistant from, the vertical line. The distance between the two crosses must be equal to the distance between the headlamp centres (A).
7   Switch the headlamps to *dipped* beam.
8   Cover the right-hand headlamp and, by carefully adjusting the horizontal adjusting screws, align the lamp so that the intersection of the horizontal and angled light pattern coincides with the vertical line on the aiming board.
9   Similarly adjust the vertical screw so that the light/dark intersection of the beam pattern coincides with the 15° line on the aiming board.
10 Cover the left-hand headlamp and adjust the right-hand lamp

35.2 Headlight rim removal

35.3 Loosening the headlight locking screws

35.4 Prise the headlight clockwise with screwdriver to clear the slotted hole

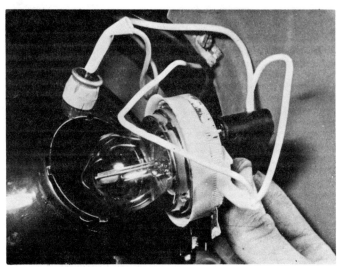

35.5 Removing the headlight bulb and holder.
Note location of sidelight bulb

39.2 Rear light bulb and socket removal (late models)

40.1 Front indicator position (late models)

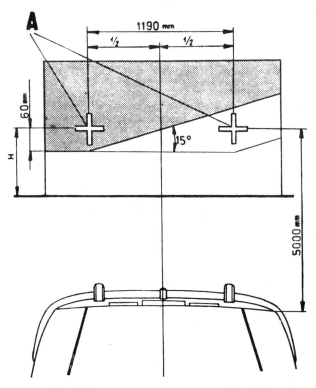

Fig. 10.10. Headlight beam adjustment (Sec. 37)

horizontal and vertical alignment in the same way as for the left-hand lamp. Switch off the headlamps.

38 Rear light unit (S models) - removal and refitting

1   This light unit is located on the rear panel. From the centre outwards the individual light units are as follows: Number plate light, reversing light, stoplight reflector, tail light and indicator light.
      With the exception of the number plate light, the right and left-hand lights are mounted on a common panel.
2   To remove the lights and panels, disconnect the respective electrical leads taking note of their fitted positions. If required, the bulbs and holders may also be removed.
3   Unscrew the panel fixing screws from inside the rear of the body and withdraw the respective units from inside, except the number plate unit with the Skoda motif imprint, which is withdrawn from outside.
4   Refitting is the reverse procedure.

39 Rear light (S models) - bulb renewal

1   If any particular bulb is to be checked or renewed, it can be removed from within the engine compartment, where the bulbs are retained in holders attached to the rear body panel.
2   To withdraw the bulb holder press and twist, then withdraw from the panel (photo).
3   Remove the bulb from the holder in the same way.
4   Refitting is the reverse procedure.

40 Direction indicator light unit, front (S models) - removal and refitting

      These models have the indicator light unit located in the front bumper channel. They are removed as follows.
1   From underneath the front bumper, pull the connecting lead from its fixing location in the light unit (photo).
2   Undo the bracket nut at the bottom and tilt the light unit to clear the bumper and remove.
3   Refitting is the reverse procedure.

41 Direction indicator light (S models) bulb renewal

1   From underneath the front bumper, pull the connecting lead from its fixing location in the light unit.
2   Twist the knurled plastic bulb socket and pull clear of the light.
3   Push and twist the bulb to remove.
4   Refitting is the reverse procedure.

42 Spotlights (S models) - removal and refitting

1   These are removed from inside the luggage compartment. Note that they do not work independently of the main headlamps and they should not be used for any length of time when stationary since they will over-heat.
2   Press and turn anticlockwise the rear cover and remove it (photo).
3   Disconnect the wiring.
4   Unscrew the retaining nuts and remove the unit complete.
5   Refitting is the reverse procedure.

42.2 Spotlight cover removal

43 Spotlight (S models) - bulb renewal

1   From inside the front luggage compartment, press and turn anti-clockwise the rear cover and remove it.
2   Before removing the bulb it should be noted that it is of halogen type and therefore the glass should not be handled with the fingers.
3   To remove the bulb twist the holder and withdraw it complete with bulb (photo).
4   Refitting is the reverse procedure.

44 Spotlight (S models) - adjustment

1   The spotlight beams are adjusted in the same way as the headlight beams.
2   Adjustment is made by loosening the adjustment screw locking nuts at the rear of the spotlight, and turning the four adjustment screws as required. The top and bottom screws adjust horizontally and the two side screws vertically.
3   When adjustment has been made, tighten the locknuts and refit the cover.

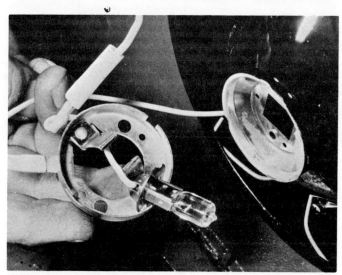

43.3 Spotlight bulb removal

45 Direction indicator flasher unit - fault diagnosis

1   The flasher unit is in a small metal container which is located on the bulkhead. The unit is adjusted by the direction indicator switch.
2   If the flasher unit fails to work or flashes faster or slower than normal, check the flasher indicator circuit before assuming there is a fault in the unit.

a) *Examine the direction indicator bulbs, front and rear, for broken filaments.*
b) *If the external flashers are working, but the internal flasher warning light has ceased to function, check the filament in the warning light bulb and replace with a new bulb if necessary.*
c) *If a flasher bulb is sound but does not work, check all the flasher circuit connections with the aid of the wiring diagram.*
d) *In the event of total indicator failure, check fuse No. 2. It will be fairly obvious if this fuse has blown as it also protects other components (See Section 19).*
e) *With the ignition switched on, check that the current is reaching the flasher unit by connecting a voltmeter between the positive terminal and earth. If it is found that current is reaching the unit, connect the two flasher unit terminals together and operate the flasher switch. If the flasher warning light comes on, this proves that the flasher unit itself is at fault and must be renewed as it is not possible to dismantle and repair it.*

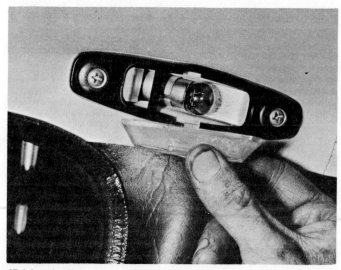

47.1 Interior light cover removal (late models)

46 Direction indicator flasher unit - removal and refitting

1 This is located on the bulkhead to the left of the dashpanel area.
2 Before removal note the lead connections and the angle at which the unit is mounted.
3 To remove, disconnect the leads and unscrew the unit tab screw from the bulkhead.
4 If the unit is to be refitted, handle with extreme care as the internal components are quite delicate.
5 Refitting is the reverse of removal.

47 Interior light - removal and refitting

1 To remove the plastic light cover, press the sides and lift from one side to withdraw it from the housing (photo).
2 If the bulb is to be checked or renewed, push it and twist anti-clockwise to remove it.
3 To remove the unit, unscrew the two crosshead screws and remove complete with unit retaining flange. Disconnect the wires.
4 Refitting is the reverse procedure.

48 Luggage compartment light - removal and refitting

1 To remove the plastic cover, push and twist, then withdraw from the unit.
2 The bulb is of festoon type and can be removed by prising from the retaining tabs.
3 If the holder unit is to be removed, remove the bulb and unscrew the two crosshead screws. Then disconnect the wiring.
4 Refitting is the reversal of dismantling.

49 Door warning lights - removal and refitting

1 To inspect or remove the door warning light unit, it is necessary to remove the door handle, window winder and armrest, then prise the door panel from the door to give access to the inner panel. Since the door will be held open for sometime thus actuating the switch, either remove the fuse or disconnect the battery earth terminals.
2 The bulb holder is removed by pushing and twisting it, to withdraw it, complete with bulb and lead. The bulb can then be removed.
3 If the light unit is to be removed undo the retaining screws and withdraw from the channel.
4 Refitting is the reverse of removal, but ensure that the light works before refitting the inner panel.

50 Dashboard instruments and lighting - general

Basically the dashboard layout and instrumentation is the same on all models except the Coupe, which has individual gauges, a different facia panel, and a central console, containing a speaker grille, spot and fog light switches with their respective warning lamps.
Removal of the switches or gauges can be achieved with the facia panels in place or removed, depending on the accessibility of the particular item to be worked on.
The various dashboard/facia panels are retained in position by screws, access to which is mainly from underneath. Before inspecting or removing any of the electrical switches or light sockets, disconnect the earth strap on the battery. Reconnect after refitting of the component removed.

51 Direction indicator and headlamp switches - removal and refitting

1 These switches are enclosed in their own separate cover panel which spans the steering column. To inspect or remove the switches it is necessary to disconnect the lower panel from the column, and this is achieved by unscrewing the two retaining screws (photo).
2 The switches are fixed to brackets and can be disconnected by undoing the retaining nut and washers from the back.
3 Make a note of the positions of the lead connections and pull away from the switch.

51.1 View showing steering column lower cover removed and indicator switch in position (110R Coupe model)

4 Refitting is a reversal of removal.

52 Dashboard switches - removal and refitting

1 There are basically two types of dashboard switch.
2 Twist type switches have a raised grip section on them (eg. wiper speed switch). To remove the knob from the switch, simply pull off.
3 The push-pull type switch knob is removed by unscrewing.
4 To remove both type of switches from the panel, remove the knob and unscrew the retaining nut from the outside of the panel.
5 Remove the switch from inside the panel.
6 Make a note of the lead connection positions and then remove them from the switch.
7 Refitting is the reverse of removal.

53 Instruments and instrument bulbs (Coupe) - removal and refitting

1 The various gauges in this particular model are individual units and can therefore be renewed as single units, if defective.
2 Removal of any of the gauges has to be achieved from the rear of the dashboard panel. The gauges are retained by 'U' shaped brackets which fit over two studs in the rear of each gauge, and are retained by nuts which, when tightened, clamp the gauge to the dash panel. Remove the battery earth strap before working on the panel.
3 To remove a gauge, it is first necessary to disconnect the bulb and socket complete with connecting cable, by pulling from the gauge direct.
4 Next remove the following connections from the rear of the relevant gauge:

    a) *Ammeter - connecting wires*
    b) *Water temperature gauge - capillary tube (unscrew retaining nut).*
    c) *Fuel gauge - connecting wire*
    d) *Speedometer - speedo cable connection.*
    e) *Rev-counter - connecting cable.*

5 Unscrew the 'U' bracket retaining nuts and remove the bracket.
6 Support the gauge face and push through from the rear to remove the gauge through the front of the panel.
7 The gauges are not repairable, and will therefore have to be renewed if defective.
8 Refitting is the reverse of dismantling.

54 Instrument panel (all models, except Coupe) - removal and refitting

1 Refer to Figs. 10.11, 10.12 and 10.13. The instrument panel is retained in the dashboard by catches, located in the rear of the panel.

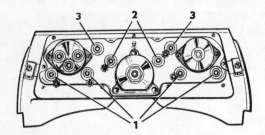

Fig. 10.11. Rear of instrument panel (MB Models) (Sec. 54)

1   Bulb socket positions for oil warning lamp, ignition light,
*   main beam light and fuel warning light.*
2   Flasher warning bulbs.
3   Speedometer, water temperature and fuel gauge lights.

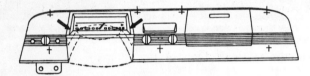

Fig. 10.12. Removal of instrument panel - position of fastening catches -
S models, except Coupe (Sec. 54)

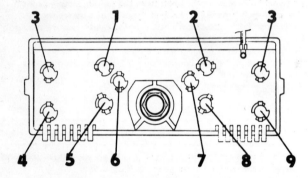

Fig. 10.13. Rear of instrument panel (S Models) (Sec. 54)

1   Speedometer and fuel gauge light.
2   Speedometer and temperature gauge light.
3   Direction indicator warning lights.
4   Spare.
5   Stoplight warning.
6   Low fuel warning light.
7   Oil pressure warning light.
8   Non-charging warning light.
9   Main beam warning light.

Simply turn the catches to remove the panel, which then allows easy
access to the bulbs and sockets, speedometer cable, oil pressure and
temperature gauge connections, together with the wiring - note
positions for reassembly.
2   Unfortunately if any of the instruments in the panel are defective
it is not possible to renew the single instrument. The complete panel
unit must be renewed.
3   Refitting is the reverse of removal.

55 Instrument warning lights - removal and refitting

1   From the underside of the dash panel, these can be removed by
twisting the bulb holders and withdrawing from the panel.
2   To remove the bulbs twist, press and withdraw from holders.
3   Refitting is the reverse of removal.

56 Hazard flasher warning light - removal and refitting

1   From the rear of the panel, pull out the holder from its socket
complete with bulb. Press and twist the bulb to remove from holder.
2   Refitting is the reverse of removal.

57 Ignition switch/steering lock - removal and refitting

1   The ignition switch is mounted on the steering column and
incorporates a circuit breaker and steering lock.
2   To remove the switch, turn the ignition key to 'O-garage' position
and then unscrew the switch clamp bolt to withdraw from the column
clamp. (Some types of switch have to be removed complete with
column clamp.
3   Make a note of the various lead connection positions and disconnect
from the switch.
4   Refit in the reverse order.

58 Courtesy light - removal and refitting

1   Disconnect the battery earth strap or relevant fuse.
2   From the side panel under the dashboard, remove sufficient
weatherstrip to peel back enough of the side panel unholstery so that
the rear of the switch is accessible.
3   To remove the switch unscrew the two retaining screws from inside
the channel, pull the switch clear and disconnect the lead.
4   Refitting is the reverse procedure.

59 Stoplight switches - removal and refitting

1   The stoplight switches are located in the front luggage compartment
under the hinged floor panel, attached to the brake master cylinder.
2   Pull off the connecting cables.
3   Unscrew the switch and carefully clean the surrounding area of the
master cylinder to ensure no dirt enters the hydraulic system. Do not
depress the brake pedal whilst the switch is removed, or air will enter
the system and you will then have to bleed it.
4   If replacing the old switch ensure it is clean.
5   Refitting is the reverse of removal.

60 Brake system failure warning lamp relay unit - removal and refitting

1   This is fitted to work in union with the brake light switches and
should a defect in the brake system occur, such as loss of pressure, it
actuates the warning light.
2   Due to the unequal pressure on the stoplight switches the warning
light may occasionally light up momentarily - this is not a defect.
However, if the light continues to stay on, the braking system should
be checked.
3   To remove the signal relay unit, disconnect the leads from their
terminals on the unit, noting which positions they were in, and unscrew
the unit retaining screw.
4   Handle the unit with care as the internal components are delicate.
5   Refitting is the reverse of removal.

61 Oil pressure light switch - removal and refitting

1   This is located on the right-hand side of the cylinder block near the
fuel pump and is screwed into the pressure/oil cooler pipes connection.
2   To remove the switch place a drain can underneath to collect spilled
oil.
3   Pull off the leads and unscrew the switch, whilst supporting the oil
return pipe (into which the switch is fitted) with a spanner, to prevent
it being loosened.
4   Refitting is the reverse procedure, but ensure the switch is clean
before fitting and top-up the engine oil level, as required.

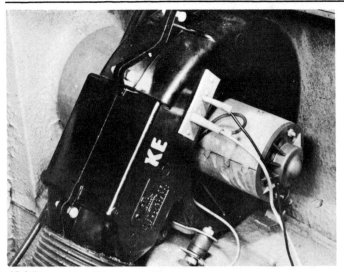

62.2 The heater unit in place in the car

62.5 Removing the heater unit intake filter

62 Heater motor unit - removal and refitting

1   This is located in the right-hand rear wing panel. Before removing disconnect the earth strap on the battery.
2   Pull off the connecting cables from the motor, and the earth cable by unscrewing the nut of the rubber cushioned connection below the motor, and also the feed cable (photo).
3   Remove the air duct hose and the connection hose to the intake channel.
4   Undo the retaining bolts to remove from the car.
5   To dismantle the electric motor from the housing, undo the respective housing flange retaining bolts and 'slit' the housing. Remove the intake filter by pulling from its recess slot (photo).
6   Refitting is the reverse of removal.

63 Heater motor unit - special note

Two types of electric motor have been fitted. The earlier type was for cars fitted with a dynamo, and the later type for cars fitted with an alternator. If renewing the motor be sure to get the correct model as the two should not be interchanged. Testing and repair of the electric motor should be entrusted to your Skoda dealer or local auto-electrician who has the specialised equipment for the job .

64 Heater and choke operating cables and levers - removal and refitting

1   The floor mounted levers are located on the central tunnel between the front seats.
2   To remove the lever unit remove the floor covering and unscrew the retaining screws, and remove with spring washers.
3   The cables are then removed from the respective lever quadrants and passed through their guides and outer cables, and can be removed from their respective connections in the engine compartment.
4   The heater water valve operating cable is also attached to, and operated from, the quadrant lever. This cable is disconnected and removed in a similar fashion to the above cables but is disconnected from the water valve connection and pulled through the outer cable. The water valve is located adjacent to the heater radiator under the rear right-hand passenger seat.
5   Refitting of these components is the reverse of dismantling, but check the adjustment of the respective cables.

65 Fault diagnosis - electrical system

Symptom	Reason/s	Remedy
Starter motor fails to turn engine		
No electricity at starter motor	Battery discharged	Charge battery.
	Battery defective internally	Fit new battery.
	Battery terminal leads loose or earth lead not securely attached to body	Check and tighten leads.
	Loose or broken connections in starter motor circuit	Check all connections and check any that are loose.
	Starter motor switch or solenoid faulty	Test and replace faulty components with new.
Electricity at starter motor: faulty motor	Starter motor pinion jammed in mesh with ring gear	Disengage pinion by pushing car in gear or remove.
	Starter brushes badly worn, sticking, or brush wires loose	Examine brushes, replace as necessary, tighten down brush wires.
	Commutator dirty, worn, or burnt	Clean commutator, recut if badly burnt.
	Starter motor armature faulty	Overhaul starter motor, fit new armature.
	Field coils earthed	Overhaul starter motor.
Starter motor turns engine very slowly		
Electrical defects	Battery in discharged condition	Charge battery.
	Starter brushes badly worn, sticking, or brush wires loose	Examine brushes, replace as necessary, tighten down brush wires.
	Loose wires in starter motor circuit	Check wiring and tighten as necessary.

Symptom	Reason/s	Remedy
Starter motor operates without turning engine		
Dirt or oil on drive gear	Starter motor pinion sticking on the screwed sleeve	Remove starter motor, clean starter motor drive.
Mechanical damage	Pinion or ring gear teeth broken or worn	Fit new gear ring, and new pinion to starter motor drive.
Starter motor noisy or excessively rough engagement		
Lack of attention or mechanical damage	Pinion or ring gear teeth broken or worn	Fit new ring gear, or new pinion to starter motor drive.
	Starter drive main spring broken	Dismantle and fit new main spring.
	Starter motor retaining bolts loose	Tighten starter motor securing bolts. Fit new spring washer if necessary.
Battery will not hold charge for more than a few days		
Wear or damage	Battery defective internally	Remove and fit new battery.
	Electrolyte level too low or electrolyte too weak due to leakage	Top up electrolyte level to just above plates.
	Plate separators no longer fully effective	Remove and fit new battery.
	Battery plates severely sulphated	Remove and fit new battery.
	Drive belt slipping	Check belt for wear, replace if necessary, and tighten.
	Battery terminal connections loose or corroded	Check terminals for tightness and remove all corrosion.
	Alternator/dynamo not charging properly	Remove and overhaul dynamo or alternator.
	Short in lighting circuit causing continual battery drain	Trace and rectify.
	Regulator unit not working correctly	Check setting, clean, and replace if defective.
Ignition light fails to go out, battery runs flat in a few days		
Dynamo not charging	Drivebelt loose and slipping, or broken	Check, replace, and tighten as necessary.
	Brushes worn, sticking, broken or dirty	Examine, clean, or replace brushes as necessary.
	Brush springs weak or broken	Examine and test. Replace as necessary.
	Commutator dirty, greasy, worn or burnt	Clean commutator and undercut segment separators.
	Armature badly worn or armature shaft bent	Fit new or reconditioned armature.
	Contacts in light switch faulty	By-pass light switch to ascertain if fault is in switch and fit new switch as appropriate.
Alternator not charging	Drivebelt loose and slipping or broken	Check, replace and tighten as necessary.
	Faulty wire connections	Check, clean and securely reconnect.
Individual electrical components are covered item-by-item in the following sub-sections:		
Fuel gauge		
Fuel gauge gives no reading	Fuel tank empty!	Refill fuel tank.
	Electric cable between tank sender unit and gauge earthed or loose	Check cable for earthing and joints for tightness.
	Fuel gauge case not earthed	Ensure case is well earthed.
	Fuel gauge supply cable interrupted	Check and replace cable if necessary.
	Fuel gauge unit broken	Replace fuel gauge.
Fuel gauge registers full all the time	Electric cable between tank unit and gauge broken or disconnected	Check over cable and repair as necessary.
Horn		
Horn operates all the time	Horn push either earthed or stuck down	Disconnect battery earth. Check and rectify source of trouble.
	Horn cable to horn push earthed	Disconnect battery earth. Check and rectify
	Fuse blown or badly connected	Check and replace if required.
Horn fails to operate	Cable or cable connection loose, broken or disconnected	Check all connections for tightness and cables for breaks.
	Horn has an internal fault	Remove and overhaul horn.
Horn emits intermittent or unsatisfactory noise	Cable connections loose	Check and tighten all connections.
	Horn incorrectly adjusted	Adjust horn until best note obtained.
Lights		
Lights do not come on	Fuse blown or badly connected	Check and replace if required.
	If engine not running, battery discharged	Push-start car, charge battery.
	Light bulb filament burnt out or bulbs broken	Test bulbs in live bulb holders.
	Wire connections loose, disconnected or broken	Check all connections for tightness and wire cable for breaks.

Symptom	Reason/s	Remedy
	Light switch shorting or otherwise faulty	By-pass light switch to ascertain if fault is in switch and fit new switch as appropriate.
Lights come on but fade out	If engine not running battery discharged	Push-start car, and charge battery.
	Light bulb filament burnt out or bulbs broken	Test bulbs in live bulb holder.
	Wire connections loose, disconnected or broken	Check all connections for tightness and wire cable for breaks.
	Light switch shorting or otherwise faulty	By-pass light switch to ascertain if fault is in switch and fit new switch as appropriate.
Lights come on but fade out	If engine not running battery discharged	Push-start car, and charge battery.
Lights give very poor illumination	Lamp glasses dirty	Clean glasses.
	Reflector tarnished or dirty	Fit new reflectors.
	Lamps badly out of adjustment	Adjust lamps correctly.
	Incorrect bulb with too low wattage fitted	Remove bulb and replace with correct grade.
	Existing bulbs old and badly discoloured	Renew bulb units.
	Poor earth	Check earth terminals, clean and tighten as necessary.
Lights work erratically - flashing on and off, especially over bumps	Battery terminals or earth connection loose	Tighten battery terminals and earth connection.
	Lights not earthing properly	Examine and rectify.
	Contacts in light switch faulty	By-pass switch to ascertain if fault is in switch and fit new switch as appropriate.
	Fuse loose in connection	Check and secure.
Wipers		
Wiper motor fails to work	Fuse blown or badly connected	Check and replace if required.
	Wire connections loose, disconnected or broken	Check wiper wiring. Tighten loose connections.
	Brushes badly worn	Remove and fit new brushes.
	Armature worn or faulty	If electricity at wiper motor remove and overhaul and fit replacement armature.
	Field coils faulty	Purchase reconditioned wiper motor.
Wiper motor works very slowly and takes excessive current	Commutator dirty, greasy or burnt	Clean commutator thoroughly.
	Drive bent or un-lubricated	Examine drive and straighten out severe curvature. Lubricate.
	Wheelbox spindle binding or damaged	Remove, overhaul, or fit replacement.
	Armature bearings dry or unaligned	Replace with new bearings correctly aligned.
	Armature badly worn or faulty	Remove, overhaul, or fit replacement armature.
Wiper motor works slowly and takes excessive current	Brushes badly worn	Remove and fit new brushes.
	Commutator dirty, greasy, or burnt	Clean commutator thoroughly.
	Armature badly worn or faulty	Remove and overhaul armature or fit replacement.
Wiper motor works but wiper blades remain stationary	Driving cable rack disengaged or faulty	Examine and if faulty, replace.
	Wheelbox gear and spindle damaged or worn	Examine and if faulty, replace.
	Wiper motor gearbox parts badly worn	Overhaul or fit new gearbox.
Heater unit		
Heater motor fails to work	Wire connections loose, disconnected or broken	Check wiring and secure connections.
	Fuse blown or bad connection	Check and replace as required.
	Brushes badly worn	Remove and have new brushes fitted.
	Armature badly worn or faulty	Have it checked and replaced if required.
	Field coils faulty	Remove and renew motor.
Motor works slowly, using excessive current	Commutator dirty, greasy or burnt	Clean commutator and check that the intake filter is clean.
	Faulty armature	Have it checked and replace if required.
Motor works but does not produce sufficient airflow	Leaky extractor pipe connections from heater	Check and refit or replace as required.
	Blocked extractor pipe from heater or intake vent	Remove and clean the heater filter.
Motor works but insufficient heat produced	Faulty thermostat	Check and replace if required.
	Heater radiator water valve shut	Check lever position. Check lever operates the valve when actuated.
	Water valve operating cable to heater unit broken	Fit new cable.

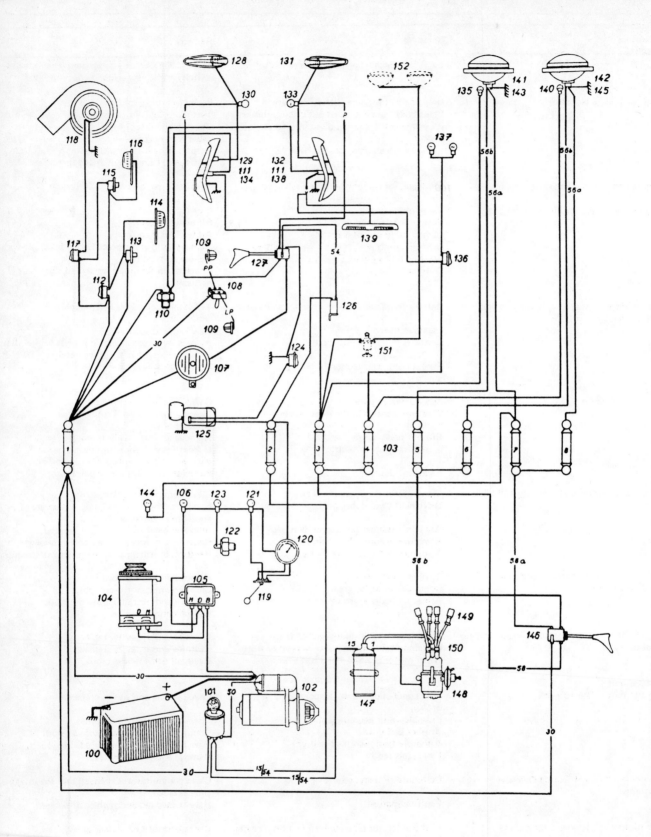

Fig. 10.14. Wiring diagram - MB Models

Key to Wiring Diagram - MB Models

100   Battery
101   Ignition switchbox
102   Electric starter motor
103   Fuses
104   Dynamo
105   Regulating switch of voltage
106   Warning light of battery charging
107   Electric horn
108   Switch of parking lights
109   Parking lights
110   Switch of stoplight
111   Stoplights
112   Switch of interior lights
113   Automatic switch of interior light (r.h. side door)
114   R.h. side lamp
115   Automatic switch of interior light (l.h. side door)
116   L.h. side lamp
117   Switch of heater
118   Electric motor of heater
119   Float of fuel level gauge
120   Fuel level gauge
121   Warning light of fuel level gauge
122   Pressure switch for lubrication tell-tale lamp
123   Warning light of lubricating system
124   Switch for windscreen wiper
125   Electric motor of windscreen wiper
126   Flasher unit
127   Switch of flashers
128   L.h. side front flasher
129   L.h. side rear flasher
130   Warning light of l.h. side flashers
131   R.h. side front flasher
132   R.h. side rear flasher
133   Warning light of r.h. side flashers
134   L.h. side tail lamp
135   Headlamp/side lamp
136   Switch for instrument illumination
137   Instrument illumination
138   R.h. side tail light
139   Number plate lamp
140   Headlamp - r.h. side lamp
141   Headlamp - l.h. side dipped beam
142   Headlamp - r.h. side dipped beam
143   Headlamp - l.h. side main beam
144   Headlamps main beam warning light
145   Headlamp - r.h. side main beam
146   Switch of main and dipped headlamps beam
147   Ignition coil
148   Distributor
149   Spark plug leads
150   Interference suppressing resistances of spark plugs
151   Foglamps   } special equipment
152   Switch for foglamps

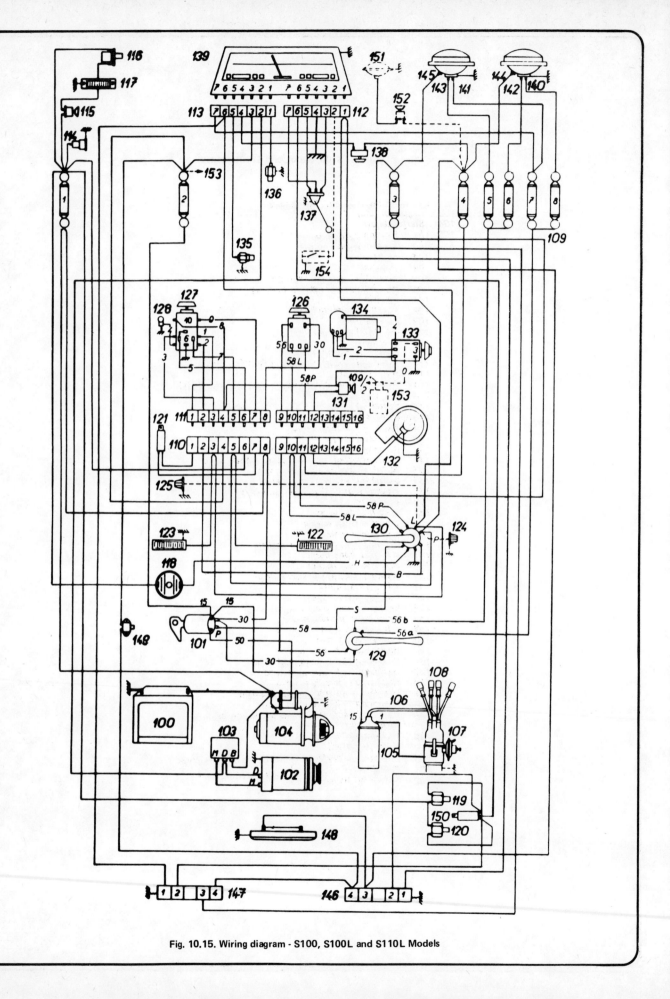

Fig. 10.15. Wiring diagram - S100, S100L and S110L Models

Key to Wiring Diagram - S100, S100L and S110L Models

100 Battery
101 Switchbox
102 Dynamo
103 Regulator relay
104 Starter motor
105 Ignition coil
106 Ignition coil cable
107 Ignition distributor
108 Spark plug cables
109 Fuses
110 Terminal board - with pin sockets
111 Terminal board - with pins
112 Instrument terminal board - red
     1 - RH flasher light, 2 - light,* 3 - fuel gauge (blue),
     4 - brake system light, 5 - fuel gauge (yellow), 6 - brake
     system light, 7 - fuel reserve light
113 Instrument terminal board - white
     1 - oil pressure light, 2 - battery charge light, 3 - positive (+)
     connecting cable, 4 - instrument light, 5 - temperature gauge,
     6 - LH flasher light, 7 - long range (main) beam light
114 Inspection lamp socket
115 Interior light switch - hand-operated
116 Interior light switch - door-operated
117 Interior light
118 Horn
119 Stop light switch
120 Brake system light switch
121 Flasher circuit breaker
122 Flasher direction indicator, front - RH
123 Flasher direction indicator, front - LH
124 Flasher direction indicator, side - RH (special extra)
125 Flasher direction indicator, side - LH (special extra)
126 Switch (trunk feeder) for dipswitch (129)
127 Disability signal light switch
128 Disability signal light tell-tale lamp
129 Dipswitch and headlamp flasher switch
130 Direction indicator and horn switch
131 Heater motor fan switch
132 Heater fan motor
133 Wiper motor switch
134 Wiper motor
135 Temperature gauge sensor
136 Oil pressure light switch
137 Fuel reserve light switch
138 Instrument light switch
139 Instrument light
140 Main beam - RH headlamp
141 Main beam - LH headlamp
142 Diplight - RH headlamp
143 Diplight - LH headlamp
144 Parking light - RH headlamp
145 Parking light - LH headlamp
146 RH tail light cluster
147 LH tail light cluster
     1 - direction indicators, 2 - stop lights, 3 - tail lights,
     4 - reversing lights
148 Number plate light
149 Reversing lights switch
150 Brake failure relay
151 Fog lamps
152 Switch
153 Electric windscreen washer
154 Switch

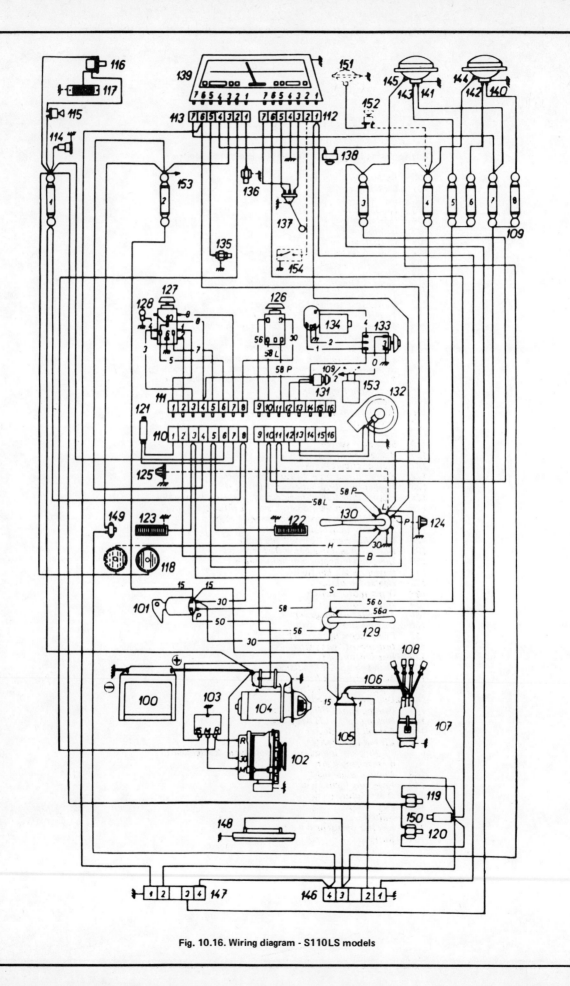

Fig. 10.16. Wiring diagram - S110LS models

Key to Wiring diagram - S110LS Models

100	Battery
101	Switch box
102	Alternator
103	Regulator relay
104	Starter motor
105	Ignition coil
106	Coil ignition cable
107	Ignition distributor
108	Ignition cables
109	Fuses
110	Terminal board - with pin sockets
111	Terminal board - with pins
112	Instrument terminal board - red

1 - RH direction indicator tell-tale light,
2 - tell-tale light*, 3 fuel gauge (blue),
4 - brake system tell-tale light, 5 - fuel
gauge (yellow), 6 - brake system tell-
tale light, 7 - fuel reserve tell-tale light

113	Instrument terminal board (white)

1 - oil pressure light, 2 - alternator function
light, 3 - positive (+) lead, 4 - instrument
light, 5 - temperature gauge, 6 - LH direction
indicator light, 7 - main beam light

114	Inspection lamp socket
115	Interior light switch - hand-operated
116	Interior light switch - door-operated
117	Interior light
118	Horn
119	Stop light switch
120	Brake system light switch
121	Flasher unit
122	Front indicator, RH
123	Front indicator, LH
124	Side direction indicator, RH (special extra)
125	Side direction indicator, LH (special extra)
126	Switch (feeder) for dipswitch (129)
127	Disability signal light switch
128	Disability signal light lamp
129	Dipswitch and headlamp flasher switch
130	Direction indicator and horn switch
131	Heater motor fan switch
132	Heater fan motor
133	Wiper motor switch
134	Wiper motor
135	Temperature gauge sensor
136	Oil pressure light switch
137	Fuel reserve light switch
138	Instrument light switch
139	Instrument (cluster) panel
140	Main beam - RH headlamp
141	Main beam - LH headlamp
142	Diplight - RH headlamp
143	Diplight - LH headlamp
144	Parking light - RH headlamp
145	Parking light - LH headlamp
146	RH tail light cluster
147	LH tail light cluster

1 - direction indicators, 2 - stop lights, 3 - tail
lights, 4 - reversing lamps

148	Number plate light
149	Reversing lamp switch
150	Brake system signalling relay
151	Fog lamps (special extras)
152	Fog lamp switch (special extra)
153	Electric windscreen washer
154	Switch *

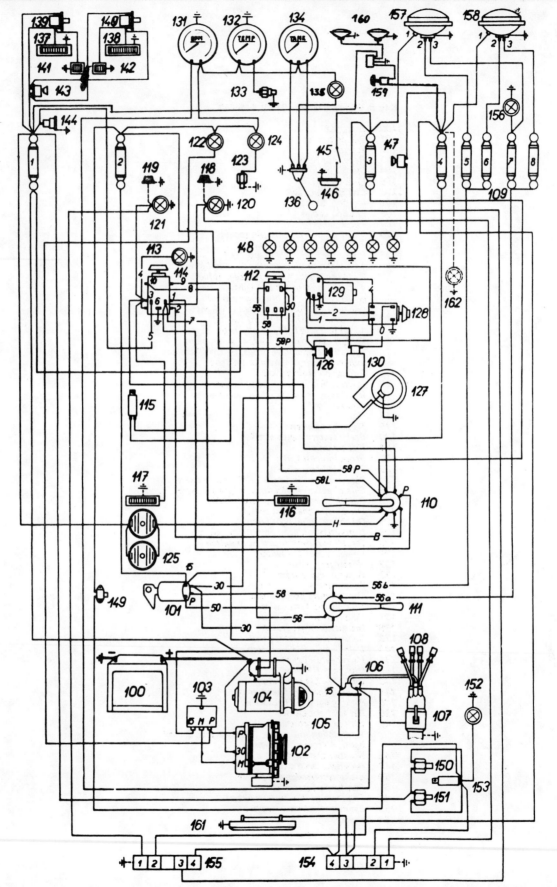

Fig. 10.17. Wiring diagram - S110R Coupe Models. (The pre-1973 models were identical but did not have the spot lights fitted as standard equipment)

Key to Wiring diagram - S110R Coupe Models

100	Battery
101	Switchbox
102	Alternator
103	Regulating relay
104	Starter motor
105	Ignition coil
106	Coil ignition cable
107	Distributor
108	Ignition cables
109	Fuses
110	Switch for direction indicators and horn
111	Switch for distance beams and flashing light
112	Feeder for the dip switch and side lamp switch
113	Switch for warning signal lights
114	Signal lights warning lamp
115	Flasher unit
116	Direction indicator - front, right
117	Direction indicator - front, left
118	Direction indicator - side, right
119	Direction indicator - side, left
120	Warning lamp of right-hand indicators
121	Warning lamp of left-hand indicators
122	Battery charging warning lamp
123	Engine oil pressure warning lamp switch
124	Engine lubrication warning lamp
125	Horns
126	Switch for heater motor fan
127	Heater fan
128	Switch for windscreen wiper motor
129	Windscreen wiper motor
130	Windscreen washer motor
131	Rev counter
132	Temperature gauge
133	Temperature gauge sensor
134	Fuel gauge
135	Fuel reserve warning lamp
136	Fuel gauge
137	Interior lamp - left-hand
138	Interior lamp - right-hand
139	Door switch - left-hand door
140	Door switch - right-hand door
141	Warning signal light - left-hand door
142	Warning signal light - right-hand door
143	Interior illumination switch (on instrument panel)
144	Inspection lamp socket
145	Luggage compartment light switch
146	Luggage compartment light
147	Switch and rheostat for instrument illumination
148	Instrument illumination
149	Reversing lamps switch
150	Stop-light switch
151	Switch for brake system warning lamp
152	Brake system warning lamp
153	Brake system signalling relay
154	Rear lamp cluster - right-hand
155	Rear lamp cluster - left-hand
	1 - direction indicators, 2 - stop lights,
	3 - tail lights, 4 - reversing lamps
156	Main beam warning lamp
157	Headlamp - left-hand
158	Headlamp - right-hand
	1 - side light, 2 - dipped beam, 3 - distance beam
159	Fog lamps switch (optional equipment)
160	Fog lamps (optional equipment)
161	Number plate light

Chapter 11 Bodywork and Fittings

Contents

1 General description

The basic body construction method on all models since the introduction of the MB series, has remained unchanged and is of all steel monocoque type, with four seats and four doors (with the exception of the 110R Coupe two door model).

All wing panels are of bolt on type, as are the front and rear panels.

The boot and engine compartment lids have internal hinges and are retained by cable operated locks. The operating lever for the engine compartment lid is located in the rear door pillar (the rear of the door pillar on the Coupe model) and the luggage compartment lid release is operated from under the dashboard.

The spare wheel is carried under the luggage compartment floor panel at the front of the car. The fuel tank is also located under the front luggage compartment and is retained by bolts, and protected from damage by an undertray.

Seatbelt anchorages are also located on stiffened areas of the bodyshell: centre door pillars, door sill channel and on the central floor structure tunnel.

As well as providing the essential strong points for seatbelts, seats and jacking, the floor structure also contributes significantly to the strength and stiffness of the bodyshell and therefore it cannot be emphasised too much that it is as necessary to keep the floor structure clean and free from corrosion, as it is to keep the upper structure and coachwork clean and corrosion free.

2 Maintenance - body and subframe

1   The condition of your car's bodywork is of considerable importance as it is on this that the second-hand value of the car will mainly depend. It is much more difficult to repair neglected bodywork than to renew mechanical assemblies. The hidden portions of the body, such as the wheel arches and the underframe and the engine compartment are equally important, though obviously not requiring such frequent attention as the immediately visible paintwork.

2   Once a year, it is a sound scheme to visit your local main agent and have the underside of the body steam cleaned. This will take about 1½ hours. All traces of dirt and oil will be removed and the underside can then be inspected carefully for rust, damaged hydraulic pipes, frayed electrical wiring and similar maladies. The car should be greased on

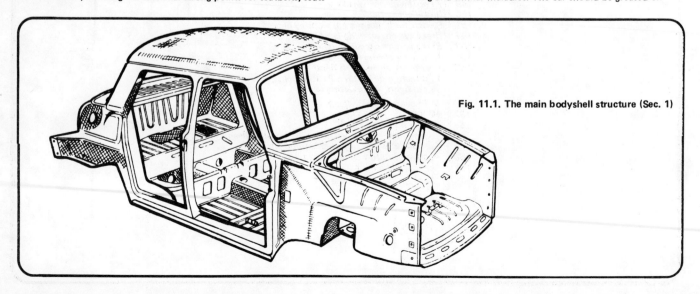

Fig. 11.1. The main bodyshell structure (Sec. 1)

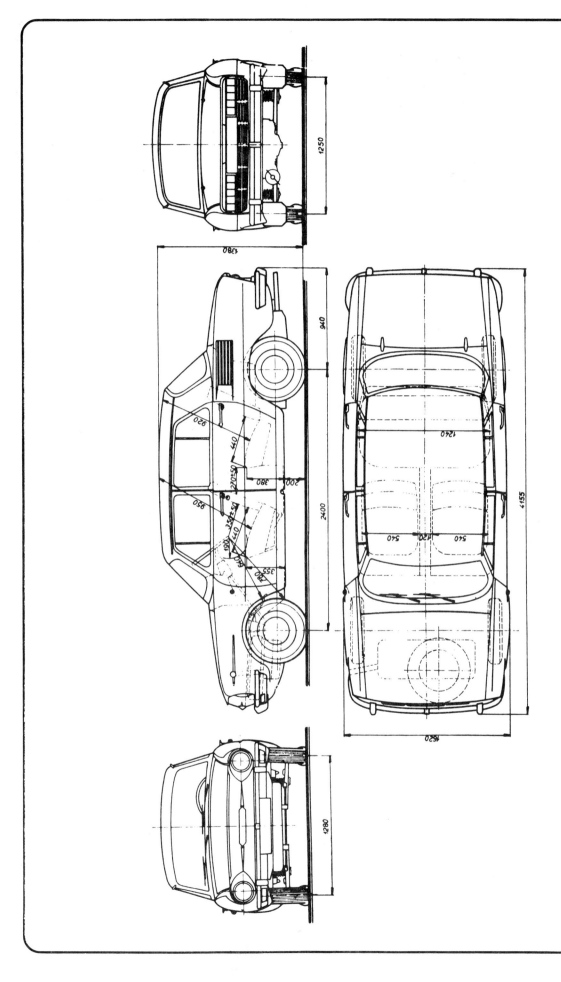

Fig. 11.2. Dimensional drawing of the body - S100, S100L, S110L and S110LS (Dimensions in millimetres)

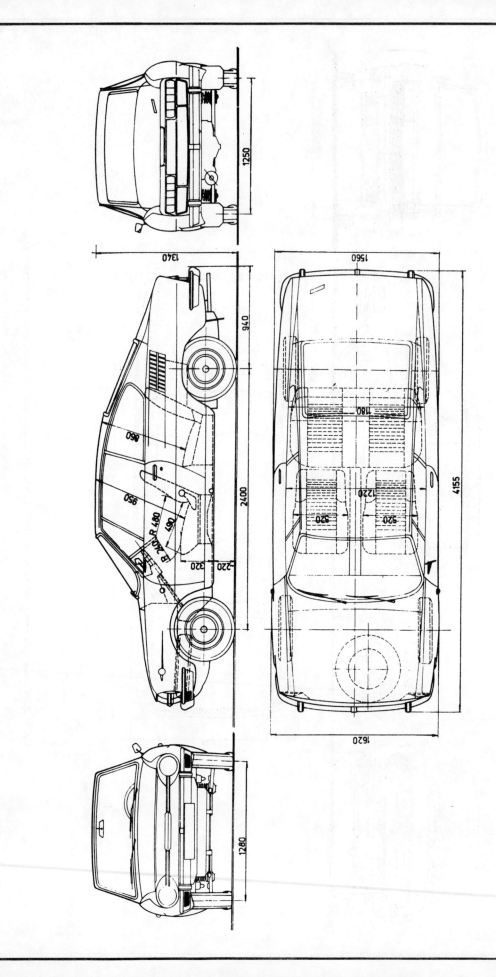

Fig. 11.3. Dimensional drawing of the body - Coupe (Dimensions in millimetres)

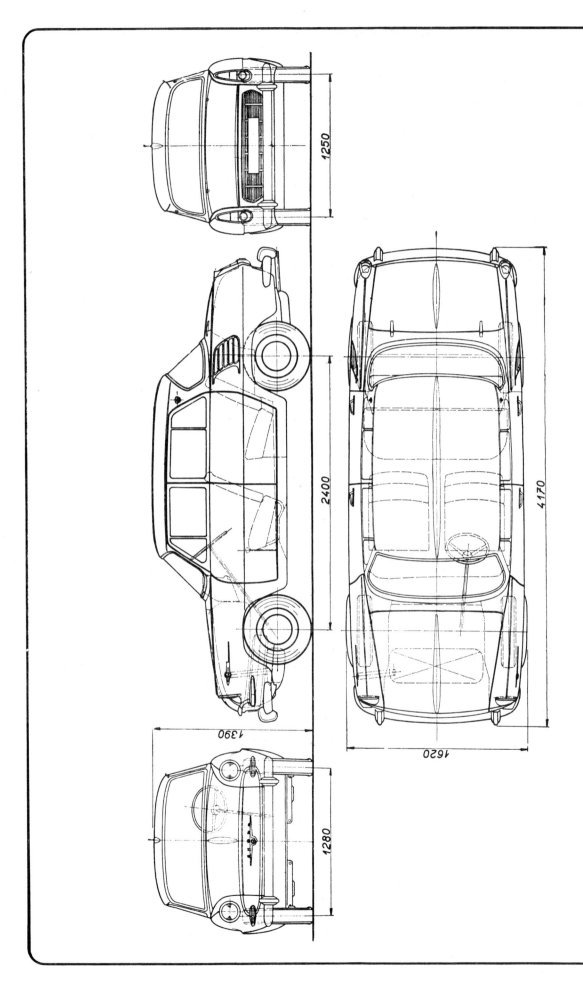

Fig. 11.4. Dimensional drawing of the body - MB Models (Dimensions in millimetres)

completion of this job.

3 At the same time the engine compartment should be cleaned in the same manner. If steam cleaning facilities are not available then brush 'Gunk' or a similar cleanser over the whole engine and engine compartment with a stiff paint brush, working it well in where there is an accumulation of oil and dirt. Do not paint the ignition system and protect it with oily rags when the Gunk is washed off. As the Gunk is washed away it will take with it all traces of oil and dirt, leaving the engine looking clean and bright.

4 The wheel arches should be given particular attention as undersealing can easily come away here and stones and dirt thrown up from the road wheels can soon cause the paint to chip and flake, and so allow rust to set in. If rust is found, clean down the bare metal with wet and dry paper, paint on an anti-corrosive coating such as Kurust, or if preferred, red lead, and renew the paintwork and undercoating.

5 The bodywork should be washed once a week or when dirty. Thoroughly wet the car to soften the dirt and then wash the car down with a soft sponge and plenty of clean water. If the surplus dirt is not washed off very gently, in time it will wear the paint down as surely as wet and dry paper. It is best to use a hose if this is available. Give the car a final wash-down and then dry with a soft chamois leather to prevent the formation of spots.

6 Spots of tar and grease thrown up from the road can be removed with a rag dampened with petrol.

7 Once every six months, or every three months if wished, give the bodywork and chromium trim a thoroughly good wax polish. If a chromium cleaner is used to remove rust on any of the car's plated parts remember that the cleaner is abrasive so use sparingly.

---

3 Maintenance - upholstery and carpets

1 Remove the carpets or rubber mats and thoroughly vacuum clean the interior of the car every three months or more frequently, if necessary.

2 Beat out the carpets and vacuum clean them if they are very dirty. If the upholstery is soiled apply an upholstery cleaner with a damp sponge and wipe off with a clean dry cloth.

---

4 Minor body damage - repair

The photograph sequence on pages 145, 146 and 147 illustrates the operations detailed in the following Sections.

Repair of minor scratches in the car's bodywork

If the scratch is very superficial, and does not penetrate to the metal of the bodywork, repair is very simple. Lightly rub the area of the scratch with a paintwork renovator, or a very fine cutting paste, to remove loose paint from the scratch and to clear the surrounding bodywork of wax polish. Rinse the area with clean water.

Apply touch-up paint to the scratch using a thin paint brush, continue to apply thin layers of paint until the surface of the paint in the scratch is level with the surrounding paintwork. Allow the new paint at least two weeks to harden; then, blend it into the surrounding paintwork by rubbing the paintwork, in the scratch area with a paintwork renovator, or a very fine cutting paste. Finally apply wax polish.

Where the scratch has penetrated right through to the metal of the bodywork, causing the metal to rust, a different repair technique is required. Remove any loose rust from the bottom of the scratch with a penknife, then apply rust inhibiting paint to prevent the formation of rust in the future. Using a rubber nylon applicator, fill the scratch with bodystopper paste. If required, this paste can be mixed with a cellulose thinner to provide a very thin paste which is ideal for filling narrow scratches. Before the stopper-paste in the scratch hardens wrap a piece of smooth cotton rag around the top of a finger. Dip the finger in cellulose thinners and then quickly sweep it across the surface of the stopper-paste in the scratch: this will ensure that the surface of the stopper-paste is slightly hollowed. The scratch can now be painted over as described earlier in this Section.

Repair of dents in the car's bodywork

When deep denting of the car's bodywork has taken place, the first task is to pull the dent out, until the affected bodywork almost attains its original shape. There is little point in trying to restore the original shape completely, as the metal in the damaged area will have stretched on impact and cannot be reshaped fully to its original contour. It is better to bring the level of the dent up to a point which is about 1/8 inch (3 mm) below the level of the surrounding bodywork. In cases where the dent is very shallow anyway, it is not worth trying to pull it out at all.

If the underside of the dent is accessible, it can be hammered out gently from behind, using a mallet with a wooden or plastic head. Whilst doing this, hold a suitable block of wood firmly against the impact from the hammer blows and thus prevent a large area of body-work from being 'belled-out'.

Should the dent be in a section of the bodywork which has a double skin or some other factor making it inaccessible from behind, a different technique is called for. Drill several small holes through the metal inside the dent area - particularly in the deeper sections. Then screw long self-tapping screws into the holes just sufficiently for them to gain a good purchase in the metal. Now the dent can be pulled out by pulling the protruding heads of the screws with a pair of pliers.

The next stage of the repair is the removal of the paint from the damaged area, and from an inch or so of the surrounding 'sound' bodywork. This is accomplished most easily by using a wire brush or abrasive pad on a power drill, although it can be done just as effectively by hand using sheets of abrasive paper. To complete the preparations for filling, score the surface of the bare metal with a screwdriver or the tang of a file, or alternatively, drill small holes in the affected area. This will provide a really good 'key' for the filler paste.

To complete the repair see the Section on filling and respraying.

Repair of rust holes or gashes in the car's bodywork

Remove all paint from the affected area and from an inch or so of the surrounding 'sound' bodywork, using an abrasive pad or a wire brush on a power drill. If these are not available a few sheets of abrasive paper will do the job just as effectively. With the paint removed you will be able to gauge the severity of the corrosion and therefore decide whether to replace the whole panel (if this is possible) or to repair the affected area. Replacement body panels are not as expensive as most people think and it is often quicker and more satisfactory to fit a new panel than to attempt to repair large areas of corrosion.

Remove all fittings from the affected area except those which will act as a guide to the original shape of the damaged bodywork (eg. headlamp shells etc.). Then, using tin snips or a hacksaw blade, remove all loose metal and any other metal badly affected by corrosion. Hammer the edges of the hole inwards in order to create a slight depression for the filler paste.

Wire brush the affected area to remove the powdery rust from the surface of the remaining metal. Paint the affected area with rust inhibiting paint; if the back of the rusted area is accessible treat this also.

Before filling can take place it will be necessary to block the hole in some way. This can be achieved by the use of one of the following materials: Zinc gauze, Aluminium tape or Polyurethane foam.

Zinc gauze is probably the best material to use for a large hole. Cut a piece to the approximate size and shape of the hole to be filled, then position it in the hole so that its edges are below the level of the surrounding bodywork. It can be retained in position by several blobs of filler paste around its periphery.

Aluminium tape should be used for small or very narrow holes. Pull a piece off the roll and trim it to the approximate size and shape required, then pull off the backing paper (if used) and stick the tape over the hole; it can be overlapped if the thickness of one piece is insufficient. Burnish down the edges of the tape with the handle of a screwdriver or similar, to ensure that the tape is securely attached to the metal underneath.

Polyurethane foam is best used where the hole is situated in a section of bodywork of complex shape, backed by a small box section (eg. where the sill panel meets the rear wheel arch - most cars). The unusual mixing procedure for this foam is as follows: Put equal amounts of fluid from each of the two cans provided in the kit, into one container. Stir until the mixture begins to thicken, then quickly pour this mixture into the hole, and hold a piece of cardboard over the larger apertures. Almost immediately the polyurethane will begin to expand, gushing frantically out of any small holes left unblocked. When the foam hardens it can be cut back to just below the level of the surrounding bodywork with a hacksaw blade.

Typical example of rust damage to a body panel. Before starting ensure that you have all of the materials required to hand. The first task is to...

... remove body fittings from effected area, except those which can act as a guide to the original shape of the damaged bodywork - the headlamp shell in this case.

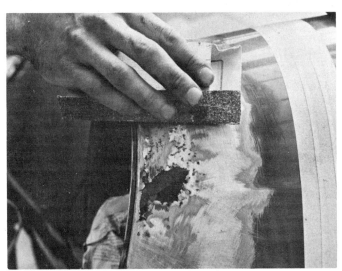

Remove all paint from the rusted area and from an inch or so of the adjoining 'sound' bodywork - use coarse abrasive paper or a power drill fitted with a wire brush or abrasive pad. Gently hammer in the edges of the hole to provide a hollow for the filler.

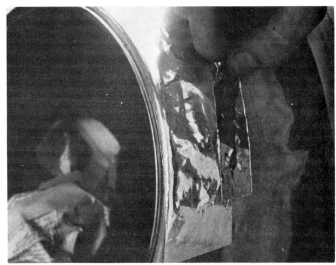

Before filling, the larger holes must be blocked off. Adhesive aluminium tape is one method; cut the tape to the required shape and size, peel off the backing strip (where used), position the tape over the hole and burnish to ensure adhesion.

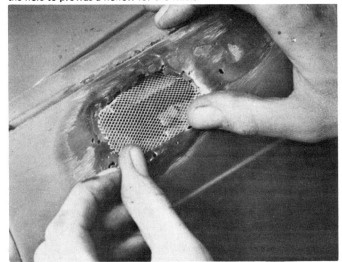

Alternatively, zinc gauze can be used. Cut a piece of the gauze to the required shape and size; position it in the hole below the level of the surrounding bodywork; then ...

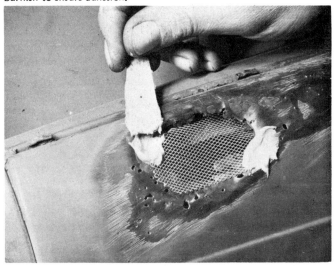

... secure in position by placing a few blobs of filler paste around its periphery. Alternatively, pop rivets or self-tapping screws can be used. Preparation for filling is now complete.

Mix filler and hardener according to manufacturer's instructions - avoid using too much hardener otherwise the filler will harden before you have a chance to work it.

Apply the filler to the affected area with a flexible applicator - this will ensure a smooth finish. Apply thin layers of filler at 20 minute intervals, until the surface of the filler is just 'proud' of the surrounding bodywork. Then ...

... remove excess filler and start shaping with a Surform plane or a dreadnought file. Once an approximate contour has been obtained and the surface is relatively smooth, start using ...

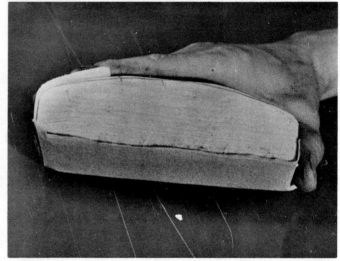

... abrasive paper. The paper should be wrapped around a flat wood, cork or rubber block - this will ensure that it imparts a smooth surface to the filler.

40 grit production paper is best to start with, then use progressively finer abrasive paper, finishing with 400 grade 'wet-and-dry'. When using 'wet-and-dry' paper, periodically rinse it in water ensuring also, that the work area is kept wet continuously.

Rubbing-down is complete when the surface of the filler is really smooth and flat, and the edges of the surrounding paintwork are finely 'feathered'. Wash the area thoroughly with clean water and allow to dry before commencing re-spray.

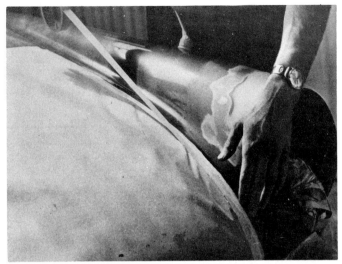

Firstly, mask off all adjoining panels and the fittings in the spray area. Ensure that the area to be sprayed is completely free of dust. Practice using an aerosol on a piece of waste metal sheet until the technique is mastered.

Spray the affected area with primer - apply several thin coats rather than one thick one. Start spraying in the centre of the repair area and then work outwards using a circular motion - in this way the paint will be evenly distributed.

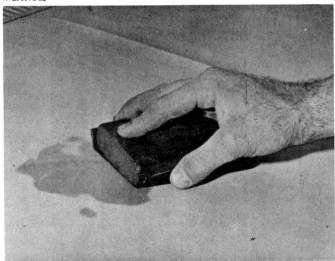

When the primer has dried inspect its surface for imperfections. Holes can be filled with filler paste or body-stopper, and lumps can be sanded smooth. Apply a further coat of primer, then 'flat' its surface with 400 grade 'wet-and-dry' paper.

Spray on the top coat, again building up the thickness with several thin coats of paint. Overspray onto the surrounding original paintwork to a depth of about five inches, applying a very thin coat at the outer edges.

Allow the paint two weeks, at least, to harden fully, then blend it into the surrounding original paintwork with a paint restorative compound or very fine cutting paste. Use wax polish to finish off.

The finished job should look like this. Remember, the quality of the completed work is directly proportional to the amount of time and effort expended at each stage of the preparation.

Bodywork repairs - filling and re-spraying

Before using this Section, see the Sections on dent, deep scratch, rust hole, and gash repairs.

Many types of bodyfiller are available, but generally speaking those proprietary kits which contain a tin of filler paste and a tube of resin hardener are best for this type of repair. A wide flexible plastic or nylon applicator will be found invaluable for imparting a smooth and well contoured finish to the surface of the filler.

Mix up a little filler on a clean piece of card or board - use the hardener sparingly (follow the maker's instructions on the packet) otherwise the filler will set very rapidly.

Using the applicator, apply the filler paste to the prepared area; draw the applicator across the surface of the filler to achieve the correct contour and to level the filler surface. As soon as a contour that approximates the correct one is achieved, stop working the paste - if you carry on too long the paste will become sticky and begin to 'pick-up' on the applicator. Continue to add thin layers of filler paste at twenty-minute intervals until the level of the filler is just 'proud' of the surrounding bodywork.

Once the filler has hardened, excess can be removed using a plane or file. From then on, progressively finer grades of abrasive paper should be used, starting with a 40 grade production paper and finishing with 400 grade 'wet-and-dry' paper. Always wrap the abrasive paper around a flat rubber, cork, or wooden block - otherwise the surface of the filler will not be completely flat. During the smoothing of the filler surfaces the 'wet-and-dry' paper should be periodically rinsed in water. This will ensure that a very smooth finish is imparted to the filler at the final stage.

At this stage, the 'dent' should be surrounded by a ring of bare metal, which in turn should be encircled by the finely 'feathered' edge of the good paintwork. Rinse the repair area with clean water, until all the dust produced by the rubbing-down operation is gone.

Spray the whole repair area with a light coat of grey primer - this will show up any imperfections in the surface of the filler. Repair these imperfections with fresh filler paste or bodystopper, and once more smooth the surface with abrasive paper. If bodystopper is used, it can be mixed with cellulose thinners to form a really thin paste which is ideal for filling small holes. Repeat this spray and repair procedure until you are satisfied that the surface of the filler, and the feathered edge of the paintwork are perfect. Clean the repair area with clean water and allow to dry fully.

5   Major body damage - repair

1   Major chassis and body repair work cannot be successfully undertaken by the average owner. Work of this nature should be entrusted to a competent body repair specialist who should have the necessary jigs, welding and hydraulic straightening equipment as well as skilled panel beaters to ensure a proper job is done.

6   Maintenance - hinges and locks

Once every six months the door, rear window, bonnet and boot hinges should be oiled with a few drops of engine oil from an oil can. The door striker plates can be given a thin smear of grease to reduce wear and ensure free-movement.

7   Door trim panels and handles - removal and refitting

1   Remove the armrest/door pull by unscrewing the retaining screws (photo).
2   Press the handle escutcheon inwards. This will reveal a pin retaining the handle to its square shaft. Push the pin out with a thin screwdriver or similar; the handle, escutcheon and spring can now be removed. This procedure is for both window winder and door handles (photo).
3   The door panel can now be removed by prising between the door and panel edges, to release it from the clips around its periphery.
4   Refitting is the reversal of removal.

8   Door locks - removal and refitting

1   Wind the window completely up.
2   Remove the door handle, window winder and armrest. Remove the door panel as described in Section 7.
3   Unscrew the inner door lock retaining bolts and withdraw the lock from the door (twist the tie-rod to the outer lock to assist).
4   Remove the outer lock bolts and also the relay lever bolt, and remove the outer lock.
5   Refitting is the reverse procedure, but be sure to replace with the levers and mechanism suitably lubricated.
6   Before trying the refitted door lock in the closed position, wind the window down to ensure freedom of movement and also as a safety precaution unlock the passenger door!

9   Quarterlight window (hinged type) - removal and refitting

1   Unscrew and remove the top hinge screw.
2   Loosen the adjuster screw of the vertical vent flap.
3   Hinge the glass clear of the sealing strip and remove.
4   Refitting is the reverse procedure.
5   Adjustment may be made by turning the adjustment screw, located in the inner panel directly below the quarterlight window, as required.

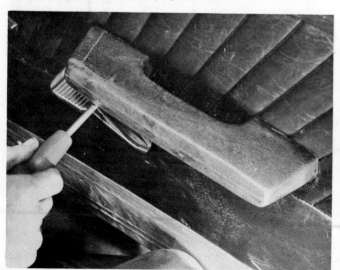

7.1 Removing the armrest/door pull

7.2 Removing the window winder handle

10 Quarterlight retaining catch - removal and refitting

1   Refer to Fig. 11.5. Drive out the cylindrical pin with a small drift, or use penetrating oil if rusted.
2   Remove the flap handle and retaining plunger and spring unit.
3   Remove the handle bracket by unscrewing and removing the retaining screw on the outside.
4   Refit in the reverse order, lubricating the working parts.

11 Quarter window (rear door) - removal and refitting

1   Remove the inner door trim.
2   Unscrew the window retaining bracket bolts, and remove with rubber pad.
3   Refitting is the reversal of dismantling.

12 Door window and winder mechanism (all models except Coupe) - removal and refitting

1   Wind the window fully up and then remove the inner panel, as described in Section 7.
2   Remove the window winder mechanism retaining bolts, and remove the winder from the support channel for the window. Withdraw the winder through the door inner panel aperture.
3   Unscrew the retaining bolt of the vertical rail at its bottom edge and push down the window, so that the guide can be removed.
4   Remove the window complete with support channel through the lower aperture in the inner door panel.
5   Refitting is the reversed procedure, but should the window need lateral adjustment, slacken the guide channel bolt and bend the channel slightly to suit.
6   Check the action of the winder mechanism to ensure freedom of movement and then replace the inner panel upholstery.

13 Hinged window, rear (Coupe) - removal and refitting

1   First disconnect the earth strap on the battery, and remove the interior light.
2   Unscrew the hinged locking and opening window location screw.
3   Remove the guide screw and withdraw the window.
4   Refitting is the reversal of removal.

14 Door window and winder mechanism (Coupe) - removal and refitting

1   Refer to Fig. 11.7. Wind the window down to its lowest position and then remove the interior door handle and winder, together with the trim panel.
2   Remove the outer seal by levering against a suitable pad.
3   Disconnect the regulating lever from the window stay, the stay step and the cable clamp.
4   Unscrew the top and bottom glass retaining screws of the front quarterlight glass, then the front glass channel retaining screws. Tilt the channel forwards to remove the glass and stay.
5   Remove the retaining screws of the window regulator and disconnect the cable from the rollers, noting carefully the cable location on the rollers, then remove the regulator.
6   Before reassembly, grease all the roller pivots. If the rollers have been removed, tighten the bolts and ensure freedom of rotation of the rollers.
7   Rewind the cable to the regulator assembly, insert into the door and relocate the cable over the respective rollers. Replace the regulator retaining screws, but do not fully tighten until the regulator has been positioned to tension the cable.
8   If it has been removed, relocate the tensioning roller.
9   Insert the rear glass channel from inside the door on the front channel from the top; retain with the relevant screws.
10 Insert the glass, complete with stay, into the channels. If the stay was removed from the glass it should be relocated 6.16 in (158 mm) from the front edge of the glass.

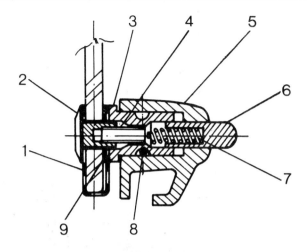

Fig. 11.5. The front quarterlight retaining catch - sectional view (Sec. 10)

1 Handle retainer	6 Retaining plunger
2 Screw	7 Spring
3 Bracket handle	8 Cylindrical pin
4 Screw	9 Pad
5 Hinged handle	

11 Hinge the front channel to the rear and locate the top screw. Wind up the glass fully and then unwind three turns. Fix the cable to the stay, ensuring that the operating lever is in the position shown in Fig. 11.7. If not, adjust as required.
12 Check the window to channels clearance and tighten if satisfactory. If not, shim the channels with washers to suit.
13 Re-insert the front quarterlight into position and relocate the outer seal.
14 Prior to reassembling the door panels and handles carefully check the door closing with the window fully wound up. The glass should clear the lower edge of the roof channel by 0.5 in (12.7 mm) and should not touch the door pillar. If it does, check the distance of the window stay from the front edge of the glass, as mentioned in paragraph 10, and adjust accordingly.

15 Door striker plate - removal, refitting and adjustment

1   If it is wished to renew a worn striker plate mark its position on the door pillar so a new plate can be fitted in the same positon.
2   To remove the plate simply undo the three crosshead screws which hold the plate in position, except the 110R Coupe which has four countersunk screws (photo). Refitting is equally straightforward.
3   To adjust the striker plate, first slacken the three screws and remove the striker plate slightly. Retighten the screws and close the door, noting the position of the door. Repeat this process until the door is 'flush' with the adjacent rear body panel. The crease in the door panel should be level with the crease in the rear body panel as well.
4   Check that the door closes easily without lifting or dropping and that on the road it does not rattle.

16 Door and door hinge - removal and refitting

1   Remove the door handles, armrest and panel trim.
2   From inside the door, unscrew the door tie-rod retaining nut to remove the rubber grommet and washer.
3   From the door hinge, unclip the snap-ring retaining the hinge pin.
4   Get an assistant to support the weight of the door and withdraw the hinge pin to remove the door.
5   The door hinges are retained by countersunk screws. If the hinges are to be removed, it is advisable to mark around the outside of the hinge so that it may be correctly repositioned on refitment.
6   Unscrew the screws to remove the hinges. It may be necessary apply some penetrating oil to assist removal.
7   Refitting is the reversal of removal.

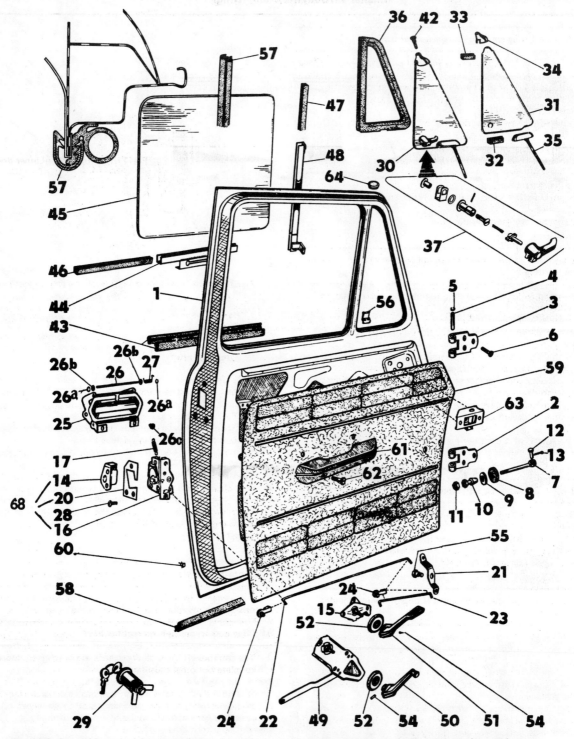

Fig. 11.6. General layout of door and window assembly for S100, S100L, S110L and S110LS Models (Sec. 12)

1 Front door assembly	16 Lock mechanism	30 Ventilating window	49 Regulator
2 Hinge (bottom)	17 Door lock spring	31 Glass	50 Crank
3 Hinge (top)	20 Lock pad	32 Bottom washer	51 Handle
4 Pin	21 Relay lever	33 Top washer	52 Cup
5 Circlip	22 Tie rod	34 Top foot	54 Pin
6 Screw	23 Tie rod	35 Control shaft	55 Screw
7 Door limiter tie rod	24 Clip	36 Rubber moulding	56 Stop
8 Tie rod ring	25 Exterior handle	37 Handle assembly	57 Weatherstrip
9 Grommet	26 Handle shaft	42 Screw	58 Weatherstrip
10 Pin	26a Ring	43 Rubber moulding	59 Trim
11 Nut	26b Adjusting shim	44 Support	60 Wire clip
12 Pin	26c Rubber buffer	45 Glass	61 Arm rest
13 Cotter pin	27 Handle spring	46 Rubber moulding	62 Screw
14 Pawl	28 Screw	47 Rubber moulding	63 Window stop
15 Transfer lock	29 Door lock	48 Guide rail	64 Plug
			68 Lock assembly

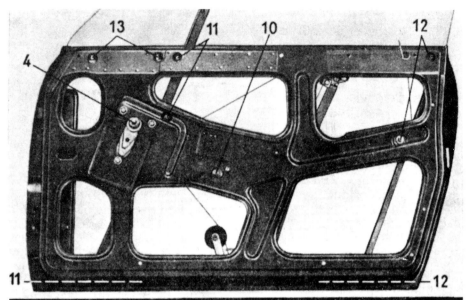

Fig. 11.7. Coupe model inner door panel showing winder mechanism (Sec. 14)

1 *Regulator lever*
2 *Regulator roller*
3 *Regulator tensioning roller*
4 *Window regulator*
5 *Front glass channel*
6 *Window stay*
7 *Stay rail stop*
8 *Rear glass channel*
9 *Door linkage lock*
10 *Linkage lock*
11 *Quarterlight retaining screws*
12 *Window channel retaining screws*
13 *Quarterlight retaining screws*

DK 1292

15.2 Coupe model striker plate

17 Door rattles - tracing and rectification

1   The commonest cause of door rattle is a misaligned, loose or worn striker plate but other causes may be:

  a) *Loose door handles, window winder handles or door hinges.*
  b) *Loose, worn or misaligned door lock components.*
  c) *Loose or worn window winder mechanism.*
  d) *Loose trim panels.*

2   It is quite possible for door rattles to be the result of a combination of the above faults, so a careful examination must be made to determine the causes of the fault.
3   If the nose of the striker plate is worn and as a result the door rattles, renew and then adjust the plate, as described in Section 15.
4   Should the inner door handle rattle, this is easily cured by fitting a rubber washer between the escutcheon and the handle.
5   If the nose of the door lock wedge is badly worn and the door rattles as a result, then fit a new lock.
6   Should the hinges be badly worn, then they must be renewed.

18 Windscreen - removal and refitting

1   If the windscreen shatters, fitting a replacement is one of the **few**

jobs the average owner is advised to leave to the experienced fitter. For the owner who wishes to do the job himself the following instructions are given.

2 Remove the wiper arms from their spindles, remove the interior rear view mirror and the visors. Cover the screen heating duct apertures and upper dash panel.

3 Next extract the trim from the outside of the screen edge rubber. This trim locks the rubber extrusion around the glass screen edge.

4 Place a blanket or suitable protection on the car bonnet to prevent scoring the paintwork with the broken screen.

5 Move to the inside of the car and have an assistant outside the car ready to catch the screen as it is released.

6 Wearing leather gloves or similar hand protection push on the glass screen as near to the edge as possible, beginning at the top corners. The rubber extrusion should deform and allow the screen to move outwards out of the screen aperture. This of course is not applicable if the screen has shattered.

7 Remove the rubber surround from the glass or alternatively carefully pick out the remains of the glass. Use a vacuum cleaner to extract as much of the screen debris as possible.

8 Carefully inspect the rubber extrusion surround for signs of pitting and deterioration. Offer up the new glass to the screen aperture and check that the shape and curvature of the screen conforms to that of the aperture. A screen will break quite soon again it the aperture and glass do not suit, typically if the vehicle has been involved in an accident during which the screen broke. A car bodyshell can be deformed easily in such instances to an extent when the aperture will need reshaping by a competent body repairer to ensure conformity with a new screen.

9 Position the new glass into the rubber extrusion surround, remember that the groove for the metal trim needs to be on the outer side of the screen assembly.

10 With the rubber now correctly positioned around the glass, a long piece of strong cord should be inserted in the slot in the rubber extrusion which is to accept the flange of the screen aperture in the bodyshell. The two free ends of the cord should finish at either the top or bottom centre and overlap each other.

11 The screen is now offered up to the aperture, and an assistant will be required to press the rubber surround hard against the bodyshell flange. Slowly pull one end of the cord, moving around the windscreen, thereby drawing the lip of the rubber extrusion screen surround over the the flange of the screen aperture.

12 Finally ensure that the rubber surround is correctly seated around the screen and then press in the metal trim strip which locks the screen in the rubber. Once the glass has been fitted satisfactorily the windscreen wipers, visors and interior mirror may be refitted.

19 Rear window - removal and refitting

1 The procedure for removal and replacement of the rear window glass is exactly the same as for the front windscreen, except that there is no interior mirror, wipers or heating duct.

20 Engine compartment lid - removal and refitting

1 To remove the engine compartment lid open it to its fullest extent.

2 Mark the position of the hinges to ensure correct alignment upon refitting.

3 Unscrew the retaining nuts and remove the lid from the car.

4 Refitting is the reverse of removal.

21 Luggage compartment - removal and refitting

The procedure for the luggage compartment lid removal is identical to that for the engine compartment lid except that the windscreen washer tubes have to be disconnected, as does the luggage compartment light (if fitted).

22 Bumpers (front and rear) - removal and refitting

1 These are retained on brackets mounted to the main body structure. Remove by unscrewing the retaining bolts on each bracket.

2 Later models have the direction indicator incorporated in the channel of the front bumpers and the wiring to this should therefore be disconnected at the start.

3 Penetrating oil may be required to free the retaining bolts of the bumper brackets.

4 Refitting is the reverse sequence.

23 Wing (front) - removal and refitting

1 Remove the front bumper, and raise the luggage compartment lid.

2 On MB models disconnect the wiring to the headlight, flasher unit and horn, also, on the right-hand wing, it is necessary to disconnect the luggage compartment lid, release cable from the handle inside the bulkhead (within the car).

3 On all models, the fuel filler neck unit must be disconnected on the right-hand wing.

4 Now remove the wing retaining bolts from within the upper drain channel, under and within the door sill, and in the front headlight area.

5 Remove the wings and also the seal strips if they are defective. Temporarily cover the exposed petrol filler pipe to prevent the ingress of dirt. Do not smoke or weld in the surrounding area!

6 Refitting of the front wings is the reverse of removal, but always replace worn or perished seal strips sticking them into place with 'Glasticon Dum Dum Putty' applied to the mating surface prior to wing assembly. This will prevent corrosion of the body joints. Before tightening the wing retaining bolts, align the wing to the correct position.

24 Wing (rear) - removal and refitting

1 Remove the bumper and raise the engine compartment lid.

2 If the left-hand wing panel is being removed, it is necessary to disconnect the engine compartment lid catch cable, from the rear panel.

3 On the MB series cars it will be necessary to disconnect the rear light/indicator wires, and remove the light cluster from the wing. Note the lead connection positions and remove the cluster unit by unscrewing the securing screws.

4 Remove the radiator and/or heater unit intake vent panel and, if fitted, the outer splash guard bolt.

5 Now unscrew and remove the wing retaining bolts from the upper channel, from the rear door pillar, from inside the side vent aperture, the rear wing to rear panel corner and the rear of the door sill (underneath).

6 Refitting is the reversed procedure to removal, but if the seal strips are badly worn or perished, replace with new ones, sticking them into place with 'Glasticon Dum Dum Putty' applied to the mating surface prior to wing assembly. This helps to prevent corrosion of the body joints. Before tightening the wing retaining bolts, align the wing to its correct position.

25 Front body panel - removal and refitting

1 Disconnect the front headlight/spotlight leads.

2 Remove the front bumper.

3 Undo and remove the front panel securing bolts to the front corner of the boot, the wheel valance under the headlight, the lower edge to the rear of the bumpers and front part of the boot lid/wings drain channels.

4 Refitting is the reversal of renewal, but if the sealing strips between the wings and front panel are damaged or badly worn, renew them.

26 Rear body panel - removal and refitting

1 From inside the engine compartment disconnect the compartment lid lock control cable.

2 Disconnect the wiring to the rear lights. On later models, the light units can be removed, if required, as described in Chapter 10.

3 Remove the rear bumper.

4 Undo and remove the rear panel retaining bolts and remove the panel by pushing to the rear.

5 Refitting is the reversal of removing, replacing any panel seal strips, badly worn or perished.

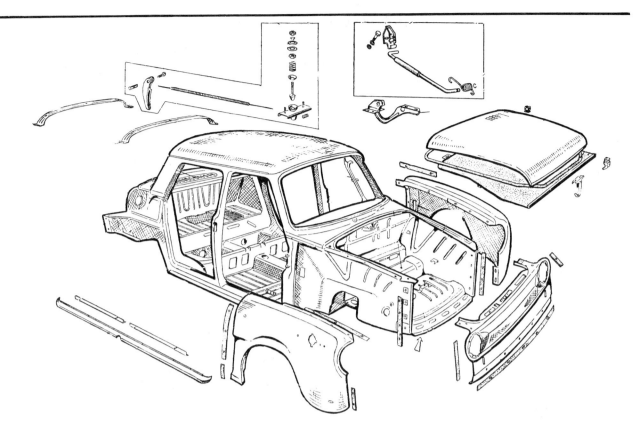

Fig. 11.8. General layout of front body panels (Secs. 23 and 25)

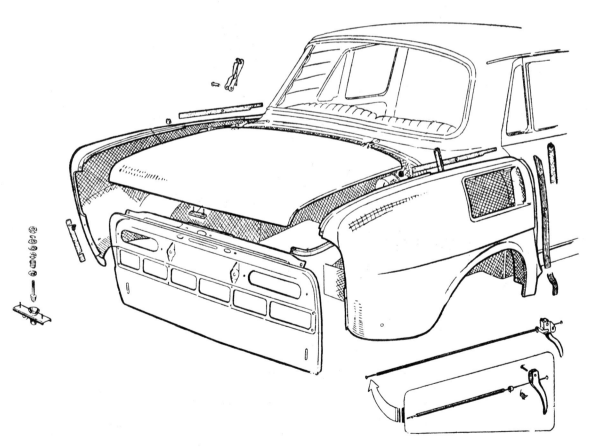

Fig. 11.9. General layout of rear body panels (Secs. 24 and 26)

27 Seats - removal and refitting

1   The front seats can be removed only in the rearwards direction.
2   From the rear of the seat runner, undo the bolt and remove the stop.
3   From underneath the seat, disconnect the recoil spring.
4   The seat can now be removed, sliding from its runners to the rear. Replace in the reverse order.
5   The rear seats are easily removed. First remove the seat cushions by lifting from their respective positons. Then from the backrests unscrew the retaining bolt, and hinge the backrest upwards, slide to the side and disconnect from the guide pins. Refit in the reverse order.

28 Heater unit distributor channels - removal and refitting

1   Refer to Fig. 11.10. The heating and cold air feed channels to the windscreen pad interior are located under the dashpanel and are fed from a central duct unit mounted on the floor. The central distribution duct has an adjustable control flap incorporated, and is operated by means of a lever on the right-hand side.
2   The car interior ducts are mounted transversely on each side of the central distribution duct, just above the foot pedals. They are an interference fit into the central duct and are removed easily by pulling from it.
3   The windscreen and directional heating feed hoses mounted in the upper dashpanel are connected to the central duct by 'Y' section distributor tubes. The feed hoses are flexible also of an interference fit.
4   The windscreen and direction heating units are located in position by screws, and bolts and nuts respectively.

29 Dashpanel (Coupe) - removal and refitting

1   Refer to Fig. 11.11. The various dashpanel - facia parts are removed by unscrewing and removing the relevant retaining screws.
2   The top panel is retained by nuts from underneath.
3   The instrument panel is removed after the removal of the surrounding facia parts. The various locating points of the dashpanel assembly are shown in Fig. 11.12.
4   Replace in the reverse order to dismantling and be sure to secure the

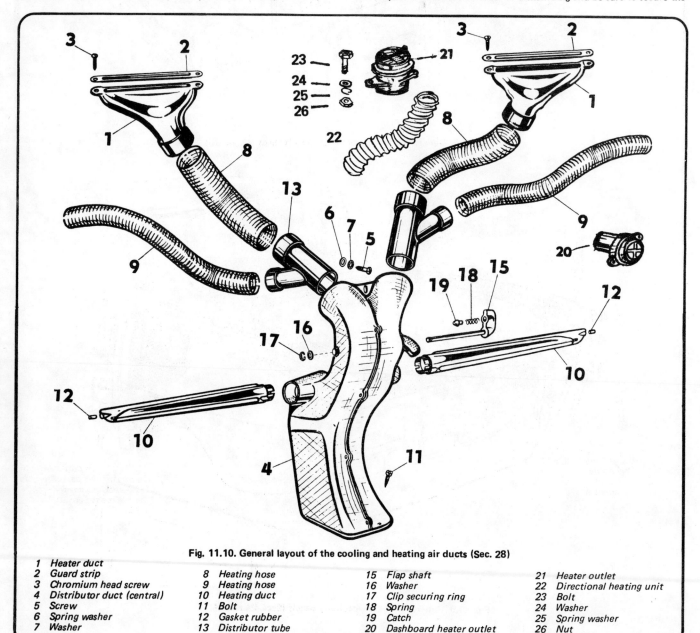

Fig. 11.10. General layout of the cooling and heating air ducts (Sec. 28)

1	Heater duct						
2	Guard strip			15	Flap shaft	21	Heater outlet
3	Chromium head screw	8	Heating hose	16	Washer	22	Directional heating unit
4	Distributor duct (central)	9	Heating hose	17	Clip securing ring	23	Bolt
5	Screw	10	Heating duct	18	Spring	24	Washer
6	Spring washer	11	Bolt	19	Catch	25	Spring washer
7	Washer	12	Gasket rubber	20	Dashboard heater outlet	26	Nut
		13	Distributor tube				

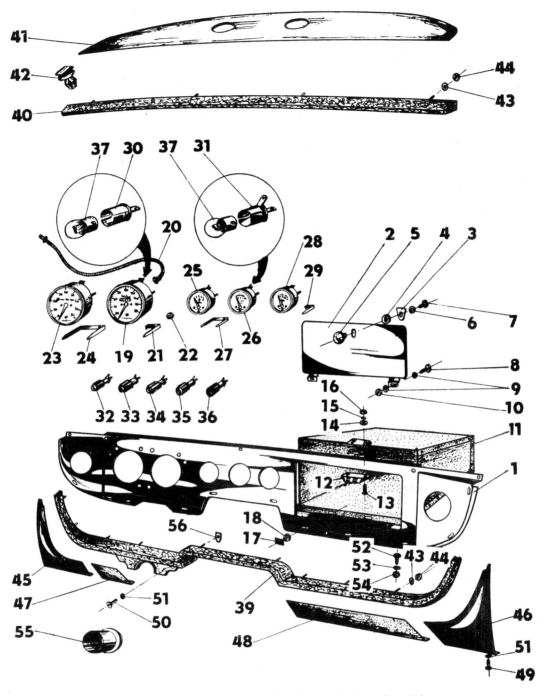

Fig. 11.11. The component parts of the dash panel - Coupe (Sec. 29)

1	Dashboard compl. painted	15	Spring washer	29	Holder	44	Nut
2	Cover assembly	16	Nut	30	Light bulb socket	45	Dashboard LH part assembly
3	Catch bracket	17	Plate	31	Light bulb socket	46	Dashboard RH part assembly
4	Catch bracket washer	18	Nut	32	Warning light - red	47	LH dashboard cover
5	Knob	19	Speedometer	33	Warning light - dark red	48	RH dashboard cover
6	Washer	20	Flexible shaft	34	Warning light - orange	49	Screw
7	Screw	21	Holder	35	Warning light - dark blue	50	Screw
8	Screw	22	Nut	36	Warning light - green	51	Washer
9	Washer	23	Revolution counter	37	Bulb	52	Screw
10	Nut	24	Holder	39	Dashboard assembly	53	Washer
11	Glove box	25	Fuel gauge	40	Dashboard (top)	54	Nut
12	Magnetic glove box lock	26	Water temperature gauge	41	Dashboard upholstered	55	Bulb socket
13	Screw	27	Holder	42	Clip	56	Thread plate
14	Washer	28	Manometer	43	Washer		

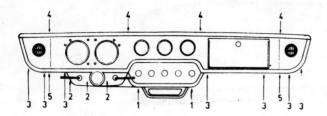

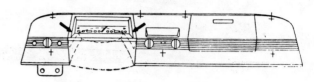

Fig. 11.12. Dashpanel location positions - Coupe (Sec. 29)

1   Bottom screws for switch holders
2   Two cap screws
3   Side and coving panel retaining screws
4   Top panel nuts
5   Bracket bolt/nuts

Fig. 11.13. Dashpanel location points - all models, except Coupe (arrows point to instrument panel retaining latches) (Sec. 30)

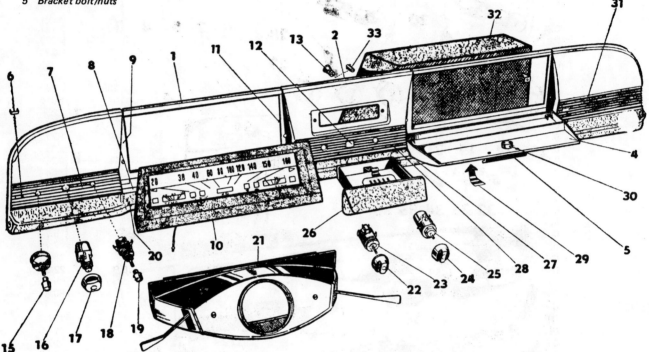

Fig. 11.14. The component parts of the dashpanel - all models, except Coupe (Sec. 30)

1 Dashboard	10 Instrument panel	19 Heater knob	27 Padded strip
2 Centre section	11 Lock	20 Short padded strip	28 Centre moulding
4 Locker lid	12 Hazard warning lamp	21 Steering column shroud	29 Decorative moulding
5 Lid handle	13 Socket of warning lamp	22 Lights knob	30 Locker lock
6 Decorative moulding clip	15 Knob	23 Main light switch	31 Outer decorative moulding
7 Decorative moulding	16 Windscreen wiper switch	24 Hazard knob	32 Dashboard locker
8 Partition	17 Knob (wiper)	25 Hazard switch	33 Warning lamp
9 Lock	18 Heater switch	26 Ashtray	

earthing cable for the instrument panel to the left-hand bracket bolt nut. For removal of instruments and lights refer to Chapter 10.

30 Dashpanel (all models, except Coupe) - removal and refitting

1   See Fig. 11.14. The complete dashpanel can be removed after the removal of the various retaining nuts, the positions of which are shown in Fig. 11.13.

2   For removal or refitting of the instruments and lights refer to Chapter 10.

3   Refit in the reverse order.

Metric conversion tables

Inches	Decimals	Millimetres	Millimetres to Inches		Inches to Millimetres	
			mm	Inches	Inches	mm
1/64	0.015625	0.3969	0.01	0.00039	0.001	0.0254
1/32	0.03125	0.7937	0.02	0.00079	0.002	0.0508
3/64	0.046875	1.1906	0.03	0.00118	0.003	0.0762
1/16	0.0625	1.5875	0.04	0.00157	0.004	0.1016
5/64	0.078125	1.9844	0.05	0.00197	0.005	0.1270
3/32	0.09375	2.3812	0.06	0.00236	0.006	0.1524
7/64	0.109375	2.7781	0.07	0.00276	0.007	0.1778
1/8	0.125	3.1750	0.08	0.00315	0.008	0.2032
9/64	0.140625	3.5719	0.09	0.00354	0.009	0.2286
5/32	0.15625	3.9687	0.1	0.00394	0.01	0.254
11/64	0.171875	4.3656	0.2	0.00787	0.02	0.508
3/16	0.1875	4.7625	0.3	0.1181	0.03	0.762
13/64	0.203125	5.1594	0.4	0.01575	0.04	1.016
7/32	0.21875	5.5562	0.5	0.01969	0.05	1.270
15/64	0.234275	5.9531	0.6	0.02362	0.06	1.524
1/4	0.25	6.3500	0.7	0.02756	0.07	1.778
17/64	0.265625	6.7469	0.8	0.3150	0.08	2.032
9/32	0.28125	7.1437	0.9	0.03543	0.09	2.286
19/64	0.296875	7.5406	1	0.03937	0.1	2.54
5/16	0.3125	7.9375	2	0.07874	0.2	5.08
21/64	0.328125	8.3344	3	0.11811	0.3	7.62
11/32	0.34375	8.7312	4	0.15748	0.4	10.16
23/64	0.359375	9.1281	5	0.19685	0.5	12.70
3/8	0.375	9.5250	6	0.23622	0.6	15.24
25/64	0.390625	9.9219	7	0.27559	0.7	17.78
13/32	0.40625	10.3187	8	0.31496	0.8	20.32
27/64	0.421875	10.7156	9	0.35433	0.9	22.86
7/16	0.4375	11.1125	10	0.39270	1	25.4
29/64	0.453125	11.5094	11	0.43307	2	50.8
15/32	0.46875	11.9062	12	0.47244	3	76.2
31/64	0.484375	12.3031	13	0.51181	4	101.6
1/2	0.5	12.7000	14	0.55118	5	127.0
33/64	0.515625	13.0969	15	0.59055	6	152.4
17/32	0.53125	13.4937	16	0.62992	7	177.8
35/64	0.546875	13.8906	17	0.66929	8	203.2
9/16	0.5625	14.2875	18	0.70866	9	228.6
37/64	0.578125	14.6844	19	0.74803	10	254.0
19/32	0.59375	15.0812	20	0.78740	11	279.4
39/64	0.609375	15.4781	21	0.82677	12	304.8
5/8	0.625	15.8750	22	0.86614	13	330.2
41/64	0.640625	16.2719	23	0.90551	14	355.6
21/32	0.65625	16.6687	24	0.94488	15	381.0
43/64	0.671875	17.0656	25	0.98425	16	406.4
11/16	0.6875	17.4625	26	1.02362	17	431.8
45/64	0.703125	17.8594	27	1.06299	18	457.2
23/32	0.71875	18.2562	28	1.10236	19	482.6
47/64	0.734375	18.6531	29	1.14173	20	508.0
3/4	0.75	19.0500	30	1.18110	21	533.4
49/64	0.765625	19.4469	31	1.22047	22	558.8
25/32	0.78125	19.8437	32	1.25984	23	584.2
51/64	0.796875	20.2406	33	1.29921	24	609.6
13/16	0.8125	20.6375	34	1.33858	25	635.0
53/64	0.828125	21.0344	35	1.37795	26	660.4
27/32	0.84375	21.4312	36	1.41732	27	685.8
55/64	0.859375	21.8281	37	1.4567	28	711.2
7/8	0.875	22.2250	38	1.4961	29	736.6
57/64	0.890625	22.6219	39	1.5354	30	762.0
29/32	0.90625	23.0187	40	1.5748	31	787.4
59/64	0.921875	23.4156	41	1.6142	32	812.8
15/16	0.9375	23.8125	42	1.6535	33	838.2
61/64	0.953125	24.2094	43	1.6929	34	863.6
31/32	0.96875	24.6062	44	1.7323	35	889.0
63/64	0.984375	25.0031	45	1.7717	46	914.4

1   Imperial gallon = 8 Imp pints = 1.16 US gallons = 277.42 cu in = 4.5459 litres

1   US gallon = 4 US quarts = 0.862 Imp gallon = 231 cu in = 3.785 litres

1   Litre = 0.2199 Imp gallon = 0.2642 US gallon = 61.0253 cu in = 1000 cc

Miles to Kilometres		Kilometres to Miles	
1	1.61	1	0.62
2	3.22	2	1.24
3	4.83	3	1.86
4	6.44	4	2.49
5	8.05	5	3.11
6	9.66	6	3.73
7	11.27	7	4.35
8	12.88	8	4.97
9	14.48	9	5.59
10	16.09	10	6.21
20	32.19	20	12.43
30	48.28	30	18.64
40	64.37	40	24.85
50	80.47	50	31.07
60	96.56	60	37.28
70	112.65	70	43.50
80	128.75	80	49.71
90	144.84	90	55.92
100	160.93	100	62.14

lb f ft to Kg f m		Kg f m to lb f ft		lb f/in^2 : Kg f/cm^2		Kg f/cm^2 : lb f/in^2	
1	0.138	1	7.233	1	0.07	1	14.22
2	0.276	2	14.466	2	0.14	2	28.50
3	0.414	3	21.699	3	0.21	3	42.67
4	0.553	4	28.932	4	0.28	4	56.89
5	0.691	5	36.165	5	0.35	5	71.12
6	0.829	6	43.398	6	0.42	6	85.34
7	0.967	7	50.631	7	0.49	7	99.56
8	1.106	8	57.864	8	0.56	8	113.79
9	1.244	9	65.097	9	0.63	9	128.00
10	1.382	10	62.330	10	0.70	10	142.23
20	2.765	20	144.660	20	1.41	20	284.47
30	4.147	30	216.990	30	2.11	30	426.70

Index

Printed by
J. H. HAYNES & Co. Ltd
Sparkford Yeovil Somerset
ENGLAND